ISBN 978-1-334-50282-8
PIBN 10747902

# 1 MONTH OF
# FREE
# READING

## at

## www.ForgottenBooks.com

By purchasing this book you are
eligible for one month membership to
ForgottenBooks.com, giving you
unlimited access to our entire
collection of over 1,000,000 titles via
our web site and mobile apps.

To claim your free month visit:

www.forgottenbooks.com/free747902

English
Français
Deutsche
Italiano
Español
Português

# www.forgottenbooks.com

**Mythology** Photography **Fiction**
Fishing Christianity **Art** Cooking
Essays Buddhism Freemasonry
Medicine **Biology** Music **Ancient
Egypt** Evolution Carpentry Physics
Dance Geology **Mathematics** Fitness
Shakespeare **Folklore** Yoga Marketing
**Confidence** Immortality Biographies
Poetry **Psychology** Witchcraft
Electronics Chemistry History **Law**
Accounting **Philosophy** Anthropology
Alchemy Drama Quantum Mechanics
Atheism Sexual Health **Ancient History**
**Entrepreneurship** Languages Sport
Paleontology Needlework Islam
**Metaphysics** Investment Archaeology
Parenting Statistics Criminology
**Motivational**

# THE REDISCOVERY

## OF

## WORDSWORTH

# THE REDISCOVERY
# OF
# WORDSWORTH

*By*

## CORNELIUS HOWARD PATTON

GORDIAN PRESS, INC.
NEW YORK
1966

Originally Published 1935
Reprinted by Gordian Press, Inc. 1966


Library of Congress Catalog Card No. 66-29467

Printed in U.S.A. by
EDWARDS BROTHERS, INC.
Ann Arbor, Michigan

*To the Memory of*

## GORDON GRAHAM WORDSWORTH
### GRANDSON OF THE POET

### THIS BOOK IS GRATEFULLY INSCRIBED

# Author's Word

IN writing this book I have had three classes of people in mind. First, those who know practically nothing about Wordsworth, but who might be drawn into the circle of his influence should the right word be said. Second, those who know enough of the Poet to realize that they should go much farther, but who lack the guiding clue. Third, those who know a great deal of Wordsworth as an honored poet of one hundred years ago, but who have not appreciated the unique significance of his message for our own particular time.

Perhaps it is fair to add that I have named the classes of hoped-for readers in the reverse order of importance, as the matter has lain in my mind. At least I have felt that the message of the Poet is the main thing, and that there is no accounting for his steadily increasing influence, evidenced in so many ways, other than on the ground that to the modern world, to use his own expression, he has become, or is becoming *A Mighty Voice*. It has been my aim to show how closely his teachings fit into our present post-war situation, and to do this in a somewhat detailed way, passing from the lower to the higher, that is from nature to man, from man to society, and from society to the ethical and philosophical principles that underlie his work. Then, in order that the totality of impression might not be missed, I have added a brief summary at the end.

In confessing the *ideas* of the Poet as my major interest, I am well aware that I shall fall foul of the critics—never more in evidence than today—to whom æsthetics is the sole criterion of successful verse. So be it. As I show in one of my chapters, the issue is as old as Matthew Arnold's reply to Leslie Stephen in the well known preface to his *Wordsworth Selections*. I can only plead that there are some good names on the Stephen side of the debate, and that in my attempt to bring Wordsworth down to date as prophet and seer, I have sought to do full justice to the sheer artistry of his work, without which his message would never have found lodgment in the human breast. It is in the rare combination of poetic idea and poetic form that I find the chief ground of confidence in respect to Wordsworth's growing power in the twentieth century world. Certainly there is small likelihood of interesting our socially-minded generation in a poet as far back as this, unless, commending him on the score of artistic merit, we can at the same time reveal him as a corrective of the false valuations, the ill-tempers and the essentially wrong attitudes of our "getting and spending" age.

Such being my aim, it has seemed best to follow the topical rather than the biographical method. If this involves a certain loss in the case of a poet whose verse is so intimately interwoven with his life, there is compensation in the fact that to so large an extent recent criticism has followed the other road. If the main facts of the Poet's career are not sufficiently known to furnish a background for intelligent reading, they can easily be ascertained. (I forbear to indicate how many of the biographers have started off with the identical sentence: "William Wordsworth was born at Cockermouth, County of Cumberland, April 7, 1770.")

At one point, however, I have been constrained to make use of the biographical approach, and that is in dealing with the Poet's unfortunate love-affair in France. Here the facts have been so recently disclosed, they are of such far-reaching significance, and they have received from critics like Herbert Read, Hugh I. Fausset and Bertrand Russel, not to mention sundry review and editorial writers, such warped and essentially unjust interpretation, that it seemed necessary, as in my tenth chapter, to discuss the *character* of Wordsworth against the background of the actualities of the Annette incident, as also in the light of this flood of recent criticism. We have reached the point where there is a call for a balanced and understanding treatment of an episode which the critics have made a stumbling-block in the path of many who have rejoiced in Wordsworth's poetry as the expression of an essentially pure and noble life. It is because Wordsworth is discussed so earnestly—so vehemently at times—that we may be confident of his influence in the modern world. When a poet is no longer discussed he is no longer read. Out of all this argument and criticism will come a truer estimate of Wordsworth's character and work. Already, from the musty philosopher-poet of the popular tradition, he has emerged as one of the most interesting figures in the history of literature. *But the time has come when we should cease thinking of Wordsworth as a problem and begin anew thinking of him as a poet.*

I wish to express my obligation to the various publishers who have allowed me to quote freely from copyrighted books. Their names are mentioned at the proper places. I gratefully acknowledge the courtesy of the *Boston Evening Transcript* in allowing the use of portions of an article on Wordsworth, published under my name, in their Book Section in 1927. I trust my indebtedness to Professor George McLean Harper is made sufficiently evident by the number of times I refer to his superb biography, *William Wordsworth, His Life, Works and Influence;* but in addition I owe him a more personal debt of gratitude for encouragement and advice offered at the time I was considering attempting a book of this character. To Professor George F. Whicher, of Amherst College, and Mr. Walter T. Field, of the Publishing House of Ginn and Company, I entertain a peculiarly deep sense of obligation. These good friends not only gave encouragement during the process of writing, but agreed to read the manuscript and to give me the benefit of their criticism. The promise was fulfilled in such a painstaking and helpful way, that I find myself at a loss to express my feelings in suitable words. Their service was as generous as it was unique.

I mention these names with the more gratitude by reason of the fact that, writing as a layman in the field of literary criticism, I have experienced no small hesitation in seeking to be heard on a theme of this kind. The best excuse I can offer is that in Wordsworth (to adopt Coleridge's well known word in regard to the Bible) there is more that "finds me" than I have experienced in all the other poets put together.

C. H. P.

Hartford, Connecticut,
August 19, 1935.

# Contents

# CONTENTS

## CHAPTER I

# "Fit Audience Let Me Find Though Few"

DURING one of the years of the World War, I was returning to Boston from a meeting at Amherst College in company with Dr. William Hayes Ward, the eminent Assyriologist, at that time editor of the *New York Independent,* and Dr. John Timothy Stone, the well-known Chicago preacher. Travelling by the branch of the Boston and Maine which traverses the wilderness of central Massachusetts, we were whiling away the time by discussing poetry. It developed that all three of us were fond of Wordsworth, and that Dr. Ward could repeat from memory the *Ode to Duty,* the *Happy Warrior,* and several others of the greater poems. Some one spoke of the sonnets as Wordsworth's finest work, and we began to recall them, one by one. We endeavored to repeat the superb sonnet beginning *The World is Too Much With Us,* and by our combined memories were able to reconstruct all but two of the lines. These two lines of the octet eluded our persistent efforts. The conversation then passed to other subjects. Sitting in front of us was a woman, apparently of the neighborhood, who, at the next stop, one of those obscure stations on the line, gathered up her belongings and proceeded to leave the train. Before doing so she turned and said, "I beg your pardon, gentlemen, but I could not help overhearing your conversation. Those lines of Wordsworth you were trying to recall are as follows:

# THE REDISCOVERY OF WORDSWORTH

> The winds that will be howling at all hours,
> And are up-gathered now like sleeping flowers.

We thanked her, and when she was out of hearing, Dr. Stone exclaimed: "Gentlemen, that thing could not have happened anywhere in the world but in New England and in Massachusetts." Whether this tribute to the culture of Massachusetts is deserved or not (I strongly suspect it is not), I venture to suggest that the incident could not have occurred in respect to any other poet than Wordsworth. There we were, an archæologist, a preacher, an executive of a mission board, and a woman who might be regarded as representative of the culture of her sex, all revealing a warm interest in this particular poet, and, of course, it was the woman who set us right when it came to recalling the elusive lines. Could Tennyson, or Browning, or Pope, or Milton, or even Shakespeare be credited with an equal devotion? Possibly Shakespeare. But there is always this difference—while we rate Shakespeare above the rest, and ungrudgingly allow that his place is unique, as a rule we think of him objectively, in admiration rather than in personal affection. Shakespeare is our Matterhorn, our Mount Everest, never the kindly peak before our door that kindled our imagination in childhood and woos our faltering steps in old age. With Wordsworth it is a matter of friendship, of soul understanding, of spiritual dependence. Matthew Arnold, in his famous preface to his *Selections from Wordsworth,* shocked his contemporaries (but not us today) by ranking Wordsworth as the third greatest English poet, surpassed only by Shakespeare and Milton. The ground of his enthusiasm is found in the poet's gift of spiritual healing.

> Time may restore us in his course
> Goethe's sage mind and Byron's force;
> But where will Europe's latter hour
> Again find Wordsworth's healing power?[1]

---

[1] *Memorial Verses—April 1850.*

Similarly, so economically minded a personage as John Stuart Mill came to feel toward Wordsworth as a man does toward the physician who has carried him through a dangerous crisis and given him a new lease of life. In his autobiography, as has often been pointed out, we are told how at a time of mental upheaval, when faith seemed falling away in every direction, the poetry of Wordsworth became as medicine to his soul.[2]

When one has entered into these more personal appreciations, the fact of the dreary wastes in the later writings of the poet become of small significance. Granted that he wrote too much; that too often his thought is obscured by prolixity; that during his golden years, 1797-1807, under the compulsion of an overworked theory of poetic diction, he produced certain pieces of doubtful propriety and worth; granted that his versification lacks the magic of Coleridge, the singing quality of Shelley, the moving sensuousness of Keats; that he was never "a dainty weaver of exquisite verse"; granted all that any reasonable critic may demand in the way of abatement and qualification; and we shall still have a body of poetical achievement of large dimensions and of supreme value in the realm of the spirit. Personally, I care little for these attempts, even when indulged in by first-class critics like Arnold, Lowell and Swinburne, to arrange the poets in a hierarchy of mathematical precision. Enough to have Shakespeare at the summit and a glad array of lesser divinities on the lower slopes of Olympus.

> If thou indeed derive thy light from Heaven,
> Then, to the measure of that heaven-born light,
> Shine, Poet! in thy place, and be content.[3]

Enough for Wordsworth that we can say with his great disciple:

---

[2] *Autobiography*, Second Edition, 1873, pp. 146 ff.
[3] Sonnet by Wordsworth.

# THE REDISCOVERY OF WORDSWORTH

Smiles broke from us and we had ease;
The hills were round us, and the breeze
Went o'er the sun-lit fields again;
Our foreheads felt the wind and rain.
Our youth returned; for there was shed
On spirits that had long been dead,
Spirits dried up and closely furl'd,
The freshness of the early world.[4]

There is much today to stimulate a fresh interest in Wordsworth. For one thing, a new crop of admirers and students has come upon the scene. No longer is it necessary to revert to Mill and Arnold, to Morley, Stephen, Swinburne and Lowell. The old-time Wordsworthians have given way to the newer critics, with their wider knowledge of the background of the Poet's life and their better understanding of the entire period of the Romantic Revival. No longer are his admirers content to enjoy him without asking questions. The praise of Wordsworth today is a well-considered praise. We have, for instance, Professor A. C. Bradley, in his *Oxford Lectures on Poetry,* saying, "There have been greater poets than Wordsworth, but none more original," in another place characterizing him as "indisputably the most sublime of our poets since Milton." In speaking of Sir Walter Raleigh's recent critique, pronounced "the best book on an English poet that has appeared for some years," Professor Bradley remarks: "That it should be a study of Wordsworth is just what might be expected. The whirligig of time has brought him full revenge." As for Raleigh himself, he considers that Wordsworth's position being secure, in view of the fact that the finest part of his work has been separated from the inferior bulk, our present concern should be not so much to judge the Poet as to understand him. From this point of view (not essentially new) Raleigh conducts us into a fellowship where we "learn courage" and feel "the visitings of a

[4]Matthew Arnold. *Memorial Verses—April 1850.*

larger, purer air, and the peace of an unfathomable sky."[5]

How wide this fellowship may be it is difficult to learn, particularly as lovers of Wordsworth have not been given, at least on this side of the water, to getting together and forming societies. The publishers have been feeling out the situation and appear to have reached the conclusion that Wordsworth is appealing to a steadily widening circle of readers, and for a variety of reasons. Having undertaken to prepare a descriptive bibliography of the Wordsworth material in the Amherst College Library, I have had occasion to examine with some care the output of books on the subject since the opening of the World War, and have found that the twenty-one years since that time have produced no less than ninety-five volumes relating to Wordsworth or his family, or having the message of this poet as a prevailing theme. In respect to authorship, or editorship, fifty-five of these may be credited to England, twenty-five to America, seven to France, four to Germany, two to Holland, one to Italy, and one to India. The publication in 1931 of *Critical Theories and Poetic Practice in the Lyrical Ballads,* by Professor Srikumar Banerjee, of the University of Calcutta, suggests the far-reach of present-day interest and also the vitality of the theory of poetic diction propounded by Wordsworth and Coleridge in 1798. The writings of Professor Emile Legouis of Paris, based upon a life-long critical study of our poet, and enriched by recent research in respect to the "Annette incident," are well known.

When we come to the scope of these post-war publications I find that sixty-five are books about Wordsworth—biography and criticism, and thirteen are reprints of the poetical works, or of particular poems. In addition, since 1914, there have been issued no less than seventeen anthologies, which would seem to suggest a revival of general

[5] *Wordsworth,* by Walter Raleigh, London, 1925.

interest akin to that created by the publication of Matthew Arnold's famous volume of Selections in 1879.

It is when we consider the authorship and character of this recent output that we begin to realize that Wordsworth is far from being the musty philosopher-poet and "back number" of popular imagination. Bradley and Raleigh have already been mentioned. But upon glancing over the list one finds such works as Professor Harper's scholarly, two-volume biography (later revised and issued in a single volume), recognized in America and England as, in many respects, a definitive work; *The Lectures and Essays* of Professor Garrod, of Oxford, inspired by Harper; *Wordsworth's Anti-Climax,* by Dean Sperry, of Harvard, with its penetrating search for personality, inspired by Garrod; the painstaking study of Professor Beatty, of the University of Wisconsin, into the philosophical background of Wordsworth and Coleridge, with especial reference to their interest in the views of the philosopher Hartley; the editing of the *Correspondence of Henry Crabb Robinson with the Wordsworth Circle,* by Miss Morley, containing much new biographical material; and the discerning and authoritative *Dorothy Wordsworth,* by Professor de Selincourt, in which not only does Dorothy, the sister, come to her own as one of the most remarkable women of the last century, but Wordsworth himself is seen in a new light of delicate and vivid minutiæ of family living.

A work of outstanding importance, also by Professor de Selincourt, truly a literary landmark, is the parallel edition of *The Prelude,* in which are printed *vis a vis* the poem as it originally came from the pen of Wordsworth in 1805, and as it was given to the public after the Poet's death in 1850. To this I shall need to revert in a later chapter.

And then there is that challenging book of Mr. Herbert Read, *Wordsworth—The Clark Lecture,* 1930, with its Freudian point of view, interpreting nearly everything in the Poet's life from the standpoint of the unfortunate love-affair in France, and full of revolt against the traditions of critics old and new—a book, one realizes, which simply *had* to be after all these years of established position and growing appreciation. On top of this has come the equally radical work by Hugh Fausset, *The Lost Leader,* in which the inner life of the Poet is attacked as spiritually unsound. These two books have at least served to uncover the attitude of a psychology-ridden public toward a poet who had risen far above the mistakes of youth. Yet even Read, appraising Wordsworth's artistry in verse, surpasses Arnold who, as we have seen, rated the Poet of the Lakes next after the sublime Milton. Even Milton, it would appear, must now give way. "Where for variety and vitality of pure poetic expression," Read inquires, "can you match the wealth of Shakespeare except in Wordsworth?" Again, however, I protest against the propensity of the critics for ranking the poets on a mathematical scale. For our present purpose it is sufficient to know, so far as recent books are concerned, that Wordsworth has a larger shelf than any English poet except Shakespeare.

But how about the living epistles of praise and blame— the men and women who read poetry but do not express their reactions in print? It is when I run across a group of men like those on the Boston and Maine train, or women like the one who treasured the finer sonnets in her heart, that I begin to realize that Wordsworth has indeed become "a Mighty Voice" in our modern world.

We know that Woodrow Wilson was a life-long student of Wordsworth and that one summer before his public career he rented a house at Ambleside, in the Lake District, so that he might be as close as possible to the scenes of *The Prelude* and of the nature-pieces which inspired so much of the Poet's work. Residents at Ambleside take pride in pointing out to visitors, especially Americans, the mansion where Wilson once lived, located in a pleasant field only a little removed from *Fox Howe,* the home of the Arnolds. Professor Harper in a personal letter informs me that it was the custom of Mr. Wilson, during his Princeton days, to read his favorite poems of Wordsworth to his family at the close of day. Not infrequently he would telephone Professor Harper that the evening was to be so employed and invite the future biographer of the Poet to join the circle.

A pleasant picture, too, is that of Woodrow Wilson in the White House, as given to the public by Ray Stannard Baker in his life of the War President. Early in his administration President Wilson invited Professor Harper and his family to become his guests, and finding themselves alone in the evening, they gathered about the open fire and enjoyed themselves in the old informal way. Quoting Professor Harper, Mr. Baker admits us to this pleasant scene:

> Mr. Wilson stretched himself out on the hearth-rug and recited poetry, as we had often heard him do. It is no mere coincidence that Wordsworth should have been the favorite poet of Wilson and Sir Edward Grey. He is the poet for statesmen.[6]

A similar scene, although somewhat less complimentary, is given to us by Owen Wister, in his life of Theodore Roosevelt, where he alludes to the late Justice Oliver Wendell Holmes of the Supreme Court. Holmes, it seems, was in the habit of spending his holidays reading poetry to his wife. At one period they took up Wordsworth and decided to read him through, omitting nothing. Several times that dullness of the Poet in his larger stretches wearied them to the point of giving him up, and just then, as the Justice put it to Wister, "The old boy would give a wiggle that connected you with the eternal."

Readers of the *Letters of Walter Hines Page* will recall his devotion to the Sage of Rydal and how he came to

---

[6] From *Woodrow Wilson—Life and Letters,* by Ray Stannard Baker, 1927, 1931, Doubleday, Doran and Company, Inc. Vol. IV, p. 465.

depend upon the steadying quality of his verse during the distracting days of the Great War. The same may be said of Viscount Grey, with whom as Foreign Secretary, Page had so much to do.[7] Speaking of Page, it is instructive to find that, as in the case of so many others, he traced his interest in poetry to the influence of a teacher at College. At Randolph-Macon College, Georgia, he became the favorite pupil of Professor Thomas R. Price, who, as a teacher of Greek, advocated the teaching of English in order that we may better understand the dead languages, thus reversing the usual point of view. With this in mind he would have young Page at his house for tea twice a week, when he would read to him from Shakespeare, Milton, Wordsworth and Tennyson, writers who became the passion of his maturer life.

What Page says of his old teacher reminds one of an even more striking experience of James T. Fields, although this, I must admit, carries us back to a generation as "antiquated" and "hopeless" as the early Victorian. In his *Yesterdays with Authors* Fields relates how, in connection with a foreign trip in 1847, he took pains to call upon the Poet Wordsworth, then living at Rydal Mount, in extreme old age, and how there was a noble tranquillity about the venerable figure that "almost awed one at first into silence." As Fields was about to leave, Wordsworth detained him with the words: "And now I must show you one of my latest presents." "Leading us up to a corner of the room," Fields goes on to say, "we all stood before a beautiful statuette which a young sculptor had just sent him, illustrating a passage from *The Excursion*. Turning to me, Wordsworth asked, 'Do you know the meaning of this figure?' I saw at a glance it was

> A curious child, who dwelt upon a tract
> Of inland ground, applying to his ear
> The convolutions of a smooth-lipped shell, etc.

---

[7] Similarly, Morley says of Gladstone that, in the midst of the cares of state, Wordsworth became one of the inspirers of his life. See *Life of Gladstone*, Macmillan. Edition of 1905, Vol. I, p. 96 and *passim*.

and I quoted the lines." "My recollection of the words,"
continues Mr. Fields, "pleased the old man, and as we
stood there in front of the figure he began to recite the
whole passage from *The Excursion,* and it was very grand
from the Poet's own lips. He repeated some fifty lines."[8]
In another book, *Notes from Fields' Essays,* edited by his
wife, we learn how the distinguished Boston publisher
came by such an intimate knowledge of Wordsworth's
poetry. From the time when, as a little child, he sat in a
"woman's school," in the city of Portsmouth, Wordsworth's poems had been familiar to him. He makes much
of the fact that at the age of five he was taught to read
from the dog-eared school reader

> Oh! what's the matter? what's the matter?
> What is't that ails young Harry Gill?

and

> Oft I had heard of Lucy Gray.

Rather good selections for the purpose in view. And what
a flood of light the incident throws upon the teaching
methods of that early time, 1821! Incidentally we have
here a commentary upon the popularity of Wordsworth
in America in a decade when the Poet was still fighting
for recognition in his own country![9]

While speaking of the use of Wordsworth in the
schools, it is worth recording that the earliest selections of
his poetry were made for educational purposes. So far as
I can learn, the first attempt may be credited to Joseph
Hine, in England in 1831—*Selections from the Poems of
William Wordsworth, Esquire. Chiefly for the Use of
Schools and Young Persons.* Mr. Hine's effort was a
worthy one and he followed a classification of his own,
beginning with poems relating to childhood and ending
*(sic)* with selections from *The Excursion.*

---

[8] *Excursion*, IV, 1132 ff.
[9] In 1835 DeQuincey wrote: "Up to 1820 the name of Wordsworth was trampled
under foot; from 1820 to 1830 it was militant; from 1830 to 1835 it has been
triumphant." Quoted by Thomas Hutchinson.

Having cited so ancient an authority as James T. Fields, I may be pardoned for speaking of the circumstances under which Aubrey De Vere came into a love of Wordsworth which gave him distinction even in the distinguished company of the *Wordsworth Society*. De Vere, in his *Essays Chiefly on Poetry*, tells how he came to his first appreciation through a chance remark to his father. Returning from the university, in the full flush of newly acquired literary enthusiasms, he happened to say, "I suppose every one knows that Byron is the greatest modern poet?" His father answered very gently, *"I do not know it."* "Then who is?" He replied, "I should say Wordsworth." "And, pray, what are his chief merits?" He answered, "I should say, majesty and pathos, as, for instance, in his *Laodamia*." That night in his room young De Vere read *Laodamia*, standing, to the last line, and was captured for life. To quote his own words, "I seemed to have got upon a new and larger planet, with

> An ampler ether, a diviner air,
> And fields invested with purpureal gleams.

One of the most discriminating students of Wordsworth with whom I have become acquainted was the late Dr. Mary Calkins, who, as a disciple of Professor James and head of the Department of Philosophy in Wellesley College, will be gratefully recalled by many. We were near neighbors in Newton, Massachusetts, and met frequently on the street. Rarely would she pass without giving some new impression she had received from the reading of Wordsworth's greater pieces. Once she remarked, "I have come to think that the word which best characterizes Wordsworth's thought is the word *penetration*"— a point of view to which we shall give attention later on. Miss Calkins confessed she was drawn to Wordsworth above others by reason of those books in *The Prelude* which describe the Poet's life at Cambridge, and those others in which he depicted his experiences as a youthful enthusiast in France during the early phases of the French Revolution. I shall not forget the light that came into her face one evening when I read to her the closing lines of the Sixth Book:

> I wanted not that joy, I did not need
> Such help; the ever-living universe,
> Turn where I might, was opening out its glories,
> And the independent spirit of pure youth
> Called forth, at every season, new delights
> Spread round my steps like sunshine o'er green fields.

"How perfectly glorious!" was her exclamation.

Professor David Morton, of Amherst College, whose sonnets are giving pleasure to so many, tells me that a few years ago a test was made as to the impressions received by students entering college from the required reading-course in English. Several thousand Freshmen were asked to name the poet who had appealed to them as the most helpful. The answers were to be handed in anonymously so that no student should be tempted to please his professor rather than express his own judgment. To the surprise of all, by a large majority the preference went not to Shakespeare, Browning, Tennyson or Keats, or even to Whitman, Kipling or Rupert Brooke, but to Wordsworth.

How are we to account for this? Are our boys, distracted by the spirit of revolt, beginning to feel the need of Wordsworth's "healing power"? Can it be that suddenly they have become students of Nature in her subtler meanings and moods? Are they losing interest in the poetry of action in favor of philosophical verse? One would have difficulty in persuading himself that such is the case. My own conjecture is that, as a result of the War, American college men have come to appreciate Wordsworth as *par excellence* the Poet of Patriotism, and of the higher ideals of nationality, and that we shall find a clue to their interest in the contemplative Poet of the Lakes when we come to consider how from a revolutionist in France he came to be a patriot in England. Yet, I am convinced, and as I hope to show later on, a still deeper reason can be found.

Americans visiting Grasmere in recent years must have been impressed by the throngs from all over England and from many foreign lands who seek out *Dove Cottage* as the leading attraction. A few years ago curiosity led me to write to the late Mr. Gordon Wordsworth, the Poet's grandson, who resided at Ambleside, and to whom I have been indebted for many favors, to learn the number of visitors registering at *Dove Cottage* in a single year. In 1911, it was 5,645; in 1923, it was 16,166; and in 1925, 18,496. Undoubtedly later years have raised the record far above twenty thousand. Mr. Wordsworth, as was natural, raised the question as to the depth of interest revealed by these figures. Tourists will be tourists, and all over the world they go where the guidebook tells them to go and usually stay about long enough to read what the guidebook says. But making all due allowance, a somewhat careful observation of the throngs entering that humble dwelling on the shores of Grasmere Lake, where William and Dorothy took up their residence in 1799, where, in 1802, Mary Hutchinson joined them as William's wife, and where the three, in intimate collaboration, produced much of the world's best poetry on Nature and on human life, has revealed a surprising number of appreciative visitors, persons who enter the wainscotted vestibule in a reverent mood, climb thoughtfully the narrow stair, linger in the drawing-room with its tiny fireplace, which Wordsworth once described as "half kitchen and half parlour fire," pause in the diminutive chamber were the Poet slept, and then pass eagerly to the much-besung orchard plot in the rear of the cottage:

> That little nook of mountain ground
> That rocky corner in the lowest stair
> Of that magnificent temple which doth bound
> One side of our whole vale with grandeur rare.

When tourists seek out the caretaker and inquire, "Where is the seat that Coleridge made? Which are the trees that Wordsworth set out? Where is the well by the side of which Dorothy planted the ferns and flowers, and where, do you suppose, was *The Green Linnet* composed?" you realize that there are people, let us believe an increasing number, to whom this is holy ground. Imagine then my combined sensations of pleasure and pain, in visiting the place for the third time, to find a *traffic officer* placed at the opening of the highway that leads to *Dove Cottage,* busily engaged in waving the big touring-cars, the motor-cycles, and especially the huge charabancs to left and right, and that another officer, resplendent in importance, was ensconced at the entrance to the Grasmere church-yard which contains the Poet's grave! We know well what Wordsworth would have said to all this. He has put it in the mouth of the Parson of Ennerdale who, in the opening lines of *The Brothers,* in addressing Jane, his wife, explodes in this fashion:

> These Tourists, heaven preserve us! needs must live
> A profitable life: some glance along,
> Rapid and gay, as if the earth were air,
> And they were butterflies to wheel about
> Long as the summer lasted: some, as wise,
> Perched on the forehead of a jutting crag
> Pencil in hand and book upon the knee,
> Will look and scribble, scribble on and look,
> Until a man might travel twelve stout miles,
> Or reap an acre of his neighbor's corn.
> But, for that moping Son of Idleness,
> Why can he tarry yonder?—In our churchyard
> Is neither epitaph nor monument,
> Tombstone nor name—only the turf we tread
> And a few natural graves.

And yet they tell us Wordsworth was without a sense of humor!

An account of my own experience in becoming interested in Wordsworth may have a certain value to fellow clergymen and also illustrate how the collection of first and rare editions may serve to sharpen one's interest in an author in a way peculiarly its own. It was my custom, when I was a pastor, each year to make a study of the works of some particular poet, with special reference to the religious message he might contain, and then, during Lent, to give my people the benefit of my studies by a series of readings. When in the course of the years I came to Wordsworth I became conscious of such a mighty appeal, and the response of my reading circle was so unmistakable, that I continued the studies into the following year. Feeling that I must have the best possible edition of the Poems, I purchased Professor Knight's eight-volume edition published in 1896. Then followed the *Prose Works* (two volumes), then the *Letters of the Wordsworth Family* (three volumes, edited by Knight), then the *Journals of Dorothy Wordsworth;* and so the stream began to flow, each book suggesting some other that simply *must* be secured.

One day the thought occurred to me that it would not be unreasonable to seek to obtain a first edition of *The Prelude,* as this particular poem, being published after the Poet's death, should be less rare and so, possibly, not beyond my means. In my caution I ventured to write to Mr. Gordon Wordsworth, explaining the circumstances and asking the size of the edition and what he would consider a reasonable price. Back came a personal letter expressing interest and saying, "Don't do anything about it until you hear again from me. My own dealer has a copy and I think the price will be satisfactory to you." Before I could reply there came another letter, stating that he had secured the copy of *The Prelude* and was mailing it to me, and that the price was nine shillings, six pence. The arrival of that faded octavo volume proved to be an event in my life. As for the price, I was amazed. Finding it so low I began to think of seeking early editions of other poems. At any rate, I would be intelligent on the subject and so began to study the bibliographies of Knight and others.

A few years later I was in London, and, as a matter of curiosity, I dropped into a well-known dealer's and inquired if he knew where a "first" of *Lyrical Ballads* could be obtained, explaining that I had no idea of purchasing so rare a book, but it would be an experience to hold a copy in my hands. "Yes," he said, *"I* have a copy," and his daughter went to a room upstairs, and brought it down. That was a thrilling hour I spent noting the sort of volume Wordsworth and Coleridge produced in collaboration when *Tintern Abbey* and the *Rime of the Ancient Mariner* were first given to the world. The book was not much to look at; it was not even preserved in a special container; but as I held the tiny volume in my hand,—"The thoughts that arose in me!" What would it mean to have that historic issue as my very own! To take it down late at night, when the family were in bed and the house was still! To show it to my friends and to quote an authority as saying, "Here is the most important publication in the English language since the appearance of *Paradise Lost!*" "And the price?" I asked, with a tremble in my voice that must have betrayed what an innocent I was. "Forty-seven pounds," was the response. In those days that meant $235, which seemed far beyond my means. Clearly such a rarity was not for the likes o' me. And so I returned the book and left the shop in a chastened mood.

But there was no getting the thought of that treasure out of my mind. *Lyrical Ballads!*—$235! I wonder if I could possibly spare such a sum. And what would my family think?—and *say?* Every collector will understand the sensation. Upon returning to America I wrote Professor Harper that I had located an original copy of *Lyrical Ballads* and that it could be had for forty-seven pounds. What did he think of the price? He replied that it was a bargain, and that if I could spare the money I should lose no time in securing the copy. I cabled that night, and a few weeks later the major contents of my savings-bank account were conveyed to London.[10] The die was cast. The Rubicon was crossed. The balance of my days (and spare cash) were to be spent in filling the gap between the *Lyrical Ballads* of 1798 and *The Prelude* of 1850. Since the second edition of *Lyrical Ballads,* 1800, is nearly as important (and as rare) as the first, on account of the famous preface on Poetical Diction, that, of course, must be secured. And since important changes were made in the third and fourth editions (Coleridge, for instance, modifying the *Ancient Mariner* in significant ways, so that the opportunity is offered to study the stages of progress in the production of one of the world's masterpieces) ; and since the four editions, side by side on a shelf, would look rather good, and constitute what Mr. Wise, the bibliographer, characterizes as "a treasureable possession"; there could be no rest until the series was complete. And then that first American edition of *Lyrical Ballads,* a reprint of the London second edition of 1800; here was the beginning of the Wordsworth vogue in our own country, a literary event of the first importance— that too must be sought and added to the collection. Eventually, of course, the field had to be broadened to include modern editions, anthologies, biography, criticism, autographs, photographs, background material, the Romantic Movement, the Lake District, books of associational interest, poetical tributes, and so forth—all that might be included under the magic term *Wordsworthiana.*

The late Professor George Herbert Palmer, of Harvard, to whom, early in the process, I had occasion to write, replied, "You have admitted a dangerous bee to your bonnet. It will never come out while life lasts, and it will ruin you if it remains." It was a fair warning from one who ought to know. About that time, noting certain

---

[10]A copy of *Lyrical Ballads* brought $1500 at the Kern sale in New York in 1929. In 1932, evidently as a result of the financial depression, a copy was offered for $800. The 1850 edition of *The Prelude* can occasionally be secured today for $10.

anxious comments from the financial genius of the family, I made the agreement that I would spend for the Wordsworth collection only such money as I could earn by writing on my own account. That seemed a reasonable arrangement; and within the family and without it has been accepted as a sufficient "alibi" even in hard times. Certainly it has proved a restricted basis of supplies. Yet— and here I am glad to bear testimony—if a man will limit himself to a single author, become fairly well acquainted with his works, and be willing to bide his time in the matter of bargains turning up, especially those to be found in the catalogues of English dealers, in the course of a few decades he can possess himself of a collection of high literary value for a surprisingly small amount of money. Naturally these remarks have no bearing upon the sort of book-collecting by the multi-millionaires, of which we read in the papers and magazines. Nor is it likely that the multi-millionaires, who often purchase libraries entire, and who, in the nature of the case, cannot have an intimate knowledge of the many authors they assemble upon their shelves, experience half the fun that has come to me in running down in out-of-the-way places volumes which have been on my *desiderata* list for years. For example, there was that day in Winchester, England, when after "doing" the Cathedral and attempting in vain to shed a few tears at the tombs of the Saxon Kings, I wandered into a second-hand book-shop, made up of narrow rooms lined to the very ceiling with the miscellany of many years. It was there on a ladder, with my head against the ceiling, in the midst of an array of inconsequential editions, that I detected a thin, green volume which I recognized at once as the first printing of *The Recluse*—not one of the rarest of Wordsworth treasures, but full of incomparably great poetry, and long needed to round out my collection. When I climbed down and asked the price, the dealer remarked dryly—"Well, considering it is a small affair, you may have it for four shillings." Such experiences, though rare, serve to keep alive the book-lover's flame.[11]

Another thing I want to say is that teachers of English miss a great opportunity when they do not arrange for their students to examine for themselves the first editions so often left idle upon the shelves of the Treasure-Rooms of Public and College Libraries. There is large inspiration in a place like the Rare-Book Room of the New York Public Library, or the Treasure-Rooms of Harvard, Yale and Cornell. Interest in a great poet of the past may be stirred in a number of ways. One is to make a pilgrimage to his home and haunts in our own or in a foreign land. But by far the best way is to read his poems in the order in which they were given to the world and in the very volumes in which they appeared. The closer one can get to the actual process of poetical creation, the stronger will be the sense of reality and the appeal to one's imagination and sympathy. Even to browse in a Treasure-Room of some great library will quicken the poetic pulse. If in such places poets are not occasionally born, they at least will feel the sprouting of their wings.

I have particularly in mind the Alice Freeman Palmer Memorial Library at Wellesley College, where in a beautiful, fire-proof room, Professor George Herbert Palmer, a few years before his death, lovingly stored for all time, humanly speaking, the treasures of English and American literature from Chaucer to the writers of our own day which he had spent a lifetime in collecting. Within those well-lined walls the inspiration is enhanced by the presence at one end of a marble bust of her whose radiant personality enriched the lives of thousands of young women, and at the other end by the presence of a superb portrait of Professor Palmer himself, whose life, so

---

[11]A personal friend upon hearing me relate the above incident, raised a question as to the ethics of the transaction. "Should you not have informed the dealer that the book was far more valuable than he supposed?" I replied that it is a dealer's business to know the value of his stock and not the business of the buyer to inform him; that if he offered the book for four shillings, he probably had acquired it for half that sum, thus making a good profit; that had I been negotiating the sale with some old lady who had produced the volume from her attic, I should have felt obliged to tell her what the book was worth to me.

gloriously prolonged, became a benediction not unlike that of the poets whom he loved and whose works he interpreted with a spiritual understanding unsurpassed in our day. It is in a spot like this that the young student is most likely to realize the beauty and force of those great lines with which Wordsworth closed the fifth book of his *Prelude*:

> He, who in his youth
> A daily wanderer among woods and fields
> With living Nature hath been intimate,
> Not only in that raw unpractised time
> Is stirred to ecstasy, as others are,
> By glittering verse; but further, doth receive,
> In measure only dealt out to himself,
> Knowledge and increase of enduring joy
> From the great Nature that exists in works
> Of mighty Poets. Visionary power
> Attends the motions of the viewless winds,
> Embodied in the mystery of words;
> There, darkness makes abode, and all the host
> Of shadowy things work endless changes,—there,
> As in a mansion like their proper home,
> Even forms and substances are circumfused
> By that transparent veil with light divine,
> And, through the turnings intricate of verse,
> Present themselves as objects recognised,
> In flashes, and with glory not their own.

# CHAPTER II

## "In Common Things That Round Us Lie"

IT IS apparent Wordsworth appeals to many minds and in many ways. Critics, economists, statesmen, jurists, preachers, educators, housewives—men and women, old and young,—such is the range of his poetic material that to each he comes with a vital and personally compelling claim. There is a good deal of truth in the remark of Mill to the effect that Wordsworth is the poet of unpoetical natures. Having this in mind, when my advice is sought as to the best approach to Wordsworth on the part of educated persons, I suggest that they begin by seeking out those poems or passages which have to do with their own special interests or points of view. If they belong in the class of Woodrow Wilson and Justice Holmes, let them begin with the *Patriotic Sonnets*. If, like F. W. Robertson, Stopford Brooke, President A. H. Strong, Dean Inge, and other preachers I could name, they are interested in the philosophy of religion, let them tackle didactic works like *Tintern Abbey* and *The Excursion*. If, with Arnold, Swinburne and Read, they value poetic artistry above the formulation of ideas, let them scan the pages of some anthology like Arnold's own, where poetic expression has been made the basis of selection. Should they belong to the now greatly expanded craft of Mill and Bagehot, they will find some interesting shop-material ready to their hands in certain poems that relate to the oppressive conditions of labor, and in those sections of *The Excursion* which have to do with the effects of the factory system, then in its infancy, as viewed by one whose devotion to Nature did not preclude the hearing "of the still sad music of humanity." The educator, of course,

would turn at once to the poems—a remarkable group—
dealing with childhood and the processes of growth.

But whatever attraction the vocational approach may
have for the interested few, if Wordsworth is to have his
chance we need to find some way of commending him to
the average man. We know it was the ambition of the
poet to make exactly that appeal. The readers he had
most on his heart were not the literati of Oxford, Cambridge and London, but the humble shepherds and dalesmen with whom he lived on terms of daily intimacy, and
whose capacity for appreciating the finer things of life he
rated extremely high, even as the material of their life—
their struggles, their sorrows, their joys, the goings-on
and fellowships of their firesides and farms became his
favorite theme. Next to that he aimed for the great
middle-class of the world of thought. Can he make a
corresponding appeal today?

Fortunately there is one poem so well known and so
great a favorite, and so typical too, that we may use it as
a key to a large body of the Poet's work. When I have
occasion to mention Wordsworth to the man, or more
likely the woman, I meet on the train, or on the piazza
of a summer hotel, I have come to expect an almost uni-
form response: "O yes, he's the old fellow, isn't he, who
wrote about the daffodils?" I have tried it a number of
times and it rarely fails. Very well, why not begin right
there? You have to begin somewhere, and what better
place than the spot where a glimmer of interest already
appears? It is something that one has read *The Daffodils*
—surely one of the most exquisite things Wordsworth
ever wrote. Personally I regard the popularity of this
poem as a rather hopeful sign, and that not only for
Wordsworth but in respect to poetry in general. It shows
that people do like the poetical description of a natural
scene—especially when it has a little preachment at the
end. And it shows that they know real poetry when they

see it. They at least recognize that *The Daffodils* is something more than a pretty thing.

Let us then take a fresh look at the familiar lines, and as we do so consider what is significant in their appeal.

I wandered lonely as a cloud
That floats on high o'er vales and hills,
When all at once I saw a crowd,
A host, of golden daffodils;
Beside the lake, beneath the trees,
Fluttering and dancing in the breeze.

Continuous as the stars that shine
And twinkle on the milky way,
They stretched in never-ending line
Along the margin of a bay:
Ten thousand saw I at a glance,
Tossing their heads in sprightly dance.

The waves beside them danced; but they
Out-did the sparkling waves in glee:
A poet could not but be gay,
In such a jocund company:
I gazed—and gazed—but little thought
What wealth the show to me had brought:

For oft, when on my couch I lie
In vacant or in pensive mood,
They flash upon that inward eye
Which is the bliss of solitude;
And then my heart with pleasure fills,
And dances with the daffodils.

Now why do we like that poem? First of all, because of the vividness and beauty of the scene—the daffodils, the lake, the trees, the waves, the breeze. By a few deft touches Wordsworth makes us see it all. He awakens our imagination. It is as if we were on the spot. The Poet's experience becomes our own. That is always the first great contribution of the poetry of Nature. In this case the effect is enhanced by the abundance of the scene. We have had potted daffodils on our tables, and we welcome them as a sign of spring; we have seen florists fill their windows with the yellow blooms; best of all, we have memories of borders of daffodils in our mother's garden. But here they are growing wild in a golden host. They stretch on and on, beneath the trees, along the shore. They dominate the landscape. Ten thousand is suggested as a good round number. By superb imagery they are compared to the milky-way with its myriads of twinkling stars. The Poet leads us quickly into the spirit of the scene, which is one of exuberant cheerfulness. This is the more effective because of the sharp contrast of the opening line. The Poet found himself in a disconsolate mood, he was a lonely wanderer when this vision of gladness burst upon his sight. It was a case of being "surprised by joy." The impression is conveyed by the presence of color, but more by the sense of motion—the fluttering and dancing of the daffodils as they yield themselves to the play of the breezes that come in from the lake. The whole scene is one of gaiety—flowers and waves in a rivalry of glee. So much for the scene. And now for the reaction. Its joy proves contagious. As the Poet takes it into his heart his mood is changed and he finds himself a part of the happy scene—in spirit he dances with the daffodils. And not only so, but memory is enriched, so that the thing of beauty becomes a joy forever. The experience will perpetuate itself through the years. What the daffodils did for him once they shall do for him again—whenever the mood of loneliness returns. By common consent the closing stanza is the best of the four, and it is interesting to have the Poet acknowledge to a friend that its two best lines:

> They flash upon that inward eye
> Which is the bliss of solitude,

were suggested by Mrs. Wordsworth. Could anything better illustrate the power of this Poet to evoke in others the emotions that stirred his own heart!

I have gone with some particularity into these lines at the cost possibly of marring the impression of the poem as a whole and detracting from the feel of the words, their emotional response, because it is an example of so many others that deal with "the common growth of mother-earth." Why stop with *The Daffodils* when Wordsworth offers us a whole garden of flowers that can make a similar appeal? People should know that with as subtle a fascination he wrote of daisies and primroses, and even of so humble a thing as the pile-wort or lesser celandine; that he has wonderful things to say about trees; that red-breasts, linnets, skylarks, nightingales and cuckoos were among his favorite themes; that butterflies and glow-worms were not beneath his poetic attention; that cataracts and brooks became the obbligato of many a favorite song. For the average reader I doubt if there can be a better introduction than the reading and the re-reading of poems like these.

Of one thing we may be confident,—such an approach would be pleasing to Wordsworth himself. One of the poems in *Lyrical Ballads,* whose beauty escaped the attention of the critics of 1798, but which is universally praised today, has to do with the Poet's conception of his own calling. It is entitled *A Poet's Epitaph.* It represents various people—politician, lawyer, physician, soldier, philosopher, and so forth, visiting a humble poet's grave, each characterized with whimsical humor not unmixed with satire. Finally a poet draws near, and in the picturing of this kindred soul Wordsworth opens wide the door of his own heart. In the midst of a number of quotable lines we find here the clue to the maze of charms by which many a lover of Wordsworth has been led:

> In common things that round us lie
> Some random truths he can impart,—
> The harvest of a quiet eye
> That broods and sleeps on his own heart.

At this point the seasoned Wordsworthian will be interposing an objection. I imagine him saying: "But you are falling into the common error, or at least encouraging it, that Wordsworth was primarily the Poet of Nature, a rôle he explicitly disavowed and which is not sustained by his poetry taken as a whole." True enough. But everything in its time. I am suggesting the best way for beginners to begin. If they think Wordsworth is exclusively or mainly the Poet of Nature, let them think so for a season. It will do them no harm, and it may result some day in their discovering that even more is he the Poet of Man, and of the mind of Man, at that. There is nothing clearer than that Wordsworth started out as a poet of Nature, pure and simple. The first four books of the great autobiographical poem, *The Prelude*, as also the matchless *Lines Composed Above Tintern Abbey*, describe how he was led along from one appreciation of Nature to another until, under her softening and personalizing influence, one day he found himself listening to

> The still, sad music of humanity.

From that it was but a step to the spiritual apprehensions that characterized his later thinking, the

> sense sublime
> Of something far more deeply interfused.

If we are content to wait for the deeper aspects of Wordsworth's message, we may know that, in a sense, we are waiting with Wordsworth himself.

And Wordsworth never outgrew his love for Nature in the minutiæ of her charms. Dorothy in her Journal tells how one day for hours she and her brother lay on their backs under the trees, neither speaking a word, as they watched the flutter of particular leaves on the topmost boughs. In *The Prelude* he speaks of a time

> When every day brought with it some new sense
> Of exquisite regard for common things.[1]

There is an interesting poem, found in nearly all the anthologies, entitled *The Primrose of the Rock*, pecu-

---

[1] *Prelude*, XIV, 261, 2.

liarly pertinent because it was written late in life when, it is claimed by many, his inspiration had departed from him. The poem is devoted to certain lessons suggested by a single primrose which one day he observed clinging to a crag on the highway from Grasmere to Rydal. It opens with these lines:

> A rock there is whose homely front
> The passing traveller slights;
> Yet there the glow-worms hang their lamps,
> Like stars, at various heights;
> And one coy primrose to that rock
> The vernal breeze invites.

I doubt if any other poet would have found such inspiration in a single flower, although this poem may well have suggested to Tennyson his *Flower in the Crannied Wall*, from which also similar lessons are drawn. With Wordsworth nothing was too small, too commonplace, for poetical attention. His poetry, especially his early poetry, abounds in references like the following, embedded in a rather prosy reflective passage, and relating to the foxglove:

> To bend as doth a slender blade of grass
> Tipped with a rain-drop.[2]

And what was true of flowers was true of trees, birds, insects, brooks and all "mute insensate things." The daffodil poem may well serve as an introduction to a score of others in which the brooding heart of the Poet discovers beauty and meaning, in the "common things that round us lie." A "pliant harebell swinging in the breeze," a "violet by a mossy stone half hidden from the eye," a mountain brook suffering the humiliation of being run through a culvert in somebody's back yard, "The little hedgerow birds that peck along the road"; a butterfly "self-poised upon that yellow flower"; a glow-worm beneath a dusky fern, "clear shining like a hermit's taper seen through a

---

[2] *Prelude*, VIII, 398, 9.

thick forest"; "bubbles gliding under ice"—alike awakened in his soul the ardor and the joy of verse.

Any one who will go through the poems of this description with an eye to their bearing upon Wordsworth's attitude toward the small things of sense will, I am convinced, reach at least three conclusions.

Standing in front of all other impressions will be this—here is a poet whose love of Nature was such that it imparted a tender feeling toward every last detail of the world lying at his feet. As we shall consider later, there are other poets of Nature; but for intensity and intimacy of feeling Wordsworth excels them all. In the second stanza of the poem misnamed *Resolution and Independence*, where the Poet is setting the scene for the weird figure of the Leech-gatherer, he flashes upon us a vision like this:

> All things that love the sun are out of doors.[3]

There is a great deal of Wordsworth in that line. And there is even more in a line of *The Prelude* where he alludes to the experience of being pent up in a gloomy house amid the narrow streets of London:

> And all my young affections out of doors.[4]

What a picture it gives us!

With hints like these, one is prepared for that wealth of understanding and sympathy which characterizes so much of the Poet's work when he is dealing with diminutive things. If these are out-of-doors, and capable of enjoying the sun, they are fit subjects for song. One bright day in April the Poet was sitting in his rustic arbor, in the tiny orchard back of Dove Cottage, when a butterfly alighted upon a yellow blossom nearby, and remained there for a considerable space of time—long enough for the observation of those keen eyes, for the sense of com-

---

[3] *Resolution and Independence* (usually known as the *Leech-Gatherer*), line 8. The entire second stanza should be read, as being full of pleasant detail.
[4] *Prelude*, VII, 76.

panionship to be aroused, and for the stirring of tender memories of childhood days. And this was the result:

> I've watched you now a full half-hour,
> Self-poised upon that yellow flower;
> And, little Butterfly! indeed
> I know not if you sleep or feed.
> How motionless!—not frozen seas
> More motionless! and then
> What joy awaits you, when the breeze
> Hath found you out among the trees,
> And calls you forth again!
> This plot of orchard-ground is ours;
> My trees they are, my Sister's flowers;
> Here rest your wings when they are weary;
> Here lodge as in a sanctuary!
> Come often to us, fear no wrong;
> Sit near us on the bough!
> We'll talk of sunshine and of song,
> And summer days, when we were young;
> Sweet childish days, that were as long
> As twenty days are now.

Here we have affection, intimacy, and a feeling of common ownership of earth and sky. There is another butterfly poem, of the same length, written the same spring, expressing the same emotion:

> Stay near me—do not take thy flight!

but more detailed in the recollection of the days when he and his sister found delight in chasing butterflies from flower to flower, and when she—girl-like—proved far more tender in her love:

> A very hunter did I rush
> Upon the prey;—with leaps and springs
> I followed on from brake to brush;
> But she, God love her! feared to brush
> The dust from off its wings.[5]

For those who seem to think that Wordsworth's sun rose and set in *The Daffodils*, I commend the reading of

---

[5] *To a Butterfly.*

the three poems on the daisy, having in mind that the English daisy is far less showy and popular than our American variety. It reveals the fertility of his genius that all three of these poems were composed in the year 1802. It is difficult to choose between them. The one beginning "In youth from rock to rock I went" carries a tincture of autobiography and is suggestive of tenderness and intimacy in such expressions as "sweet Daisy," "The Poet's darling." In this poem, too, are the lines

> The homely sympathy that heeds
> The common life our nature breeds.

Throughout there is a suggestion of Burns, who, in his well-known *To a Mountain Daisy* had already immortalized this flower, as had Chaucer long before him. The poem beginning "Bright flower, whose home is everywhere," is one of Wordsworth's gems, especially if printed without the last stanza, and is pertinent as suggesting a companionship of feeling between the daisy and the observing Poet:

> Methinks that there abides in thee
> Some concord with humanity,
> Given to no other flower I see
> The forest thorough!

In the third poem, *To the Same Flower*, appreciation of the at-hand things of daily life finds expression in the lines:

> Thou unassuming Common-place
> Of Nature, with that homely face,
> And yet with something of a grace
> Which love makes for thee!

It is in this poem that the Poet reveals his affection by an extraordinary use of similes, the Daisy being likened in turn to "A nun demure of lowly port," "Or sprightly maiden of Love's court," "A queen in crown of rubies drest," "A starveling in a scanty vest," "A little Cyclops with one eye," "A silver shield with boss of gold," "Yet like a star, with glittering crest"—a literary *tour de force* which one forgives without effort as conveying a tenderness that can be playful as well as deep.

For Wordsworth's appreciation of trees, one should read *When to the Attractions of the Busy World*, which refers to the grove of firs near Dove Cottage to which Wordsworth's brother John, who was lost at sea, loved to resort, and which was known in the family as "John's Grove." But above all read the poem entitled *The Yew Trees*, written in 1803, in which the Poet celebrates the famous yews of Borrowdale:

> . . . those fraternal Four of Borrowdale,
> Joined in one solemn and capacious grove;
> Huge trunks! and each particular trunk a growth
> Of inter-twisted fibres serpentine
> Up-coiling and inveterately convolved.

The poem throughout is rich in the suggestion of intimacy and understanding, but even more of Wordsworth's power to convey the magic atmosphere of secluded and eerie spots. Ruskin spoke of *The Yew Trees* as "the most vigorous and solemn bit of forest landscape ever painted."[6] Nor was this love of trees confined to a few like the fir and yew. In a single book of *The Excursion* (VII) we find references of realistic charm to elms, oaks, sycamores, mountain ash, fir, cedar—a veritable arboretum in verse.

For Wordsworth's love of birds there is a wide range of choice, but for the purpose in view, as indeed for pure artistry of form, *The Green Linnet* outshines them all. The opening stanza is idyllic in its picturing of the Poet seated in his orchard in the companionship of the birds and the blossoms which he loved.

> Beneath these fruit-tree boughs that shed
> Their snow-white blossoms on my head,
> With brightest sunshine round me spread
> Of spring's unclouded weather,

---

[6] *Modern Painters*, Part III, Sec. II.

> In this sequestered nook how sweet
> To sit upon my orchard-seat!
> And birds and flowers once more to greet,
>     My last year's friends together.

To this, one may well add those lines from the poem beginning, "I heard a thousand blended notes:"

> The birds around me hopped and played,
> Their thoughts I cannot measure:—
> But the least motion which they made,
> It seemed a thrill of pleasure—

And on no account should one miss *The Sparrow's Nest,* in which, in lovely simplicity, is set forth the Poet's childhood delight in everything pertaining to bird-life, together with his often quoted tribute to his sister in whose company the nest of the sparrow, with its "bright blue eggs together laid" had been visited with reverent timidity:

> The Blessing of my later years
> Was with me when a boy:
> She gave me eyes, she gave me ears;
> And humble cares, and delicate fears;
> A heart, the fountain of sweet tears;
>     And love, and thought, and joy.

It has been said of the poet William Browne that "pleasing cadences came to him in full measure from moorland rills." What the rills of Devon were to this too-little-known poet of Nature in far-off Elizabethan days, the brooks of Westmoreland and Cumberland were to Wordsworth. And even more—if we may take literally his favorite characterization of the Poet:

> He murmurs near the running brooks
> A music sweeter than their own.[7]

Certainly Wordsworth's association with the brooks and rivers of his native country must be regarded as one of the leading inspirations of his life.

---

[7] *A Poet's Epitaph.*

One of the *Miscellaneous Sonnets* begins with the address: "Brook! whose society the Poet seeks."[a] The three Yarrow poems will occur to any one at all familiar with Wordsworth, but for the sense of intimacy there is no poem like the first in the series *Poems on the Naming of Places*, the one beginning: "It was an April morning: fresh and clear."

> Up the brook
> I roamed in the confusion of my heart,
> Alive to all things and forgetting all.
> At length I to a sudden turning came
> In the continuous glen, where down a rock
> The stream, so ardent in its course before,
> Sent forth such sallies of glad sound, that all
> Which I till then had heard appeared the voice
> Of common pleasure: beast and bird, the lamb,
> The shepherd's dog, the linnet and the thrush,
> Vied with this waterfall, and made a song
> Which, while I listened, seemed like the wild growth
> Or like some natural produce of the air,
> That could not cease to be.

A worthy companion piece to this is the twenty-sixth sonnet in the *River Duddon* series:

> Return, Content! for fondly I pursued,
> Even when a child, the Streams—unheard, unseen;
> Through tangled woods, impending rocks between;
> Or, free as air, with flying inquest viewed
> The sullen reservoirs whence their bold brood—
> Pure as the morning, fretful, boisterous, keen,
> Green as the salt-sea billows, white and green—
> Poured down the hills, a choral multitude!
> Nor have I tracked their course for scanty gains;
> They taught me random cares and truant joys,
> That shield from mischief and preserve from stains
> Vague minds, while men are growing out of boys;
> Maturer Fancy owes to their rough noise
> Impetuous thoughts that brook not servile reins.

The second impression, I think, will be that of accuracy of observation and representation in respect to everything

---

[a] *Miscellaneous Sonnets*, Part II, XXXI.

pertaining to the natural scene. Here we have something close to the scientific spirit of our own age, a habit of mind which should commend Wordsworth to those who feel that the search for truth must begin with the things beneath their feet. If we use the word in the ordinary sense, Wordsworth was no scientist. In *The Excursion* he prays to be saved from the condition of being

Lost in a gloom of uninspired research.

There comes to mind also the oft-quoted characterization:

One that would peep and botanize
Upon his mother's grave.

Yet he was a scientist in the deeper significance of the word. His passion was for reality, for truth in both the inward and outward parts. He was a naturalist as well as a Poet of Nature. Addicted to flights of fancy and imagination, he never allowed these to warp the hard facts of sense. Wordsworth's earth was a good solid earth, his sky was a real sky, his trees were actual trees growing in the vales. When a certain painter was introducing a tree into his landscape and was asked what tree, he replied, "Oh, just the ordinary tree." To Wordsworth that would not have been a tree at all.

Wordsworth's knowledge of the natural world was accurate and full, and here he may be contrasted favorably with certain other poets. Goethe, with all his zeal for science and the natural order, appears to have had slight knowledge of the details upon which true science is built. Eckermann, in his *Conversations* indicates that the supposedly omniscient Goethe was a child in some fields of knowledge. One day Goethe asked Eckermann if the yellow-hammers and sparrows in the hedge were larks. To Eckermann, who was a good deal of an ornithologist, this was truly shocking. Wordsworth and the German biographer would have been good companions on a walk. An interesting book has been written by the English ornithologist, Wintringham, entitled *The Birds of Words-worth,* in which he deals with fifty-one species of birds which are described or mentioned in the poems, some of them many times. The author bears witness to the particu-larity and fidelity of the Poet in every one of these references. Viscount Grey, whose love for birds was well known, and who throughout his life was a close observer of bird-life on his estate at Falloden in the North of England, speaks of the nightingale and compares Keats's Ode and Wordsworth's poem on this universal favorite among English songsters. The famous Ode of the younger poet, Grey points out, "touches heights of poetry that the lines of Wordsworth do not attempt." Yet he finds in Wordsworth's lines "the authentic nightingale." John Burroughs, in his impressions of the English countryside, analyzes the effect of the nightingale's song and finds it perfectly expressed in the lines:

> These notes of thine—they pierce and pierce;
> Tumultuous harmony and fierce.

So far as I know, Wordsworth has never been caught in a careless or inaccurate description. Some one was bold enough to challenge the line in *The Prelude* in which he alludes to the enlarged appearance of sheep when seen through a screen of mist. It happens that my friend, Mr. Charles E. Walmsley, of Ambleside, who knows the Lake District by heart, has sent me a confirmation of this very line. In speaking of a recent walk he had taken through the Kirkstone Pass, and of the strange effect produced by the mountain mist, he says: "The mist called up from the depth of memory a scene from my boyhood when my father, near this same summit, on a misty day, let me peep through a hog-hole (the hole in a wall between two fields or from the road leading to a field so that the shepherd may not have recourse to the gates). Over the opening a large slab of stone stands. As I peeped through the hole, I saw in a depression of the adjoining field a shepherd with his sheep. They were grotesquely exaggerated by the mist, and ever since then I have entered into the spirit of Wordsworth's description of such a scene in *The Prelude*,

His sheep like Greenland bears."

In the famous preface to the 1800 edition of *Lyrical Ballads*, Wordsworth states that it was his habit to write "with his eye on the object," and the evidence for this is found in a thousand deft touches of delineation scattered through his verse. In no place is it more apparent than when he is dealing with the subtler facts and charms of natural phenomena—those that the average eye fails to detect. As Morley brings out in his admirable essay, when Wordsworth describes the daisy casting the beauty of its star-shaped shadow on the smooth stone, or the boundless depth of the abysses of the sky, or the clouds made vivid as fire by the rays of light, every touch is true; not the copying of a literary phrase, but the result of direct observation.

In no way does Wordsworth show more fineness of perception than in the sense of sound. To appreciate this, we need to see him not only sitting in his orchard plot, listening to the twittering of birds and the hum of bees, but also reclining by some woodland stream or mountain beck, catching the faintest murmur and allowing the music to sink into his soul. Apparently no voice of Nature escaped those preternatural ears. It was more than the exercise of a talent. There were times when the penetrating of the intricate labyrinth of sound became a passionate desire. This is well exampled in a passage from *The Prelude* relating to school-time habits of thought:

For I would walk alone,
Under the quiet stars, and at that time
Have felt whate'er there is of power in sound
To breathe an elevated mood, by form
Or image unprofaned; and I would stand,
If the night blackened with a coming storm,

> Beneath some rock, listening to notes that are
> The ghostly language of the ancient earth,
> Or make their dim abode in distant winds.[9]

In a still earlier passage he speaks of the echo from the hills across the frozen lake in winter; and any one who in boyhood has listened at night to the crash and roar of a field of ice expanding under intense cold, will appreciate his reference to his skating experience during his school-days at Hawkshead:

> From under Esthwaite's splitting fields of ice
> The pent-up air, struggling to free itself,
> Gave out to meadow-grounds and hills a loud
> Protracted yelling, like the noise of wolves
> Howling in troops along the Bothnic Main.[10]

There is a poem on *The Power of Sound* which contains many good lines, but it is too particularistic and encyclopedic to warrant classification with the greater pieces. One gains a finer appreciation from incidental references scattered through the nature poems. Here are a few examples:

> Ye brooks
> Muttering along the stones, a busy noise
> By day, a quiet sound in silent night.[11]

> No sound is uttered,—but a deep
> And solemn harmony pervades
> The hollow vale from steep to steep,
> And penetrates the glades.[12]

> Now here, now there, an acorn, from its cup
> Dislodged, through seer leaves rustled, or at once
> To the bare earth dropped with a startling sound.[13]

> And the bleak music from that old stone wall.[14]

> Where music dwells
> Lingering—and wandering on as loth to die.[15]

---

[9] *Prelude*, II, 302-310.
[10] *Ibid.*, I, 539-543.
[11] *Ibid.*, XII, 18-20.
[12] *Evening of Extraordinary Splendour.*
[13] *Prelude*, I, 83 f.
[14] *Ibid.*, XII, 319.
[15] Sonnet: *Inside of King's College Chapel.* The reference is to the effect of organ music in a Gothic church.

Most exquisite of all is the reference to the songbirds in the thickets of Grasmere Valley in contrast with the "lordly birds" which send down voices from the sky:

> And thickets full of songsters, and the voice
> Of lordly birds, an unexpected sound
> Heard now and then from morn to latest eve,
> Admonishing the man who walks below
> Of solitude and silence in the sky.[16]

These last lines were greatly admired by Pater.

In all these exactitudes of sight and sound it is to be remembered that Wordsworth, throughout a large part of his career, depended in no small measure upon his sister Dorothy, whose senses were as keen as her heart was true. Of them both Professor Harper has well said: "The depth of their feelings can be measured by the truth of their perceptions. The precision of their expressions was due to the intensity of their experience, and this was intense because it was simple.[17]

To all this devotion to the details of the natural scene we are to add Wordsworth's sense of the orderliness of the universe, of the reign of universal law, his unwillingness (reluctantly achieved) to admit of any arbitrary intervention. This is of the essence of the scientific mind. It is my conviction that were he living today, the writer of the *Ecclesiastical Sonnets* would find himself at home in the laboratories of Oxford, Harvard or Johns Hopkins. And, if more is needed to reveal his identity with the modern world, I venture to think that in the whirl of electrons Wordsworth would be discovering not the evidence of chance, but

> Authentic tidings of invisible things;
> Of ebb and flow, and ever-during power;
> And central peace, subsisting at the heart
> Of endless agitation.[18]

---

[16] *The Recluse.*
[17] *William Wordsworth,* one volume edition, Scribners, p. 367.
[18] *Excursion,* IV, 1144-1147.

Those who charge Wordsworth with being essentially out-of-step with the progress of science, overlook a striking passage in his *Preface* to *Lyrical Ballads,* in which he links the poet and the scientist as joint-partners in the search for truth. His words should be familiar to all readers of his poetry.

> Poetry is the first and last of all knowledge—it is as immortal as the heart of man. If the labours of men of science should ever create any material revolution, direct or indirect, in our conditions, and in the impressions which we habitually receive, the poet will sleep then no more than at present; he will be ready to follow the steps of the man of science, not only in those general indirect effects, but he will be at his side, carrying sensation into the midst of the objects of the science itself. The remotest discoveries of the chemist, the botanist, or mineralogist will be as proper objects of the poet's art as any upon which it can be employed. . . . If the time should ever come when what is now called science, thus familiarized to men, shall be ready to put on, as it were, a form of flesh and blood, the poet will lend his divine spirit to aid the transfiguration, and will welcome the being thus produced as a dear and genuine inmate of the household of man.

When we recall that this was written in 1800, it must appear as one of the most forward-looking utterances of literature. It marks Wordsworth as both broad-minded and prophetic in his outlook upon the world of knowledge. We may congratulate ourselves if, after all these years, we even approximate his conception of poetry and science walking hand in hand.[19]

Along with the impressions I have mentioned will come a third, which needs only a passing reference, as it will recur in later chapters, especially those dealing with Nature in her grander forms and with the meaning of Nature as a whole. I refer to the fact that with Wordsworth each object—no matter how obscure—opens on to illimitable depths of meaning. Nature everywhere is glowing and alive. He could speak of *"splendour* in the

---

[19] In contrast with Wordsworth, Keats held that the inevitable advance of science would be the death of poetry. See: *Science and Poetry,* by the distinguished critic, I. A. Richards, p. 8.

grass, of *glory* in the flower." If more than others he dealt with the commonplace of the external world, it was because at every point the veil of the commonplace had been pierced, because his was the rare gift of transfiguring the simple experience, the simple scene and turning it toward a larger and higher, because an infinite significance. Everywhere you get the impression that more is than seems.

The *River Duddon Sonnets,* which describe the course of one of the Poet's favorite streams, are of unequal merit, but the closing number, entitled *Afterthought,* is one of the noblest things that fell from his pen, finely suggestive of the larger meaning of Nature's common sights and sounds.

> I thought of Thee, my partner and my guide,
> As being past away.—Vain sympathies!
> For, backward, Duddon! as I cast my eyes,
> I see what was, and is, and will abide;
> Still glides the Stream, and shall forever glide;
> The Form remains, the Function never dies;
> While we, the brave, the mighty and the wise,
> We Men, who in our morn of youth defied
> The elements, must vanish;—be it so!
> Enough, if something from our hands have power
> To live, and act, and serve the future hour;
> And if, as toward the silent tomb we go,
> Through love, through hope, and faith's transcendent dower,
> We feel that we are greater than we know.

Of even deeper reach are the familiar lines with which the Poet brought to a close the greatest of his odes:

> To me the meanest flower that blows can give
> Thoughts that do often lie too deep for tears.

# CHAPTER III

# "Of All the Mighty World of Eye and Ear"

TO A larger degree than is true of any other English poet, Wordsworth is the exponent of a particular locality. Throughout his life he bore the stamp of the district in which he was born and in which he spent by far the larger part of his poetical career. And upon that district he placed an indelible stamp. One of the surest signs of his immortality is the fact that quite generally, on both sides of the Atlantic, the English Lake District is spoken of as "The Wordsworth Country." A well-known book has been written entitled *Wordsworthshire* in which the author deals with the lake country as the scene of the majority of Wordsworth's poems, and as bearing today the impress of his genius.[1] So intimate has the association become that when some event in the district, like the building of a bridge or the opening of a road, or more often the threatened encroachment of some commercial enterprise, gets into the newspapers the reporter without fail will work in some reference to what the Poet Wordsworth had to say about the spot in question. In every edition of the complete works since 1815, the first poem is the one beginning "Dear native regions," this being an extract from a much larger piece composed in anticipation of leaving school at Hawkshead, when the Poet was sixteen years of age. *Dear Native Regions* occupies its place of honor by the Poet's own choice; and how much of sentiment is carried by the opening line is indicated by the fact that years after, in composing *The Prelude,* he recurred to the phrase and its biographical suggestion in a passage beginning:

[1] *Wordsworthshire,* by Rev. Eric Robertson, for many years rector of St. John's at Ambleside. A better known book is that of Rev. H. D. Rawnsley, of Keswick, *Literary Associations of the English Lakes,* in which Wordsworth occupies the leading place.

Dear native regions, wheresoe'er shall close
My mortal course, there will I think on you;
Dying, will cast on you a backward look.[2]

Of no other poet can it be said that to the same extent
a locality becomes the key to interest and understanding.
For this reason to know Wordsworth at all intimately it
is necessary to visit the Wordsworth country, a privilege
which, as we have seen, is being enjoyed by Americans and
others in a steadily increasing stream. From many points
of view the reward is great, since for variety and charm,
combined with compactness and accessibility, possibly no
other scenic area equals that of the English Lakes. It is
indeed

A universe of Nature's fairest forms.[3]

For the American or Canadian who cannot cross the
ocean, the best comparison, possibly, is the Adirondack
wilderness in the northeastern section of New York State.
Here the combination of lakes and mountains, conjoined
with richness of vegetation, are pleasantly suggestive of
the English district. Lake Champlain, with the wide views
made possible by its location between the Green Mountains on the east and the Adirondacks on the west, surpasses Windermere in grandeur, as it does in length; but
must yield when it comes to grace and charm in the nearer
view. Lake George, considered by some the most beautiful body of water in the United States, is scarcely equalled
by Ullswater which it closely resembles in form; but few
would claim that it makes the same poetic appeal. Lake
Placid may best be likened to Derwentwater, the queen of
all the English Lakes, with Whiteface standing at the
head of the one and Skiddaw at the foot of the other. The
mountain peaks of the Adirondacks average considerably
higher than those of the English district; but, on account
of the greater elevation of the valleys, this superiority is
not as important as would appear. In the case of the

---

[2] *Prelude*, VIII, 468 ff.
[3] *Ibid.*, IV, 8.

Adirondacks, as with the White Mountains of New Hampshire, the extensive forests of evergreens and deciduous trees, with their dense and varied undergrowth, must be considered an unrivalled attraction, since in England the mountain forests have long since yielded to a covering of turf, reaching in many cases to the very summit of the peaks. Even Wordsworth regretted the passing of timber forests in a country where he sang the praise of many a tree. Of New England generally it may be said that it possesses a certain advantage over the mother country by reason of its many varieties of trees. Whereas England has but one kind of oak, we have sixteen. This perhaps is a fair offset to England's wonderful turf and the impression of greenness received in nearly every section and nowhere more than in the northwest corner.

Historically the English region has the advantage of reaching back to Roman days, and of possessing those fascinating place-names and topographical terms which reflect the Norse settlements of a thousand years ago.[*] But the Adirondacks have a fair offset in associations connected with the struggle between France and England for possession of the New World during the middle of the eighteenth century, with its romantic warfare of Indian tribes, so effectively presented by Parkman and Cooper.

In two respects the English district has an advantage all its own. I refer to the picturesqueness of its human habitations, and to the literary associations of the Lakes. The diminutive cottages of mountain stone, with their rough slate roofs, and their rounded chimney-tops, scattered here and there through the vales or snuggled against some friendly slope, belong to the English lakeland almost as much as do the trees and shrubs. Here Nature

---

[*]One has in mind such names as Windermere, Patterdale, Gowbarrow, Helvellyn, Silverhow, Langdale, Glen-redding, Ladore, and such terms as force, beck, tarn, fells, nabs, pikes, ghyll, scar, hawes, etc. Some of these are being adopted by Americans for their own nomenclature, and always with the idea of imparting a certain romantic flavor and charm.

has not been desecrated by the hand of man, as is so often the case in the American countryside.

> Well may'st thou halt—and gaze with brightening eye!
> The lovely cottage in the guardian nook
> Hath stirred thee deeply; with its own dear brook,
> Its own small pasture, almost its own sky![5]

The same may be said of the walls of rustic stone which separate the pastures, running hither and yon over the mountains in such delightful irregularity and framing many a pleasant picture of cattle and sheep. Even Robert Frost, with his charming characterizations of the old farms of Vermont, can offer nothing like this. It is interesting to note that Woodrow Wilson, upon writing to his wife at the time of his first visit to the Lake District in 1896, dwelt upon the charm of the dwellings rather than upon the literary associations.

> One who knows nothing of the memories and the poems associated with these places might well bless the fortune that brought him to a region so complete, so various, so romantic, so irresistible in its beauty, where the very houses seem suggested by Nature and built to add to her charm.[6]

In the matter of literary associations, it is doubtful if any district of approximate size, in the old world or the new, can compare with the English Lakes. The term "Lake Poets" may no longer be regarded as sufficiently accurate for the use of careful writers, but merely to name such authors as Wordsworth, Southey, the Coleridges (father and son), DeQuincey, Christopher North, Ruskin, Dr. Arnold, and Harriet Martineau, is to lay upon this region a distinction as alluring as it is unique.

In this chapter I want the reader to think of Wordsworth as an interpreter of the larger aspects of Nature, "the mighty world of eye and ear," in distinction from the smaller things—Nature's commonplace, which have

---

[5] *Admonition*, in *Miscellaneous Sonnets*.
[6] *Woodrow Wilson—Life and Letters*, by Ray Stannard Baker, Doubleday, Doran and Company, 1927, 1931. Vol. IV, p. 465.

been occupying our attention. This, for the region under survey, means lakes, mountains and skies. What has Wordsworth to say about these?

Very little, so far as particular lakes are concerned. In the poems they are taken for granted rather than described. There are references enough to this or that detail of lake scenery—the daffodils of Ullswater, the single green island of Grasmere, the crumbling ruins of the hermitage on St. Herbert's Island of Derwentwater, the evolutions of a flock of water-fowl over the surface of Rydal Mere, the path around the meandering shores of Esthwaite—but of the lakes as lakes he has little to say. And in this he is thoroughly true to his art, since the poet, as also the painter, prefers bits of scenery or aspects of view, rather than totality of impression. Fortunately, Wordsworth once consented to write a guidebook to the Lake Country and in this may be found a treatment of Windermere, Conniston, Wastwater, Ullswater and all the rest, which is as authentic as it is discriminating and original. The student of Wordsworth should not miss this superb piece of prose.[7]

In one respect, however, the Poet has opened his heart and given us an interpretation of the Lakes as a whole. To him, apparently, these bodies of clear, fresh water, nestling among the hills, found their highest meaning as reflectors of the glory of mountain, wood and sky. In the *Guide* he makes much of the value of the inverted image of a landscape as mirrored in the tarns, especially at sunset, or under conditions where the blaze of light is softened and the "surface of the lake will reflect before the eye correspondent colours through every variety of beauty, and through all degrees of splendour." Wordsworth argued that it is much more desirable that lakes

---

[7] *A Guide Through the District of the Lakes in the North of England,* fifth and final edition in 1835. The *Guide* has recently been republished, with valuable introduction and notes, by *Prof.* de Selincourt, London, 1926. It may also be found in the *Prose Works.* The *Guide,* during Wordsworth's life, had a large circulation, being popular with tourists. The tale is told of how one day Wordsworth met a tourist who asked him if he had written anything else besides *"The Guide to the Lakes."* Humbly enough Wordsworth replied, "Yes, I have written some verses also."

should be numerous and small than fewer and larger. He preferred the diminutive mountain tarns of Cumberland to the extensive lakes of Scotland and Switzerland as affording greater variety and a recurrence of the reflected glory of the hills.[8] And in this he appears to have the consent of our modern landscape architects, who have nothing better (lacking the real thing) than to introduce a small body of water which shall mirror a graceful tower or well-composed clump of trees, as visitors to the Bok Tower in Florida and the Lincoln Monument in Washington will recall with satisfaction. Long before this the builders of India sought the same effect by a basin of water reflecting the incomparable Taj Mahal. What the architect has especially in mind is the effect of increased depth produced by the duplicated scene. To Wordsworth the advantage arises rather from the inversion of the image, the softening of the impression of color and form, the blending of lights and shades, these combining to produce a mystic effect which acts powerfully upon the imagination. And always you will find a resultant mood of quietness or exultation expressed. Possibly the best illustration is from *There Was a Boy*. In this exquisite bit of work, written in 1798, a schoolboy friend of the Poet is pictured as standing by the lake at night mimicking the hootings of an owl, and in moments of silence receiving solemn impressions.

> The visible scene
> Would enter unawares into his mind
> With all its solemn imagery, its rocks,
> Its woods, and that uncertain heaven received
> Into the bosom of the steady lake.[9]

These lines were greatly admired by Coleridge, who in

---

[8] In *Our Old Home*, where Hawthorne gives his impressions of the Lake District, he complains (good naturedly) that when he came to *Rydal Water*, the surface was ruffled by a breeze, and he remarks: "Now the best thing these small ponds can do is to keep perfectly calm and smooth, and not attempt to show off any airs of their own, but content themselves with serving as a mirror for whatever of beautiful or picturesque there can be in the scenery around them."

[9] For a more detailed description of a mountain landscape mirrored in a lake, see the passage in the *Recluse* beginning:
"How vast the compass of this theatre."

his *Biographia Literaria* remarked, "Had I met these lines running wild in the deserts of Arabia, I should have instantly screamed out 'Wordsworth.'"

In the second book of *The Prelude* there is a picture of the Hawkshead schoolboys having an uproarious time on a picnic by the shore of Windermere and of the impressions the young Wordsworth received as, quieting down, they rowed home in the late afternoon:

> But, ere nightfall,
> When in our pinnace we returned at leisure
> Over the shadowy lake, and to the beach
> Of some small island steered our course with one,
> The Minstrel of the Troop, and left him there,
> And rowed off gently, while he blew his flute
> Alone upon the rock—oh, then, the calm
> And dead still water lay upon my mind
> Even with a weight of pleasure, and the sky,
> Never before so beautiful, sank down
> Into my heart, and held me like a dream![10]

Probably most of us have come to realize with Wordsworth that the value of all sights and sounds is enhanced on the bosom of a still lake at night, that

> Waters on a starry night
> Are beautiful and fair.

Possibly we have yet to learn that such impressions sink deepest when we are alone. To how many of us has there come an experience of a scene like this:

> There sometimes does a leaping fish
> Send through the tarn a lonely cheer;
> The crags repeat the raven's croak
> In symphony austere;
> Thither the rainbow comes, the cloud,
> And mists that spread the flying shroud,
> And sunbeams, and the sounding blast.[11]

It was Byron who remarked that Wordsworth had taught him how to look at a mountain. Well, how *should*

---

[10]*Prelude*, II, 164 ff.
[11]*Fidelity*.

we look at a mountain? Just what may Byron have had in mind? It will be no slight task to learn the Wordsworth way. There will need be a careful reading of the *Guide* (as instructive today as when it was written) and a searching of the longer poems like *The Recluse, The Prelude, The Waggoner,* and *The Excursion.*

Perhaps the first impression one receives is that Wordsworth is more interested in the details of mountain scenery—in modern parlance "the close-up" view—than he is in the distant and general effects. For theatrical effects he has small regard. We find him dwelling lovingly upon the mountain brook, the tiny waterfall or cataract. In the *Guide* he contends it is a mistake to suppose that waterfalls are scarcely worth being looked at except after much rain, "that the more swollen the stream, the more fortunate the spectator," and his argument here is a revelation of his sense of the subtle charm of rocks, herbs and flowers as they "glisten with moisture diffused by the breath of the precipitous water." Mosses, ferns and lichens (the "foliage of the rocks") were Wordsworth's delight. A characteristic bit of description is this:

> And the mountains over all, embracing all,
> And all the landscape endlessly enriched
> With waters running, falling or asleep.[12]

Wordsworth's sense of color led him to an appreciation of the beauty in things too often passed by in our rambles, as when in the *Guide* he speaks of "that mellow tone and variety of hues by which mountain turf is distinguished." And even when he deals, as of course he often must, with pikes and sharp declivities, his interest appears to be less in the bold and terrible than in the softened and quietly beautiful outlines of the crags.

Nevertheless, mountains are mountains, and we are more interested in what the Poet has to say of them in the mass. He considers it of the first importance that we

---

[12]*Prelude,* VIII, 95 ff.

should study a group of mountains as a system before we attempt to know them as separate peaks. For this purpose he urges the ascent of a central peak from which something like a bird's-eye view can be obtained. For the Lake District he suggests Great Gable or Scafell, with a subsequent climb of Helvellyn. In the *Guide,* he takes us in imagination to the top of these peaks, and, beginning with Windermere, shows how eight valleys diverge from the point on which we are supposed to stand, "like the spokes from the nave of a wheel."

In this connection one recalls the fine treatment of the sensation of looking off into unmeasured space in every direction from a mountain-top—the sensation of height and distance—in Wordsworth's poem *To ——, Her First Ascent of Helvellyn:*

> Lo! the dwindled woods and meadows;
> What a vast abyss is there!
> Lo! the clouds, the solemn shadows,
> And the glistenings—heavenly fair!
>
> And a record of commotion
> Which a thousand ridges yield;
> Ridge, and gulf, and distant ocean
> Gleaming like a silver shield.[13]

Having a good general view of the district, Wordsworth would have us familiarize ourselves with the leading valleys by rambles starting at the outer rim of his wheel and working toward the center, thus following the course of the streams to their source and passing from the tamer to the wilder scenes. Each valley has its distinct and separate character, and each needs to be surveyed in varying lights and shades and from points of vantage, found here and there among the foot-hills, at the bend of a stream, or in the bay of a lake. He loves to point these

---

[13]For a more detailed treatment of a mountain view, see the poem, *View from the Top of Black Comb,* said to be the most extensive prospect in England. And by no means should the reader miss the opening lines of the last book of *The Prelude,* in which we have that magnificent description of a view from the summit of Snowden at night, above the mists and under the full light of the moon. It is too long for quotation here.

out, and is eager that no visitor to the region shall miss the prospects which were dear to his own eyes. He would have you look at a mountain again and again, taking pains to revisit each favorite site, since the view is never twice the same. And he is even bold enough to hope that you will visit his beloved vales at different seasons of the year. Tourists, as a rule, he tells us, choose the worst season of all, mid-summer, when the rains are most frequent and when Nature offers fewer of her subtle charms. To him the finest of the seasons is autumn, with winter and spring following close behind.

We owe it to Wordsworth, possibly more than to any other nature-writer, that we have come to appreciate the effect of haze, mists, clouds and night as the most beautiful aspect of mountain scenery. He tells us how, in early youth, Nature revealed her soul to him

> . . . in lights and shades
> That marched and countermarched about the hills
> In glorious apparition.[14]

And to the end of his days, if we may judge from the fact that his poem *To the Clouds* was not published until 1842, he found in the phenomena of the sky in their relation to mountain scenery the source of some of his greatest inspirations. In the *Guide* are a number of references to the effect of clouds as they cling to the mountain peaks as by some loving affinity, an effect to which the English region, the true "cloud-land" of the world, is peculiarly susceptible, but which will be appreciated also by all who have tarried in the moist valleys of the White Mountains or the Adirondacks, or, in fact, in any part of the Appalachian system. Here, Wordsworth admits, one finds large compensation for being compelled to visit the Lakes in mid-summer.

Days of unsettled weather, with partial showers, are very frequent; but the showers, darkening or brightening, as they

---

[14] *Prelude*, XII, 96 ff.

fly from hill to hill, are not less grateful to the eye than finely interwoven passages of gay and sad music are touching to the ear. Vapours exhaling from the lakes and meadows after sunrise, in a hot season, or, in moist weather, brooding upon the heights, or descending towards the valleys with inaudible motion, give a visionary character to everything around them. . . . Akin to these are fleecy clouds resting upon the hill-tops; they are not easily managed in picture, with their accompaniments of blue sky; but how glorious are they in Nature! how pregnant with imagination for the poet! . . . Such clouds, cleaving to their stations, or lifting up suddenly their glittering heads from behind rocky barriers, or hurrying out of sight with the speed of the sharpest sledge—will often tempt an inhabitant to congratulate himself on belonging to a country of mists and clouds and storms.

With these quotations in mind, we can understand why Wordsworth advocated climbing mountains with reference to the sunrise and sunset. He recognizes that the precipitous sides of the mountains, and the neighboring summits, may be seen with fine effect under any atmosphere which allows them to be seen at all, "but he is the most fortunate adventurer who chances to be involved in vapours which open and let in an extent of country partially, or, dispersing suddenly, reveal the whole region from centre to circumference." Of incomparable beauty are the misty mornings on the hills.

In *The Excursion* Wordsworth speaks of the effect upon his friend, whom he calls the Wanderer, of night impressions of the hills:

> In solitude returning, saw the hills
> Grow larger in the darkness; all alone
> Beheld the stars come out above his head,
> And travelled through the wood, with no one near
> To whom he might confess the things he saw.[15]

*The Excursion* abounds in descriptions of mountain scenery and mountain life, but of them all there is nothing finer than the picture of the Langdale Pikes, the "two huge peaks" which from another vale "peered into" that

---

[15] *Excursion*, I, 127 ff.

in which the "Solitary" lived. The emphasis here is upon
the sense of *companionship* as day by day the people in
the vales listen to the "wild concert" of the winds, streams
and cataracts, and from their cottage windows watch the
play of sunlight and cloud upon the towering heights. The
passage must be quoted in full if one would appreciate
both the delicacy and the splendor of its depiction.

> In genial mood,
> While at our pastoral banquet thus we sate
> Fronting the window of that little cell,
> I could not, ever and anon, forbear
> To glance an upward look on two huge Peaks,
> That from some other vale peered into this.
> "Those lusty twins," exclaimed our host, "if here
> It were your lot to dwell, would soon become
> Your prized companions.—Many are the notes
> Which, in his tuneful course, the wind draws forth
> From rocks, woods, caverns, heaths, and dashing shores,
> And well those lofty brethren bear their part
> In the wild concert—chiefly when the storm
> Rides high; then all the upper air they fill
> With roaring sound, that ceases not to flow,
> Like smoke, along the level of the blast,
> In mighty current; theirs, too, is the song
> Of stream and headlong flood that seldom fails;
> And, in the grim and breathless hour of noon,
> Methinks that I have heard them echo back
> The thunder's greeting. Nor have nature's laws
> Left them ungifted with a power to yield
> Music of finer tone; a harmony,
> So do I call it, though it be the hand
> Of silence, though there be no voice;—the clouds,
> The mist, the shadows, light of golden suns,
> Motions of moonlight, all come thither—touch,
> And have an answer—thither come, and shape
> A language not unwelcome to sick hearts
> And idle spirits:—there the sun himself,
> At the calm close of summer's longest day,
> Rests his substantial orb;—between those heights
> And on the top of either pinnacle,
> More keenly than elsewhere in night's blue vault,
> Sparkle the stars, as of their station proud.

> Thoughts are not busier in the mind of man
> Than the mute agents stirring there:—alone
> Here do I sit and watch.—"[16]

In the phrase "Your prized companions" we are to find the best answer to Byron's remark, conveying as it does the sense of identity of life which Byron himself discovered, and which, thanks to Wordsworth, he reflects in the nature-worship of the hills which characterizes the descriptions of the third canto of *Childe Harold*. It was in his later, chastened mood, and when he found himself alone among the Alps, that Byron wrote:

> I live not in myself, but I become
> Portion of that around me; and to me
> High mountains are a feeling—
> . . . . . . . . . . . . .
> Are not the mountains, waves, and skies a part
> Of me and of my soul, as I of them?

Wordsworth, too, was fond of human companionship on his mountain walks, and his poetry bears evidence of how greatly his mind was enriched in this way. On this account it is hardly necessary to say that he preferred walking to riding. What would be his opinion of our modern way of tearing through a landscape in motor-cars, one can easily imagine. There are, of course, practical advantages in this mode of travel, but it is fairly certain that Wordsworth would have seen only its disadvantages. In this connection one recalls the passage in *The Excursion* where he and the Wanderer are trudging along on their way to the home of the Recluse:

> The wealthy, the luxurious, by the stress
> Of business roused, or pleasure, ere their time,
> May roll in chariots, or provoke the hoofs
> Of the fleet coursers they bestride, to raise
> From earth the dust of morning, slow to rise;
> And they, if blest with health and hearts at ease,
> Shall lack not their enjoyment:—but how faint
> Compared with ours! who, pacing side by side,

---

[16] *Excursion*, II, 688-725.

> Could, with an eye of leisure, look on all
> That we beheld; and lend the listening sense
> To every grateful sound of earth and air;
> Pausing at will—our spirits braced, our thoughts
> Pleasant as roses in the thickets blown,
> And pure as dew bathing their crimson leaves.[17]

Imagine what such a walk would mean in the company of Coleridge, or the keen-eyed Dorothy, or his poetically-minded brother John! There was that great day when Sir Walter Scott was visiting the Wordsworths at Dove Cottage, and when the two poets, joined by the scientist, Sir Humphrey Davy, climbed Helvellyn together. Imagine the conversation along the way, the sharing of sensations on the summit!

Even more was Wordsworth given to roaming the mountains alone. How many pictures he gives of beauties, meanings and mysteries borne into his soul when contemplating Nature in the intensity of solitary observation! The boy Wordsworth clinging to a wall of slippery rock, arrested in his plundering of a bird's nest as he listens to the strange mutterings of "the loud dry wind"; or the boy Wordsworth rowing out upon the lake under the stars in a stolen boat, becoming terrified and conscience-stricken by "a huge peak, black and huge," which "upraised its head from behind that craggy steep"; the young man Wordsworth returning from a night of revelry and finding himself confronted with the glory of the rising sun, and in the fullness of the moment dedicating himself to poetry and truth; the man Wordsworth, on "an evening of extraordinary splendour and beauty," standing uncovered, as in a transport of love, drinking in "the gleam, the shadow and the peace supreme"! When reading of experiences like these we have no difficulty in understanding how the Poet could speak of the "souls of lonely places," of "the self-sufficing power of solitude."

Both the poems and the *Guide* reveal how intimate was

---

[17] *Excursion*, II, 97-110.

the Poet's knowledge of the entire region of the Lakes. There was no mountain he had not climbed, there was scarcely a brook that, alone, or with Dorothy, he had not traced to its source. I ran across an amusing illustration of this one day in looking through the five volumes of the 1827 edition of his works (now in the Amherst College collection), which were the personal property of the Poet. On the margin of the poem *The Idle Shepherd Boys,* opposite the lines describing the rock which spanned the chasm of Dungeon-Ghyll, evidently a dangerous spot, in the penciled hand-writing of Mrs. Wordsworth are the words, "William walked over it."

Wordsworth reaches sublime heights when dealing with atmospheric effects and the influence of the sky. No poet, outside of the Bible, is his rival when he sings of sunrise, sunset, storms, thunder and lightning, stormy night, the moon among the clouds. Shelley has his *Clouds,* which we read and reread with delight—so full of melody and of delicate suggestion; but Wordsworth lifts us up; we feel that we are part of the cosmic scene,

> Lodged in the bosom of eternal things.

This was the aspect of Wordsworth's work which especially appealed to Keats, and which he celebrates in one of the Sonnets addressed to Haydon:

> Great spirits now on earth are sojourning;
> He of the cloud, the cataract, the lake,
> Who on Helvellyn's summit, wide awake,
> Catches his freshness from Archangel's wing.

One reason is that Wordsworth is always connecting the sky with the earth; never are we left suspended in thin air; but we sense the unity of the spot on which we stand with the heavenly spectacle. In the *Tintern Abbey* poem, in expressing his joy over finding himself once more on the banks of the River Wye, he gives us a clue—quite unconsciously, I suspect—to a characteristic attitude in respect to Nature's larger realm:

> Once again
> Do I behold these steep and lofty cliffs,
> That on a wild secluded scene impress
> Thoughts of more deep seclusion; and connect
> The landscape with the quiet of the sky.[18]

Whether Wordsworth is singing of sunsets, rainbows or skylarks, he leaves us with the sense of being commingled with the universe as a whole.

Along with Thomson, Cowper, Crabbe, and poetic spirits as far removed as the Hebrew Psalmists and Zoroaster, Wordsworth celebrated the splendor of the sun. But here again we must look for the passing reference rather than for complete expression. His poetic response to the sun, it appears, began while he was yet a lad at Hawkshead:

> Already I began
> To love the sun; a boy I loved the sun,
> Not as I since have loved him, as a pledge
> And surety of our earthly life, a light
> Which we behold and feel we are alive;
> Nor for his bounty to so many worlds—
> But for this cause, that I had seen him lay
> His beauty on the morning hills, had seen
> The western mountain touch his setting orb,
> In many a thoughtless hour, when, from excess
> Of happiness, my blood appeared to flow
> For its own pleasure, and I breathed with joy.[19]

These lines are typical of many others which are full of the sunrise-sense of wonders yet to be.

And yet the moon appears to have made even a stronger, or at least a tenderer appeal. Following immediately after the above quotation are the lines:

> And, from like feelings, humble though intense,
> To patriotic and domestic love
> Analogous, the moon to me was dear;
> For I could dream away my purposes,

---

[18] *Lines Composed a Few Miles Above Tintern Abbey.*
[19] *Prelude*, II, 177 ff.

> Standing to gaze upon her while she hung
> Midway between the hills, as if she knew
> No other region, but belonged to thee,
> Yea, appertained by a peculiar right
> To thee and thy grey huts, thou one dear Vale!

We have the advantage of two poems devoted exclusively to the moon—both worthy pieces, although written in his "uncreative period." One was composed by the seaside, and deals with the moon as "The Sailor's Friend"; the other was composed at Rydal Mount and is more general in its appreciation. The two may be considered as a single work, even as they bear the same title, *To the Moon*. In these pieces the Poet gives expression to his favorite conception of Nature as performing a healing function for the mind—a subject that will occupy us in a later chapter. In the earlier poem we have:

> . . . a fitness in thy sway
> To call up thoughts that shun the glare of day,
> And make the serious happier than the gay—

Also this:

> Let me a compensating faith maintain;
> That there's a sensitive, a tender part
> Which thou canst touch in every human heart,
> For healing and composure.

In the second piece we have the expression:

> The moral intimations of the sky.

I find that I have marked so many moon passages and references in my Wordsworth that it is out of the question to cite even a small proportion of them; but the exquisite comparison in *The Prelude* between Spenser and the moon must not be passed by:

> Sweet Spenser, moving through his clouded heaven
> With the moon's beauty and the moon's soft pace.[20]

Nor can we realize what the "skiey influences" meant

---

[20] *Prelude*, III, 280, 281.

to Wordsworth unless once more we consider him on those long walks at night, gazing at the stars and listening to the weird voices of the wood and stream. As with the hills, so now with the stars, there arose within him a sense of intimacy and of understanding love; there was a community of interest between him and the worlds of space. The dawning of this companionship with the universe as a whole, he dated quite definitely from the summer vacation which, as a student at Cambridge, he spent among his native hills:

> But now there opened on me other thoughts
> Of change, congratulation or regret,
> A pensive feeling! It spread far and wide;
> The trees, the mountains shared it, and the brooks,
> The stars of Heaven, now seen in their old haunts—
> White Sirius glittering o'er the southern crags,
> Orion with his belt, and those fair Seven,
> Acquaintances of every little child,
> And Jupiter, my own beloved star![21]

And so at every point, as we travel in Wordsworth's "mighty world of eye and ear," we find ourselves dealing with the materials of infinitude. In the sixth book of *The Prelude* there is a passage in which the ground we have traversed thus far is presented in lines universally recognized for their majesty and strength. These have to do not with the Lake District, but with the Alps.

> The immeasurable height
> Of woods decaying, never to be decayed,
> The stationary blasts of waterfalls,
> And in the narrow rent at every turn
> Winds thwarting winds, bewildered and forlorn,
> The torrents shooting from the clear blue sky,
> The rocks that muttered close upon our ears,
> Black drizzling crags that spake by the way-side
> As if a voice were in them, the sick sight
> And giddy prospect of the raving stream,

---

[21] *Prelude*, IV, 239 ff.

The unfettered clouds and region of the Heavens,
Tumult and peace, the darkness and the light—
Were all like workings of one mind, the features
Of the same face, blossoms upon one tree;
Characters of the great Apocalypse,
The types and symbols of Eternity,
Of first, and last, and midst, and without end.[22]

[22]*Prelude*, VI, 624 ff.

# CHAPTER IV

# "Of Something Far More Deeply Interfused"

WE COME now to the main thing in Wordsworth's poetry of Nature, an attitude more challenging to present-day thought, more inherently important than all we have considered thus far. Had Wordsworth done nothing more than fix our gaze upon the minutiæ of the outer scene with a new intensity, a new delight, arousing a love of Nature for her own sake, he would have gained a title to distinction and gratitude. But this is not the heart of his message, it touches but the outer rim of his meaning for us today. There were nature-poets before Wordsworth, and even if on the score of fidelity of observation and artistry of expression we award him the leading place, we leave him without his peculiar mark of greatness. We are not to forget that the author of *Tintern Abbey* came in the goodly succession of Thomson, Gray, Cowper and Burns, and that seventy years before *Lyrical Ballads* was offered to an unappreciative world, the reaction from the artificialities of Pope and his school had set in.

The "Back-to-nature" movement in literature may be said to have been launched on the day when the young Scotsman, James Thomson, arrived in London with the manuscript of a poem called *Winter* in his bag, this being the first installment of what the world came to know as *Thomson's Seasons.* It was in 1725. This was followed by the publication of *The Castle of Indolence,* in which, under Thomson's intimate touch, the charms of Nature took on an almost seductive grace. Then came Gray with his immortal *Elegy,* probably the best known and best loved poem in the English tongue. Then appeared the sensitive Cowper, roaming the meadows of the placid

Ouse, or dreaming under the shade of an ancient beech, and producing a huge poem of six books, bearing the prosaic name of *The Task,* but so crammed with Nature's secret ways that it was thought to mark a new era in English verse. If for nothing else, Cowper's poem will be remembered for the line:

> God made the country, and man made the town.

Finally the rollicking and sentimental Burns, with his heart-warming pictures of farmyard and field in the Scottish Lowlands, and his *To a Mouse* and *To a Mountain Daisy,* so suggestive of Wordsworth himself.

Nor did the poetic treatment of Nature have to wait until these forerunners of the Romantic Revival appeared upon the scene. *The Shepherd's Calendar* of Spenser, somewhat artificial and conventional in its description of bucolic life, is yet full of grace and charm, running the gamut of the sylvan months and in a way anticipating Thomson by one hundred and fifty years. Scattered through the plays of Shakespeare are pastoral scenes of idyllic beauty and bits of out-door description which reveal how close was Nature to the great poet's heart:

> Sweetest Shakespeare, Fancy's child,
> Warble his native wood-notes wild.

Back of all—some will say best of all—stands Geoffrey Chaucer, whose love of Nature in her brightest and freshest hues is reflected not only in the *Prologue,* whose opening lines the college student is proud to repeat, but throughout the *Canterbury Tales.* What delight to meet a passage like this!:

> The bisy larke, messager of day,
> Salueth in hir song the morne gray;
> And fiery Phebus riseth up so brighte,
> That al the orient laugheth of the lighte,
> And with his stremes dryeth in the greves
> The silver droppes hangyng on the leves.[1]

---

[1] *The Knight's Tale.*

The fact is, as President Neilson has so clearly brought out in his book on Robert Burns, after Chaucer the love of Nature in all her forms became a tradition in English poetry, so that we need not be surprised at its outcropping in any age. None knew this better than Wordsworth himself, who on more than one occasion expressed his obligation to the older nature-poets, especially Chaucer, Milton, and Cowper. Over his dining-room fireplace at Rydal Mount there hung five portraits—Chaucer's, Spenser's, Shakespeare's, Bacon's and Milton's—in a line. Of perhaps equal significance is the fact that in writing a whimsical poem on the erratic comings and goings of Coleridge in the Grasmere home, he bestowed upon it the title: *Stanzas Written in My Pocket-copy of Thomson's Castle of Indolence.*

What, then, is the real distinction of Wordsworth's work? Where are we to find the greater meaning of his nature-verse? It is in the "Something far more deeply interfused" of the *Tintern Abbey* lines, where, more than in any other composition, we are to look for the inner and abiding essence of his thought. We are to find it in the fact that, in distinction from all the others, Wordsworth had a *philosophy of Nature,* and that this philosophy arose from the sentiment of Being, or Personality, pervading the universe as a whole, and in such things as flowers, birds, crags, clouds, streams, pebbles and drops of dew breaking out into something correspondent to the consciousness of man.

The classic passage is the one from *Lines Composed a Few Miles Above Tintern Abbey,* referred to above, undoubtedly the favorite of the majority of readers who pass beyond the elementary stage. The passage, although familiar—possibly *because* it is familiar—needs to be read with thoughtful attention and with something more than a general sense of its sublimity and charm. *Tintern Abbey* was written in 1798, when the poet was twenty-eight years of age. The very day of composition is men-

tioned in the title—July 13; and the meaning is that, unlike many of his longer pieces over which he labored for
weeks and months, and in contrast with much of his
poetry which was subjected to lifelong revision, these
glowing lines were struck off in a single heat of inspiration, and remained unaltered through all the years.[2]

In his old age the Poet dictated to Miss Fenwick, his
neighbor and intimate friend, this account of the composition:

> No poem of mine was composed under circumstances more
> pleasant for me to remember than this. I began it upon leaving
> Tintern, after crossing the Wye, and concluded it just as I was
> entering Bristol in the evening, after a ramble of four or five
> days with my sister. Not a line of it was altered and not any
> part of it written down until I reached Bristol.[3]

All the circumstances point to the spontaneity and finality
of *Tintern* as an expression of Wordsworth's deepest
intuition of Nature's meaning and of her power both to
kindle and soothe the heart of man. The central idea is
contained in these lines:

> And I have felt
> A presence that disturbs me with the joy
> Of elevated thoughts; a sense sublime
> Of something far more deeply interfused,
> Whose dwelling is the light of setting suns,
> And the round ocean and the living air,
> And the blue sky, and in the mind of man:
> A motion and a spirit, that impels
> All thinking things, all objects of all thought,
> And rolls through all things. Therefore am I still
> A lover of the meadows and the woods,
> And mountains; and of all that we behold
> From this green earth; of all the mighty world
> Of eye, and ear,—both what they half create

---

[2] This assertion is made on the strength of the statement of the Poet himself, quoted
below. In the library of Yale University, among the *Longmans Manuscripts*, there is
an autograph letter of Coleridge, addressed to the publishers of *Lyrical Ballads*, 1800,
asking that three changes be made in the *Tintern Abbey* poem as printed in 1798. I
have examined these changes and find that they relate to single words or letters, not
at all affecting the sense. Very likely the alterations were made by Coleridge on his
own authority.

[3] See Fenwick notes in the Knight and other editions of the poems.

And what perceive; well pleased to recognise
In nature and the language of the sense
The anchor of my purest thoughts, the nurse,
The guide, the guardian of my heart, and soul'
Of all my moral being.

After this classical utterance, one should turn to the famous passage in the first book of *The Prelude* beginning:

Wisdom and Spirit of the universe!
Thou Soul that art the eternity of thought—

noting especially the lines:

Ye Presences of Nature in the sky
And on the earth! Ye Visions of the hills!
And Souls of lonely places!

In a way these last lines are more personalistic than those of *Tintern Abbey,* in that he capitalizes the words "Presences," "Visions" and "Souls"—a detail of composition to which the Poet gave careful attention. The theory is set forth explicitly, and in philosophical form, in the opening lines of the ninth book of *The Excursion,* where, speaking through the voice of the Wanderer, the Poet commits himself to the idea of an "Active Principle" pervading the universe and communicating good on every side:

"To every Form of being is assigned,"
Thus calmly spake the venerable Sage,
"An *active* Principle:—howe'er removed
From sense and observation, it subsists
In all things, in all natures; in the stars
Of azure heaven, the unenduring clouds,
In flower and tree, in every pebbly stone
That paves the brooks, the stationary rocks,
The moving waters, and the invisible air.
Whate'er exists hath properties that spread
Beyond itself, communicating good,
A simple blessing, or with evil mixed;
Spirit that knows no insulated spot,
No chasm, no solitude; from link to link
It circulates, the Soul of all the worlds.

> This is the freedom of the universe;
> Unfolded still the more, more visible,
> The more we know; and yet is reverenced least,
> And least respected in the human Mind,
> Its most apparent home."

If it be urged that this is nothing less than Greek and Latin mythology in modern dress, we have what amounts to a disavowal in the sonnet beginning: "Brook, whose society the Poet seeks," especially the lines:

> I would not do
> Like Grecian Artists, give thee human cheeks,
> Channels for tears; no Naiad shouldst thou be,—
> Have neither limbs, feet, feathers, joints, nor hairs:
> It seems the Eternal Soul is clothed in thee
> With purer robes than those of flesh and blood.

And yet Wordsworth did not hesitate to attribute a moral function, or what he considered a moral function, to natural objects, and that in a most particularistic way. The following passage from *The Prelude* is fairly startling in its boldness:

> To every natural form, rock, fruit, or flower,
> Even the loose stones that cover the highway,
> I gave a moral life: I saw them feel,
> Or linked them to some feeling: the great mass
> Lay bedded in a quickening soul, and all
> That I beheld respired with inward meaning.[4]

In *Stray Pleasures* he attributes a sense of happiness to leaves and to waves:

> Each leaf, that and this, his neighbour will kiss;
> Each wave, one and t'other, speeds after his brother;
> They are happy, for that is their right!

One of the most exquisite sonnets is the one beginning,

> It is a beauteous evening, calm and free,

in which the personality of ocean takes on a divine semblance:

---

[4] *Prelude*, III, 127 ff.

> The gentleness of heaven broods o'er the Sea:
> Listen! the mighty Being is awake,
> And doth with his eternal motion make
> A sound like thunder—everlastingly.

Even the mountains are conceived of as possessing souls, and they are made to converse across the valleys, and to look on as man goes about his pleasure and toil. In the second book of *The Excursion*, Wordsworth has the Solitary characterize the mountains that hemmed in his retreat as "prized companions" not only of himself but of the winds, and as consciously engaging in "wild concert" during the days of storm. In *Loud is the Vale*, after picturing the tumult of the streams following a violent storm, by an exquisite touch he introduces the thought of peace from far-off space, through the lifting of the eye to the sky:

> Yon star upon the mountain-top
> Is listening quietly.

Similarly in the great *Ode* we have the lines:

> The Moon doth with delight
> Look round her when the heavens are bare.

The most definite of all the references—one that brings the sense of Being into the realm of flowers and birds in an almost creedal way, is that in the poem beginning, "I heard a thousand blended notes," one of the loveliest things Wordsworth ever wrote:

> Through primrose tufts, in that green bower,
> The periwinkle trailed its wreaths;
> And 'tis my faith that every flower
> Enjoys the air it breathes.
>
> The birds around me hopped and played,
> Their thoughts I cannot measure:—
> But the least motion which they made,
> It seemed a thrill of pleasure.[5]

---

[5] It was through the reading of this poem that the eminent Shakespearean scholar, Henry Hudson, came to his love of Wordsworth.

Quotations like these might be greatly extended, but the foregoing should be sufficient to show how different was the attitude of Wordsworth from that of Burns and the other nature-poets. It is true, some of Wordsworth's references to self-consciousness in Nature—possibly some of the above—may be attributed to mere personification, the device by which, from most ancient times, poets have sought to heighten the effect by addressing Nature as though she possessed a mind and voice. The Bible is full of this sort of thing—"The mountains and the hills shall break forth before you into singing, and all the trees of the field shall clap their hands";[6] "When the morning stars sang together, and all the sons of God shouted for joy."[7] Wordsworth, of course, would not forego so beautiful a device.[8] But after allowance is made, it will be found that so many passages are built upon a definite sense of Nature as a living, breathing and feeling whole that we must face the fact of a philosophy which appears to run counter to the dictates of common sense.

Before attempting to pass judgment we need to examine more closely some of the terms which Wordsworth was accustomed to use, especially the word "Presence." This was the Poet's favorite characterization, one of the key-words of his thought. At different times we find him referring to the inner life of Nature as "Being," "Soul," "Visions," "Active Principle," and "Presence"; but his fondness for the final term is apparent. Just what did he mean by "Presence"? It is one of those elusive terms which poets love but which philosophers, as a rule, avoid. Since Wordsworth was both poet and philosopher we may expect that the word will take on at least a semblance of the word, the intensive and the non-intensive signifi- of definiteness. There is the higher and the lower meaning cance. When we use the term presence instead of per-

---

[6] Isaiah 55: 12.

[7] Job 38: 7.

[8] For an illuminating discussion of the value of poetic personification, see I. A. Richard's *Practical Criticism*, pp. 199 ff.

sonality, ordinarily it is to strengthen the idea, to convey the impression of wholeness of being—all there is of body, mind and soul. Along with this concept is also that of dignity, or at least of power, and the sense of nearness. The use of the term "The Presence" as an epithet for the King or Emperor is a case in point. Even the space containing such a personage reflects the pervasiveness of the idea, and we speak of the "Presence-chamber." But frequently the word is used in quite another sense for the purpose of conveying a lessened or more tenuous impression of personage, as when we speak of a ghostly presence, or a faint sensing of reality in person or thing. In such use it is the shadow rather than the substance that we feel.

Without entering into a detailed discussion of Wordsworth's use of the word Presence, which might weary the reader (he employs the term no less than ninety-five times), I will say that an examination of this usage brings a certain amount of relief in that in the crucial passages he seems to imply something less than personality in the full content of the term. Personality was an aspect of Nature which he felt rather than discerned. It rested upon a certain awareness rather than upon clear apprehension. It was the atmosphere rather than the substance of places and things. It had to do with attributes like beauty, tranquillity, joy and peace, rather than with full and self-conscious sense of being. When, in *The Recluse,* he speaks of "Beauty—a living Presence of the earth," he gives us a clue to his ascription of personal quality to Nature as a whole. So also in the great *Ode,* when he deals with the intuition of immortality in the mind of the child as a "Presence which is not to be put by," as something that "broods like the day." Similarly we have in *Vaudracour and Julia,*

> Earth breathed in one great presence of the spring.

If this appears to be a watering-down of the obvious

meaning of personality, it is to be kept in view that associated with it, in Wordsworth's mind, was a strong, at times an overwhelming sense of dignity and worth. The Presence that disturbed him with the joy of elevated thoughts was one of infinite beauty and strength. The Spirit of Nature, which the Poet at times seems almost to have worshipped, was a Holy Spirit. That which he found shadowed forth in meadows, woods and mountains commanded the sentiments of reverence and devotion. Thus in the great *Tintern* passage, in the same breath he could speak of Nature as "a presence," a "something far more deeply interfused," "a motion and a spirit." It was because of the "sense sublime" that he could

> recognize
> In nature and the language of the sense
> The anchor of my purest thoughts, the nurse,
> The guide, the guardian of my heart, and soul
> Of all my moral being.

I am reserving for the next chapter the consideration of what Nature came to mean in the detail of Wordsworth's experience and response, and what, arising from this fact, may be his special message to our time; but it is well at this point to note that those high appreciations upon which I have dwelt arose in large measure from the Poet's sense of kinship with Nature as possessing both sense and soul. Nothing can be common that participates in the universal life, that shares in the "all-sanctifying Presence." The divine spark may be small, its glow too dim for ordinary perception, but there it is for those who have eyes to see and hearts to feel. If "in common things that round us lie" and throughout "the mighty world of eye and ear," Wordsworth discovered a glory beyond that which others felt, it was because to him was given the power to evaluate the scene in terms of personal worth. Here also lies the secret of his sense of companionship with Nature. It was the thrill of *life* that he felt on every side—in animal, flower, tree, brook, mountain, sun, moon, and stars—in the universe too as a whole. When he spoke of the mountains as his friends, it was more than a figure of speech. It was actual kinship, his habit of entering into "the secret sympathies of things." This, as one might expect, went out most easily to the brute creation, especially the domestic animals, "those charming companions of our humanity." On just two pages of *The Recluse* I have marked the following illustrations: "the small gray horse that bears the paralytic man"; "the famous sheep-dog, first in all the vale"; "Friends shall I have at dawn, blackbird and thrush"; "Helvellyn's eagles —I shall be free to claim acquaintance"; "The owl that gives the name to Owlet-Crag—a chosen one of my regards"; "The heifer in yon little croft, and the mother cow." How clear it becomes that Wordsworth, above all poets who went before, and possibly above all who have come after, although some may claim a like distinction for Shelley, dwelt in a living, breathing, self-conscious, and responsive world. It was not so much that Nature had a soul, as that the soul *was* Nature. Perhaps, too, we shall find here the explanation of the fact that to some Wordsworth primarily is the Poet of Nature, and to others the Poet of Man. He is both. And for the reason that, more than either, he is the *Poet of Personality*.[9]

Naturally such idealistic views have not gone without challenge. Probably the majority of readers, while admiring Wordsworth's interpretations of Nature in terms of personality as *poetry*, are content to let it go at that. It is recognized that his was a highly sensitive mind, that vividness of feeling, boldness of utterance, inventiveness of imagination were his temperamental stock in trade. It was to be expected that phantasy and romance would color his thinking on the higher levels of apprehension. Here, as among the Greeks, we have the "freshness of

[9]For the most thorough and satisfactory discussion of Wordsworth's theory of nature, see *Naturalism in English Poetry*, by the Rev. Stopford Brooke, a book so eloquently written that it has become a classic. Originally printed in 1902, it is now published in the series, *The King's Treasuries of Literature*, E. P. Dutton & Co., N. Y. See also Principal Shairp's *The Poetic Interpretation of Nature*, 1877.

the early world." Here, too, is the naïveté of childhood in its outlook upon the charm of a newly discovered creation; or, to employ Wordsworth's own familiar lines, the afterglow of

> a time when meadow, grove, and stream,
> The earth, and every common sight,
> To me did seem
> Apparelled in celestial light,
> The glory and the freshness of a dream.[10]

Those who offer this explanation would probably hold that, whether we accept the Wordsworth philosophy or not, we should rejoice in its promulgation because of what it meant to the Poet himself. Whether the idea of Nature as a living being is true or not, it was true to Wordsworth, at least during the period of his finest verse, and this is warrant enough. Under any lesser view there would have been no *Lines Written in Early Spring*, no *Tintern Abbey*, possibly no first book of *The Prelude*. After all, poetry is not science, and one may be permitted to leave theories at home when journeying in the land of romance. We can imagine Matthew Arnold elaborating a lucid and altogether delightful defense of Wordsworth on this score.

A more prosaic explanation is that what Wordsworth has done is to project his own personality into the heart of Nature, imputing to her the powers by which his own reactions were reached. Nature, an echo of himself. This is a process in which we all indulge when, in our dealings with the higher animals, we love to assume an intelligence responding to our own. Wordsworth went the whole way, sensing a similar response in trees and flowers and bits of stone. This appears to have been the opinion of Coleridge —at least at the time he wrote his ode to *Dejection*, where we have the well-known lines:

---

[10] *Immortality Ode*, Stanza I.

O Lady! we receive but what we give,
And in our life alone does Nature live:
Ours is her wedding garment, ours her shroud,
    And would we aught behold, of higher worth,
Than that inanimate cold world allowed
To the poor, loveless, ever-anxious crowd,
    Ah! from the soul itself must issue forth
A light, a glory, a fair luminous cloud
    Enveloping the Earth—
And from the soul itself must there be sent
    A sweet and potent voice, of its own birth,
Of all sweet sounds the life and element!

There is a passage in *The Prelude* which might be quoted as an approximation to such a view on the part of Wordsworth himself:

                    An auxiliar light
Came from my mind, which on the setting sun
Bestowed new splendour; the melodious birds,
The fluttering breezes, fountains that run on
Murmuring so sweetly in themselves, obeyed
A like dominion, and the midnight storm
Grew darker in the presence of my eye:
Hence my obeisance, my devotion hence,
And hence my transport.[11]

These are an authentic Wordsworth utterance, but the lines do not convey the idea of imputed personality. They show rather a personality responsive to Nature's initial call. The light of his mind is an "auxiliar light." It is a "new splendour" which his thought bestowed on "the setting sun." As Brooke, in defense of Wordsworth, so well puts it: "We do not receive what we give; we give and receive back something wholly different. It is not the reflection of ourselves which we have from Nature, it is the friendship of another than ourselves."[12] What Wordsworth contends for is a separate life in Nature and Man.

In respect to both of these theories the major question is as to the reality of the wonderful things which Words-

---

[11]*Prelude*, II, 368 ff.
[12]*Naturalism in English Poetry*, p. 161.

worth found written on Nature's face. Do sense-objects, such as mountains, trees and flowers, have faculties or attributes which entitle them to be classed and dealt with (poetically or otherwise) as though they are possessed of Being?

If we leave the decision to the scientists—at least the scientists of a few years ago—we shall receive an emphatic negative for our answer. By no accepted test, they assure us, can consciousness, or intelligence, or feeling be attributed to matter as such. The line between animate and inanimate Nature may be difficult, if not impossible to determine, but that the faculties of sense and feeling lie on the hither side only a poet or a dreamer could doubt. "A mountain range," remarks an American geologist of note, "is usually the result of a crushing of a geosyncline by tangential pressure, and a mountain peak is generally a remnant left in the erosion which has removed an immense mass of rock around it. Consequently we [geologists] do not believe that the mountain has a spirit with which we can enter into conversation." This authority, evidently having Wordsworth and his defenders in mind, adds facetiously: "In fact, we prefer the oreads and dryads and naiads and nereids and all the other 'ads' and 'ids' of classical mythology, to the new mythology of æsthetic critics."[13] Very clever—and, of course, convincing, if we have solely in mind those utterances which express the idealizing fervor of our Poet in its extremer forms, such as in *Lines Written in Early Spring*. But in dealing with the "Presence" passages, in which Wordsworth appears to have expressed his deeper convictions, the thoughtful reader today will probably find himself in a more tolerant mood, or at least inclined to hold his judgment in reserve.

Perhaps the geologists are not to have the final word. Perhaps the physicists and the biologists may have some-

---

[13] Prof. William N. Rice, in *The Poet of Science*, pp. 30, 31. Prof. Rice argues in favor of Tennyson as the true Poet of Science, as distinguished from Wordsworth and others of the Romantic School.

thing to offer. Better still, perhaps the modern philosopher, appraising and interpreting both poetry and science —not to mention religion—may be coming to the rescue of the more personalistic view of the universe to which poets like Wordsworth gave their allegiance.

Here, for instance, is no less an authority than Professor A. N. Whitehead, of Harvard, in his widely read *Science and the Modern World,* devoting an entire chapter to the Romantic Movement in literature for the sake of showing how Wordsworth and Shelley, especially the former, by their theory and treatment of Nature, prepared the way for the modern objectivist view of matter which finds in Nature an organism, or rather finds Nature to be an organism, functioning in ways which we must recognize as kindred to those of personality. The argument is highly philosophical and I will make no attempt to reproduce it here. But in brief, it recognizes that every bit of matter must be considered in relation to the totality of matter, which totality is found to possess the attributes of "change, value, eternal objects, endurance, organism, interfusion." Characteristics like these, Whitehead maintains, may be identified with the evidence of Being which Wordsworth found pervading every detail of the natural scene. Whitehead calls attention to the fact that both Wordsworth and Shelley bear witness that Nature cannot be divorced from its æsthetic values, and that "these values arise from the cumulation, in some sense, of the brooding presence of the whole on to its various parts." Put in a nutshell, it is the doctrine that matter is alive.[14] If this philosophy of objectivism falls somewhat short of the full notion of personality in Nature, it at least serves to modify the old antithesis between mind and matter, since matter itself is found to have something akin to mind; and it certainly gives pause to those who hold that the only accurate approach to Nature is that of science. With an authority like White-

---

[14] *Science and the Modern World,* Chap. V.

head maintaining that the poetical approach, that is "the approach through imaginatively exalted sensibility," is as necessary to the full apprehension of Nature as the scientific processes of observation and experiment, the "matter-of-fact" critic, or the man of affairs, may well hold in check his tendency to relegate to the limbo of moonshine the findings of a Wordsworth, a Shelley or a Keats. Rather must we not maintain that science and poetic intuition are two parallel roads to reality?

And how about the "etherealization" of matter, under the discoveries of scientists like Soddy, Rutherford and Moseley? With atoms reduced to electrons and protons, and these in turn reduced to electrical energy and spoken of as a series of events, the atom becomes a "ghostly structure," and old-time substance appears to lose its particularistic meaning.[15] It is interesting to conjecture what would be the reaction of a Wordsworth to such revolutionary discoveries as these. Would he feel more or less at home in such a universe as ours? Would the "sense sublime of something far more deeply interfused," the "Presence that disturbs me with the joy of elevated thoughts," appear more or less rational than in the days when he and Dorothy roamed the Wye Valley in a mood of exalted sensibility? Who can say? My guess is that Wordsworth would find the vitality, the beauty and the solemnity of his world vastly enhanced. Certainly, as never before, the affinity of our modern men of science appears to be with the poets whose faculty is imagination.

The religious bearing of Wordsworth's theory of Nature must not be overlooked, and this comes to the front in connection with the criticism that, in the *Tintern Abbey* passage quoted on a previous page, we have nothing less (and nothing more) than the pantheistic view of the world. The charge has been made again and again, each new critic pouncing upon the passage with the verve of a

---

[15] *Cf.* Eddington's conception of the whole universe as composed of "mind-stuff," and Jeans's suggestion that the universe is a thought in the mind of God.

fresh and dreadful discovery. Thus the late Professor Herford, of the University of Manchester, in a recent book, calmly assumes that at the time of writing *Tintern Abbey* the Poet was a convinced pantheist.[16] Similarly the late Professor Irving Babbitt, of Harvard, argues eloquently against what he calls "The Primitivism of Wordsworth" on the assumption that the Poet was a pantheist at heart.[17] Oddly enough, the taint of pantheism has been detected not by theologians and preachers, who might be supposed to be well-informed and somewhat sensitive on the subject, but by the literary men. Clergymen as a rule, have found deep satisfaction in the disputed passage, and probably no lines of Wordsworth are more quoted by them; certainly no lines have sunk deeper into the heart of the thinking public in England and America.

The pantheistic objection has been carefully considered and effectively answered by Principal Shairp of Edinburgh, Reverend Stopford Brooke, President Augustus Strong, of the Rochester Theological Seminary, Dean Inge, Professor E. Hershey Sneath, of the Yale Divinity School, and Miss Margaret Sherwood, of Wellesley College.[18] In a question of this kind one needs to be careful as to his definitions, and not to be misled by popular usage, or general impressions of philosophical trend. Pantheism is the identification of the universe with God, or, in its more extreme form, the identification of God with the universe. Under either concept there is a denial of the personality of God in any sense which could have value or significance to the average man. All is substance, and substance is all. If the reader will re-examine the *Tintern* passage with these distinctions in mind, he should have

---

[16] *Wordsworth*, by Prof. C. H. Herford, Dutton, N. Y.

[17] *The Primitivism of Wordsworth*, in the *Bookman*, Sept. 1931. So also I. A. Richards in his *Principles of Literary Criticism*, 1930, Oliver Elton in his *Wordsworth*, 1924, de Selincourt in the preface to his *variorum* edition of *The Prelude*, and Prof. Melvin M. Rader in his *Presiding Ideas in Wordsworth's Poetry*, p. 180.

[18] The titles of the works referred to above, and in the same order are: *Studies in Poetry and Philosophy*, 1872; *Theology in the English Poets*, 1874; *The Great Poets and Their Theology*, 1897; *Studies of English Mystics*, 1906; *Wordsworth, Poet of Nature and Poet of Man*, 1912; *Under-currents of Influence in English Romantic Poetry*, 1935.

no difficulty in establishing the theistic trend, if not the theistic content, of the Poet's thought.

Miss Sherwood, referring to the Wordsworth passages which deal with rapt moments of insight into the ultimate meaning of Nature, has this to say:

> These passages have led to Wordsworth being called both pantheist and mystic; man could hardly be both. If the pantheist is one who believes "that there is no God but the combined forces and laws which are manifested in the existing universe," Wordsworth is no pantheist. The consciousness in *Tintern* of the immanence of the divine, "A motion and a spirit that rolls through all things," is no denial of transcendence, no affirmation that spirit is matter-bound, as in the pantheist's thought, but suggests a more quick and vital way of drawing near the power impelling all things. Those who claim that Wordsworth was a pantheist forget that the spirit which "rolls through all things" has its dwelling place in setting suns, in the living air and in the mind of man, but is not bounded by them. No one is coincident with his dwelling place.[19]

Professor Harper acquits Wordsworth (as must any painstaking reader) of being a pantheist in his later years; but on the strength of the *Tintern Abbey* passage, he maintains that such was the Poet's belief in 1798, when the poem was written. The change, he holds, came between the writing of this poem and the composition of *The Prelude,* which was finished in 1805, *The Prelude* itself being witness, since it was intended as a renunciation of the earlier view. Professor Harper's language is as follows: "One of the purposes of *The Prelude,* painfully and redundantly achieved, is to renounce this pantheism, for it is nothing less."[20] This is a very interesting view, full of possible significance as to the motive and content of *The Prelude.* Certain difficulties, however, would seem to stand in the way of its acceptance. For one thing, the time between the composition of the two poems seems rather short for so fundamental a change of faith. For

---

[19] *Under-currents of Influence in English Romantic Poetry,* Harvard University Press, 1935, p. 152. Prof. Sneath meets the pantheistic objection in an even more particularistic way, and with unanswerable logic. *Op. cit.,* pp. 130, 131.
[20] *William Wordsworth,* one volume edition, p. 452.

while *The Prelude* was not finished until 1805, we know it was begun in 1799, and that the underlying purpose was in the Poet's mind from the outset. More to the point is the fact that *The Prelude* contains a passage strikingly parallel to that of *Tintern Abbey,* possibly even more suggestive of a pantheistic view. Although it describes the reactions to Nature which began in the seventeenth year of the Poet's life, the object clearly is to establish the origin of an attitude which became a permanent possession, viz., the sense of Being diffused through the external world. The lines, taken from the second book, are as follows:

> I was only then
> Contented, when with bliss ineffable
> I felt the sentiment of Being spread
> O'er all that moves and all that seemeth still;
> O'er all that, lost beyond the reach of thought
> And human knowledge, to the human eye
> Invisible, yet liveth to the heart;
> O'er all that leaps and runs, and shouts and sings,
> Or beats the gladsome air; o'er all that glides
> Beneath the wave, yea, in the wave itself,
> And mighty depth of waters.[21]

Wordsworth must have had the *Tintern Abbey* passage in mind when he wrote those words. They certainly express the same point of view. As giving color to Professor Harper's position, it may be said that following the above passage are lines which temper the impression by pointing to faith in the "Uncreated" as being worthy of adoration and love. These are the additional lines, following immediately upon the others:

> Wonder not
> If high the transport, great the joy I felt
> Communing in this sort through earth and heaven
> With every form of creature, as it looked
> Towards the Uncreated with a countenance
> Of adoration, with an eye of love.

---

[21] *Prelude*, II, 399 ff.

> One song they sang, and it was audible,
> Most audible, then, when the fleshly ear,
> O'ercome by humblest prelude of that strain,
> Forgot her functions, and slept undisturbed.[22]

But, let it be noted, these tempering lines were not in the original *Prelude*. An examination of de Selincourt's *variorum* edition will reveal that they were written subsequent to 1805; therefore the bare passage, with its pantheistic suggestion, seemed appropriate to Wordsworth at that date; he was still in the mood of the *Tintern Abbey* piece. The natural explanation of the subsequent lines is that they were added (as were many other orthodox references) to prevent a misconception of the Poet's views. Some one—very likely Coleridge—informed Wordsworth that he was being accused of pantheism, and that these lines of *The Prelude* would serve to strengthen the impression. Evidently he took the hint. And while I am dealing with this matter, it perhaps is worth mentioning that the evidence is indisputable that Wordsworth was not in the slightest degree pantheistic in 1805. *The Prelude* in its original form contains numerous references to the deity, the term "God" being used again and again, and nearly always with full theological significance. An examination of the de Selincourt *Prelude* will show that in not a single instance was this term inserted as the result of later revision; one and all they are found in the manuscript of 1805.

To my mind Professor Harper's theory will find difficulty with the fact that the *Tintern Abbey* passage, in spite of its known pantheistic suggestion, was left unchanged and unexplained throughout the Poet's life. If it suited him in 1798, as expressing a correct and helpful view of deity, it suited him also in 1850, the year of his death. In *Hart-Leap Well*, written in 1800, we have an even earlier indication of Wordsworth's essentially theistic view. I refer to the well-known stanza:

---

[22]*Prelude*, II, 409 ff.

> The Being that is in the clouds and air,
> That is in the green leaves among the groves,
> Maintains a deep and reverential care
> For the unoffending creatures whom he loves.

As a matter of fact, in a letter to his friend, Mrs. Clarkson, written in 1814, Wordsworth distinctly and indignantly disavowed any pantheistic import to anything he had composed. A lady had written to Mrs. Clarkson claiming that Wordsworth identified God with Nature. His reply was: "She condemns me for not distinguishing between Nature as the work of God and God himself. But where does she find the doctrine inculcated? Whence does she gather that the author of *The Excursion* looks upon Nature and God as the same?"[23]

It is of course well known that after his dip into the rationalism of William Godwin and his school, following his sojourn in France, Wordsworth experienced a religious change amounting almost to a conversion, and that ultimately he settled down in the orthodox faith of the English Church, of which he became an ardent defender. But since, theologically considered, *Tintern Abbey*, *The Prelude* and *The Recluse*—the master-poems of the early period—are all of a piece, it is clear that his change of belief must be dated prior to 1798.

What shall we say then is the message of Wordsworth to our time, arising from his theory of Nature? His message is of the importance of *Natural Religion*. The need today is for a fresh discovery of God in the light of the

---

[23] What the teachers of literature and the critics generally almost uniformly overlook is that the employment by poets of philosophical language akin to pantheism is often no more than the attempt to express a spiritual experience so intimate and profound that only by the use of the most passionate terms can the essence be conveyed. In the very purpose and process of the conveyance the poet reveals the separateness and identity of his being. As to my contention that at the time of the writing of *Lyrical Ballads* Wordsworth was essentially theistic in his point of view, fresh and convincing evidence comes from the *Unpublished Letters of Coleridge*, issued in 1933 (Vol. I, p. 76). In a letter to his friend Rev. John P. Estlin, of Bristol, who had been sending certain of his sermons to Coleridge for criticism, the latter wrote referring not only to his own but also to Wordsworth's opinion—"He admires your sermon against *Payne* much more than your last; I suppose because he is more inclined to Christianity than to Theism simply considered." The letter bears the date June 1797. This at least is a fair offset to the oft-quoted characterization of Coleridge who, in writing to Thelwall, remarked that Wordsworth was "at least a semi-atheist." Coleridge was notoriously careless and gossipy in referring to the views of his friends.

steadily expanding universe of physical science. We need a return to that type of thinking which recognizes forces, values, meanings in the external world which the eye of the scientist does not, and cannot detect; to the conception of Nature as the dwelling-place of Divinity, the meeting-place of God and man. Wordsworth is the prophet of "the great apocalypse of the God who lives in the order of his cosmos." In these days, when the line between the natural and the supernatural is less sharply drawn, we hear little of the old distinction between Natural and Revealed Religion. Theologians today are content with discussing, "What *is* revelation?" Nevertheless the distinction remains valid and useful when we are confronted by the ultimate facts of experience; and it is to a poet like Wordsworth that the thoughtful man is likely to turn as he endeavors to harmonize the two. In his thinking Wordsworth began with Nature, and it was out of Nature that he built up his faith. It was not that he ruled out the more intimate and compelling approach of God to men, which we associate with the term Revealed Religion—we know that he did not. Rather, he felt constrained to stress that sphere of revelation in which he found himself most at home. Connecting as he did, every phenomenon with God, his poetry became "one long protest against the banishment of God from His universe." And it is just at this point that he speaks comforting words to the thinking people of our time. If through the close study of Nature many have lost the sense of God, then through the closer study of Nature shall many find a way of return. For those who find themselves in this state of mind it is the poet rather than the theologian who is likely to become a guide.

Sir J. Arthur Thomson, in his book *The Riddles of Science,* has a striking passage in which he argues that educated men who are seeking for a religious basis of thought and life must consent to become mystical in their outlook upon the world.

We are writing for men and women, like ourselves, who are dissatisfied and ill at ease without some belief in a spiritual meaning behind it all. We cannot help trying to make some sense of our experience as a whole (that is philosophy), and we personally cannot make any sense without belief in a Divine Purpose (that is religion). We are taking religion to mean a sending forth of tendrils towards a supersensuous or mystical reality, personalized in God, a reality which gives some meaning to the world and man's place in it. So far as we understand the question, religion is not worthy of the name unless it transcends the scientifically measurable or definable. Educated men today have to choose between a mystical religion or none at all.[24]

A better interpretation of the present-day quest for a religious faith it would be difficult to find, and the statement leads directly to the Wordsworthian point of view.

As showing that Sir Arthur Thomson does not stand alone among men of advanced scientific thought, we need but remind ourselves that from Eddington, Jeans, Pupin and Millikan we have had utterances in similar vein. When Dr. Millikan received the Roosevelt Gold Medal in 1932, his *spiritual conceptions* were stressed as the basis of the award. In the citation he was declared to be "a prophet of the new time, bearing to bewildered man, alike from atom and from star, news of the presence and the goodness of God." A new time indeed appears to impend, a time when the attitude of wonder and of reverent humility, which in so large measure characterized the older scientists, like Kepler, Newton, Faraday and Tyndall, and which both Wordsworth and Tennyson made glorious in verse, will again find its way into the heart of a truth-seeking generation. And yet it is not so much new as old, since in the early dawn of the Christian revelation there was an Apostle who wrote: "For the invisible things of him since the creation of the world are clearly seen, being perceived through the things that are made, even his everlasting power and divinity." At an even earlier date there was a *poet* who sang:

---

[24]*The Riddles of Science*, Sir J. Arthur Thompson, 1932, Liveright Publishing Corporation, New York

# OF SOMETHING FAR MORE DEEPLY INTERFUSED

The heavens declare the glory of God,
And the firmament showeth his handiwork.

## NOTE

Prof. Beatty, of the University of Wisconsin, in his *William Wordsworth—His Doctrine and Art,* page 29, with approval, quotes Hazlitt as holding that Wordsworth was a necessitarian, this on the basis of the well-known passage in *Tintern Abbey* which ends with the lines:

A motion and a spirit, that impels
All thinking things, all objects of all thought,
And rolls through all things.

Hazlitt's comment *(Philosophical Necessity, Works, XI, 277)* is as follows: "Perhaps the doctrine of what has been called philosophical necessity was never more finely expressed than in these lines." Let us examine that statement. The two verbs used by Wordsworth are: "impels" and "rolls." Neither of these need be taken as carrying the idea of necessity. To impel means to urge, to incite to action, which, when applied to the impact of God upon man, accords with Wordsworth's conception of divine influence expressed in many places. The word "rolls," which has given offense to so many critics as conveying the notion of pantheism and necessity, need not and should not be taken in that sense. Wordsworth's use of the word is clearly indicated in the poem *To My Sister,* written in the same year as *Tintern Abbey,* 1798, and upon the same theme, the influence of nature. The stanza to which I particularly refer is the following:

And from the blessed power that rolls
About, below, above,
We'll frame the measure of our souls:
They shall be tuned to love.

Here we have language strikingly similar to that of the *Tintern Abbey* passage, and an employment of the word "rolls" in which freedom of choice is clearly implied.

# THE REDISCOVERY OF WORDSWORTH

Prof. Gingerich in his *Essays in the Romantic Poets* calls attention to the fact that in the same passage in *Tintern Abbey* the idea of freedom is implied in the phrase, "both what they half create and what perceive," referring to the impression of eye and ear.

Prof. Beatty, not content with reading into *Tintern Abbey* the idea of necessity, makes bold to quote a passage from *The Excursion* as supporting the same view—

> So build we up the Being that we are;
> Thus deeply drinking-in the Soul of Things,
> We shall be wise perforce. . . .
> (Book IV, lines 1264-1266)

The quotation is incomplete, and as a result absolutely misleading. Had Prof. Beatty taken the pains to complete the sentence from which the above lines are extracted, he would have found that so far from teaching necessity it inculcates exactly the opposite. The balance of the sentence reads as follows:

> and, while inspired
> By choice, and conscious that the Will is free,
> Shall move unswerving, even as if impelled
> By strict necessity, along the path
> Of order and of good.

The idea of the passage as a whole is that voluntarily yielding to the persuasions of nature and accepting her pure principle of love, *one forms the habit of benevolence.* The necessity of which the poet speaks is self-imposed, arising from within. If the reader has any further doubt, he should read the ninth book of *The Excursion,* where in a noble passage freedom is taught in the most explicit fashion. See lines 206-240. I have found no evidence that at any period after 1798 Wordsworth accepted the idea of determinism, although passionate phrases here and there, taken out of their connection, might seem to give color to such a view.

# CHAPTER V

# "The Harvest of a Quiet Eye"

IN the consideration of Wordsworth as the Poet of Nature, it is important to keep in mind that his philosophy, in all its larger implications, was the result of his own experience. It was the seasoned interpretation of profound changes in his inner life, the fruitage of a life-long exposure to Nature's restoring and educating power. In this respect Wordsworth differs materially from the other outstanding interpreters of Nature, who, from the time of Plato down, have started with the idea rather than with the impact of life. After all, the characteristics of Nature are valid only for the characteristics which they excite. It is for this they exist. It is for this they offer their appeal to the mind of man. It is when we consider the effect that Nature had upon the character and work of a genius like Wordsworth that we realize the profundity of her life and her capacity for the perennial fertilizing of the soul. A suitable text for all I have to say on this subject may be found in that great passage in *The Prelude* beginning "Wisdom and Spirit of the Universe," in which the poet expresses a profound sense of satisfaction in the fact that from earliest childhood he had been reared in the midst of scenes which served to purify and ennoble the soul:

> Not with the mean and vulgar works of man,
> But with high objects, with enduring things—
> With life and nature—purifying thus
> The elements of feeling and of thought,
> And sanctifying, by such discipline,
> Both pain and fear, until we recognise
> A grandeur in the beatings of the heart.[1]

---

[1] *Prelude*, I, 408 ff.

I have alluded to Wordsworth's experience as a life-
long one, but there was one experience which transcended
all the others. I refer to the transformation of those six
portentous years between his return from France in the
autumn of 1792, and the publication of *Lyrical Ballads*
in the autumn of 1798. There can be no understanding of
the essential Wordsworth without a realization of what
those years meant in the formation of his religious views
and of his outlook upon the world. At this point biography and criticism should walk hand in hand, and for
those who would penetrate to the influences which fix
character and determine the trend of a life, I strongly
recommend the reading of the modern biographies, especially those of Harper and Legouis which are built upon
the significance of these early years. Aside from the
temporary residence in London, Racedown and Alfoxden,
there is little of outward event to record; but in the
soul of the young Poet there were mighty transactions
and in these Nature played a leading part.

At the beginning of the period we find the youthful
Wordsworth in a state bordering upon panic. Three
events had served to shatter his peace of mind. The first
was his affair with Annette—the fact of the unmarried
mother and her child left perforce in France, which to a
sensitive and chivalrous soul like Wordsworth must have
brought a torment of brooding, alternating between pity
and self-blame. We know now that heart-breaking letters
were being sent by Annette, and that in the autumn of
1793, during the Reign of Terror, at the peril of his
life, Wordsworth made an attempt to rejoin her at
Blois, journeying as far as Paris.[2] The second event was
his prolonged indecision as to a congenial calling in life.
The strong desire of his relatives was that he should
take orders in the Church. Against this he rebelled, yet
with no clear leading in any other direction. The demoral-
izing effect of a situation like this, extending through a

---

[2] See Harper's *William Wordsworth*, edition of 1929, pp. 150 ff.

series of years, is easily understood. Finally, and more disrupting than either of the above, was his sorrow over England's attitude toward the France of his affections and dreams. To the mind of Wordsworth, during the period in question, the cause of freedom had become involved in the success of the French Revolution, which, in spite of certain excesses beginning to appear, held out a mighty hope for the race. A reading of *The Prelude,* especially Books IX, X and XI, and of the poem *French Revolution,* will reveal with how much enthusiasm and hope the young English poet had committed himself to the cause of the Republic.

> Bliss was it in that dawn to be alive,
> But to be young was very heaven! . . .
>
> . . . . . . . . . . . . .
> Not favoured spots alone, but the whole earth,
> The beauty wore of promise . . .[3]

And yet, in the winter of 1793, shortly after his return, England declared war against France. The shock to Wordsworth's nature was terrific. To the end of his life he spoke of it as amounting to a moral tragedy. The pillars of his social thinking were broken down. The very foundations of faith appeared swept away. It was at this time, during his sojourn in London, that Wordsworth was drawn into the circle of free-thinkers and radicals, known locally as "English Jacobins," who foregathered in the home of William Godwin, and when, to the thought of some of his friends, he was rated as "a semi-atheist." Two of his works, not otherwise significant, reflect the distraction of his mind during the same period—the poem *Guilt and Sorrow,* completed in 1793-94, and the drama *The Borderers,* composed in 1795-96. Of both works it may be said that not only are they tragic in conception and treatment, but they produce a distinctly depressing effect. In the poem and the drama alike we find a strong element of remorse. There is no mistaking the autobiographic sig-

---

[3] *French Revolution,* lines 4 ff.

nificance of these pieces when once the key is in our hands.
How self-revealing are lines like these:

> Three sleepless nights I passed in sounding on,
> Through words and things, a dim and perilous way.[4]

Altogether, it is a very much upset young man that we
discover in the Wordsworth of this period—dispirited,
restless, gloomy, pessimistic, wounded in his affections,
shattered in his ideals, considering that the times were
out of joint, and more than half suspecting that he was
out of joint himself. Six years later we see him emerge
strong and buoyant, a man of courage and faith, happily
settled upon poetry as his calling, and determined that
his poetry shall convey a message of optimism and cheer
not only to England but to a war-weary and disillusioned
world.

What happened? Did space permit it would be pertinent to trace the process by which joy and peace were
reborn in the soul of this young poet. The recital would
take us to Racedown and Alfoxden in the south of
England, where, after years of separation, he was joined
by Dorothy, where, under her gentle persuasions, he was
led back to Nature as his first love, and where the peace
of a newly discovered world crept into his soul. It would
introduce us for the first time to Coleridge, "the lofty
one, of the god-like forehead," who, in the brilliance of
his intellect and the richness of his affection, could give
and receive in equal measure, and into whose eager ears
Wordsworth poured the broodings of his wounded soul.
Best of all, the story would take us on long tramps with
that immortal three, through the gorse and broom of the
Somerset downs, over the ridges and peaks of the Quan-
tock Hills, and along the banks of "The Sylvan Wye,"
where Nature became the transparent veil of divinity, and
where, in a moment of high inspiration, he indited the
*Lines Composed Above Tintern Abbey,* which, better

---

[4]*Borderers,* Act IV.

than any poem we can name, uncover the foundations of his peace. All this and more should be in the possession of the reader who would receive the full message of Wordsworth into his heart. And these six crucial years were the introduction to a life-long experience of Nature's power not only to heal, but also to educate, refine and satisfy the soul.

Looking at the matter in a more detailed way, what was it that Nature gave to Wordsworth and that he in turn has given to the world? What were the elements of his satisfaction? What the sources of his strength? We have heard him characterizing his calling in words like these:

> In common things that round us lie
> Some random truths he can impart,—
> The harvest of a quiet eye
> That broods and sleeps on his own heart.

What *are* these "truths"? Where are we to look for that "harvest of a quiet eye"? The central message of Wordsworth as a poet of nature confronts us at this point.

First of all, the sense of joy. When Dr. Henry van Dyke, in a volume of essays, sought to express in a single phrase Wordsworth's mission to his age he chose this: "The Recovery of Joy." First the Poet, he shows us, after the wrecking of his hopes in France, recovered joy for himself, and thus by the same sign became the apostle of joy to an age too much given over to melancholy and despair.[5] The same might be said, perhaps with greater force, of the strength of Wordsworth's influence today. Certainly there is no missing of the joy-element as we read his nature-poems, both those of the period of *Lyrical Ballads* and those that followed. The impression meets us on almost every page.

One day in March, after the settlement in Grasmere, Wordsworth was resting on the stone bridge at the

---

[5] *The Recovery of Joy*, an essay by Henry van Dyke, in *Companionable Books*.

foot of the little lake below Kirkstone Pass, known as "Brother's Water." Dorothy had gone for a stroll along the path on the western side of the lake, leading to Dove Dale—scene of the exquisite poem:

> She dwelt among the untrodden ways
> Beside the springs of Dove.

When Dorothy returned to the bridge the Poet handed her these lines:

> The Cock is crowing,
> The stream is flowing,
> The small birds twitter,
> The lake doth glitter,
> The green field sleeps in the sun;
> The oldest and youngest
> Are at work with the strongest;
> The cattle are grazing,
> Their heads never raising;
> There are forty feeding like one!
>
> Like an army defeated
> The snow hath retreated,
> And now doth fare ill
> On the top of the bare hill;
> The Ploughboy is whooping—anon—anon;
> There's joy in the mountains;
> There's life in the fountains;
> Small clouds are sailing,
> Blue Sky prevailing;
> The rain is over and gone!

The poem is not without its faulty lines. (A Shelley or a Tennyson would never have been content with "And now doth fare ill On the top of the bare hill.") Yet it is a marvel of compressed expression. In a single picture, set before us in twenty short lines, we have offered to view the following objects: the crowing cock, the flowing stream, the twittering birds, the glittering lake, the green fields, the sleep-inducing sun, the busy farmers, the grazing cattle, the vanishing snow, the whooping ploughboy, the mountains, the fountains, the clouds, the sky and the disappearing rain—each, by statement or suggestion, and with an extraordinary accumulation of effect, conveying the sense of deep-seated and pervasive happiness. The picture of the cattle, with their noses deep in the lush grass, "Their heads never raising," "forty feeding like one," is a master-stroke. And this was in March—of all months! And the lines were struck off in haste!

One day, reflecting upon this aspect of his work, my curiosity got the better of my judgment—if it be that—and turning to the Wordsworth Concordance I counted the number of times he had used the word "Joy" and its derivatives, and I found it to be 468. After such an investigation one is not surprised to find the Poet in one place characterizing himself as "joy-smitten."

It is significant that the deeper meanings of the joy he discovered in the external world are best set forth in an early poem like *Tintern Abbey*. Nothing could better attest how far he traveled toward faith and hope in those six critical years. Here we find him speaking of "the *deep* power of joy," and of how under its direction we reach the inner harmonies and penetrate to the sources of truth —"We see into the life of things."

Here also we learn that there is an ascending scale of joys, and once we have caught the inspiration we may be lifted above the ugly facts of selfishness and insincerity and all that otherwise would drag us into gloom.

> Knowing that Nature never did betray
> The heart that loved her; 'tis her privilege,
> Through all the years of this our life, to lead
> From joy to joy: for she can so inform
> The mind that is within us, so impress
> With quietness and beauty, and so feed
> With lofty thoughts, that neither evil tongues,
> Rash judgments, nor the sneers of selfish men,
> Nor greetings where no kindness is, nor all
> The dreary intercourse of daily life,
> Shall e'er prevail against us, or disturb
> Our cheerful faith that all which we behold
> Is full of blessings.

And so too in respect to the experiences of sorrow and loss which are sure to come in future days—it is in the memory of happy scenes on the River Wye that he exhorts his sister to find as her portion "healing thoughts of tender joy." It is with this note that the great poem closes.

Thus we find that Wordsworth became the purveyor of joy to his age because, as a result of struggle, he acquired serenity of spirit in those very fields that wrecked the faith and hope of many. We turn to him today because he found in Nature the element we need, and sometimes crave above all others—not pleasure, not even happiness, but joy—something deep and vital, something that can satisfy and fortify the soul. It is at this point, I am inclined to think, that we shall find the inwardness of Wordsworth's peculiar hold upon the youth of our time. With an instinct as sure as it is heartening we see them turning to him as the exponent of

> Spontaneous wisdom breathed by health,
> Truth breathed by cheerfulness.[6]

Of almost equal significance to Wordsworth was the experience of the tranquillity which came to him out of Nature's heart. We may say that tranquillity is one of the key-words of his message. If the prevalence of joy in the outer world put to flight his early gloom, it was in the quietude of this same world that he found the remedy for his restlessness and distraction of spirit. The evidence for this hovers like a benediction over much of his finer verse. No better illustration can be found than the closing stanza of that little-known poem *Memory*, written in 1823:

> With heart as calm as lakes that sleep,
> In frosty moonlight glistening;
> Or mountain rivers, where they creep
> Along a channel smooth and deep,
> To their own far-off murmurs listening.

Of this stanza F. W. Myers remarks: "What touch has

---

[6] From *The Tables Turned.*

given to these lines their impress of an unfathomable peace? For there speaks from them a tranquillity which seems to overcome one's soul; which makes us feel in the midst of toil and passion that we are disquieting ourselves in vain; that we are traveling to a region where these things shall not be; that 'so shall immoderate fear leave us, and inordinate love shall die.' "[7]

One would have to quote a score of poems to show how Wordsworth became possessed of the idea that peace lies at the very heart of Nature's life and that through its transmission man comes to his true self. In the poem *Song at the Feast of Brougham Castle,* he describes in exquisitely tender lines how the proud Lord Clifford, through adversities which forced him to a shepherd's life, became at length subdued to the peace at Nature's heart:

> Love had he found in huts where poor men lie,
> His daily teachers had been woods and rills,
> The silence that is in the starry sky,
> The sleep that is among the lonely hills.

In another place he speaks of "the peace of an unfathomable sky." This peace he pictures as brought down by the mountains:

> There is an Eminence,—of these our hills
> The last that parleys with the setting sun;
> We can behold it from our orchard seat;
> And, when at evening we pursue our walk
> Along the public way, this Peak, so high
> Above us, and so distant in its height,
> Is visible; and often seems to send
> Its own deep quiet to restore our hearts.[8]

It was a happy thought of Dorothy to bestow her brother's name upon this peak. Indeed, it was for the most part a longing for a seasoned life of tranquillity that led the Poet and his sister, after their years of wandering, to

---

[7] *Wordsworth*, English Men of Letters Series, The Macmillan Company, edition of 1925, p. 183.

[8] *Poems on the Naming of Places*, III.

settle upon Grasmere as their permanent home. The vale appealed to them as a paradise of seclusion.

The profoundest passage is the one in *The Excursion* where "The Solitary" betrays his yearning for peace:

> What but this,
> The universal instinct of repose,
> The longing for confirmed tranquillity,
> Inward and outward; humble, yet sublime:
> The life where hope and memory are as one;
> Where earth is quiet and her face unchanged
> Save by the simplest toil of human hands
> Or season's difference; the immortal Soul
> Consistent in self-rule; and heaven revealed
> To meditation in that quietness![9]

In all this, be it noted, Wordsworth stands in interesting contrast to Emerson, who, in his essay on *Nature* emphasizes motion or change as the first secret of the external world—the "aboriginal push" and the projection of internal energy; man identified not so much with Nature's poise as with Nature's excess. "Typically American!" one might easily exclaim. More typically scientific, would be the correct rejoinder. Yet to the mind of Wordsworth these two aspects of Nature—motion and rest—are to be conceived of not as antithetic, but rather as complementary phases of a deeper life.

We come now to a third principle in Nature for which Wordsworth stands out as *par excellence* the prophet and seer, and that is the principle of love. And here we shall find ourselves walking in a truly religious atmosphere. According to St. Paul, love, joy and peace are marks of the Kingdom of God. According to Wordsworth, they are also marks of the Kingdom of Nature. The principle of love and self-sacrifice, which others have found reflected in Nature's face, Wordsworth found written deep in Nature's heart. It was to him the inner secret of her power over the heart of man. We see this most clearly in the character of the Wanderer in *The Excursion*,

[9] *Excursion*, III, 397 ff.

where Wordsworth gives us his conception of a man of natural nobility, impressed by the thought of Nature's beauty and power, led into the deeper and tenderer feeling of love, and in this experience finding the conquest of doubt and fear.

> In his heart,
> Where Fear sate thus, a cherished visitant,
> Was wanting yet the pure delight of love
> By sound diffused, or by the breathing air,
> Or by the silent looks of happy things,
> Or flowing from the universal face
> Of earth and sky. But he had felt the power
> Of Nature, and already was prepared,
> By his intense conceptions, to receive
> Deeply the lesson deep of love which he,
> Whom Nature, by whatever means, has taught
> To feel intensely, cannot but receive.[10]

In the character of Peter Bell we have presented the opposite type—a man of brutal instincts, licentious, cunning, impudent, devoid of the sense of beauty:

> A primrose by a river's brim
> A yellow primrose was to him,
> And it was nothing more.

In this much abused poem, marred, as we must admit, by diffuseness and the introduction of unworthy lines, we have the story of how this "ruffian wild" came under the power of Nature's love and fidelity in the form of an ass who watched by the dead body of his master during four starving days. The absurdity of certain elements in the tale need not blind us to the profundity of its message:

> And now is Peter taught to feel
> That man's heart is a holy thing;
> And Nature, through a world of death,
> Breathes into him a second breath,
> More searching than the breath of spring.

More attractive than either of these is the picture of

[10] *Excursion*, I, 184-196.

Wordsworth and his sister yielding themselves to the sweet influences of a spring day:

> Love, now a universal birth,
> From heart to heart is stealing,
> From earth to man, from man to earth;
> —It is the hour of feeling.

> One moment now may give us more
> Than years of toiling reason;
> Our minds shall drink at every pore
> The spirit of the season.

> Some silent laws our hearts will make,
> Which they shall long obey;
> We for the year to come may take
> Our temper from today.

> And from the blessed power that rolls
> About, below, above,
> We'll frame the measure of our souls:
> They shall be tuned to love.[11]

It was through experiences like these, even more through his later brooding upon them, that the Poet could speak of "Nature's holy plan," and welcome every out-door experience as the opportunity

> To feed the spirit of religious love
> In which I walked with Nature.[12]

This impression he carried down to every last detail of the natural scene. In April mornings "fresh and clear," in flowers and birds and waves, in the bright speed of brooks as they emerge from their mountain cradles, in the cool of the forest glade, in the lush green of the meadows, in "the soul of happy sound," in the splendor of the "full shining moon," in the "witchery of the soft blue sky," even in "summer's storms and winter's ice," Wordsworth traced the opulence of love breathing from Nature's inner soul. The higher expression of this principle, naturally, he found in the mother-love of the domestic animals and the

---

[11]From *To My Sister*.
[12]*Prelude*, II, 357-358.

intercommunions and sacrificial devotion of family life. Creation itself was to him "the birth of universal love."[13]

Joy, tranquillity, love—such are the principles of Nature that stand out with special distinctness in the poetry of Wordsworth, as possessing educational and healing power. But they are not to be thought of as detached and independent in their workings upon the mind. Rather we are to regard them as a cycle of influences tending to stimulate and purify the elements of thought and feeling. Back of the observer, the dreamer, the mystic, stands the man—the full-orbed man, with reason enthroned as the central element in his being. And it is the man as a whole that Nature, by the totality of her process, leads into pathways of peace and power.

To understand Wordsworth's thought at this point— arising, let us never forget, from his own experience— one needs to read the first two books of *The Prelude,* where he deals with his childhood and school-time; *Tintern Abbey,* of course, where he gives us an intensive view; and the fourth book of *The Excursion,* where the "Wanderer" takes the "Solitary" in hand and shows him how he may be eased of his despondency by undergoing the Nature-cure. To these might be added the first book of *The Excursion,* since there we have an account of the "Wanderer's" own education, and of how he achieved so sublime a trust. Here also is set forth the mighty influence of mountains upon his religious faith:

> But in the mountains did he *feel* his faith
> All things, responsive to the writing, there
> Breathed immortality, revolving life,
> And greatness still revolving; infinite:
> There littleness was not; the least of things
> Seemed infinite; and there his spirit shaped
> Her prospects, nor did he believe,—he *saw.*[14]

Even better is the passage in *The Prelude,* where Words-

---

[13] If this be regarded as too idealistic for the modern mind, it may be noted that the eminent physicist, Michael Pupin, out of the researches in the laboratory drew "concrete physical evidence that God loves the soul of man."
[14] *Excursion,* I, 225 ff.

worth bears witness to the influence of mountains, lakes, cataracts, mists and winds upon his own character and his outlook upon the world:

> If in my youth I have been pure in heart,
> If, mingling with the world, I am content
> With my own modest pleasures, and have lived
> With God and Nature communing, removed
> From little enmities and low desires,
> The gift is yours; if in these times of fear
> This melancholy waste of hopes o'er-thrown,
> If, 'mid indifference and apathy,
> And wicked exultation when good men
> On every side fall off, we know not how,
> To selfishness, disguised in gentle names
> Of peace and quiet and domestic love,
> Yet mingled not unwillingly with sneers
> On visionary minds; if, in this time
> Of dereliction and dismay, I yet
> Despair not of our nature, but retain
> A more than Roman confidence, a faith
> That fails not, in all sorrow my support,
> The blessing of my life; the gift is yours,
> Ye winds and sounding cataracts! 'tis yours,
> Ye mountains! thine, O Nature! Thou hast fed
> My lofty speculations; and in thee,
> For this uneasy heart of ours, I find
> A never-failing principle of joy
> And purest passion.[15]

To these stately lines might be added also the lighter touch which we find in the poem *The Tables Turned,* in which in playful mood, conversing with his old-time teacher and companion on many a walk, the Poet contrasts the education of Nature with the education of books:

> Books! 'tis a dull and endless strife:
> Come, hear the woodland linnet,
> How sweet his music! on my life,
> That's more of wisdom in it.

[15] *Prelude,* II, 427 ff.

And hark! how blithe the throstle sings!
He, too, is no mean preacher:
Come forth into the light of things,
Let Nature be your Teacher.

She has a world of ready wealth,
Our minds and hearts to bless—
Spontaneous wisdom breathed by health,
Truth breathed by cheerfulness.

One impulse from a vernal wood
May teach you more of man,
Of moral evil and of good,
Than all the sages can.

And now it is necessary to consider an objection of so basic a character that, if it can be sustained, the main structure of Wordsworth's attitude and argument crumbles to the ground. It is the objection of a selective and partial view of the forces that rule the world, a view that conveys an essentially false impression of Nature as a whole. Wordsworth, it is contended, deals exclusively, or almost so, with the gentler aspects of Nature as found in "the pretty pastoralism" of the English landscape. His poetry reflects the glory of grass and flowers and singing birds, the quiet beauty of sequestered vales, the calm of embosomed lakes. Where, it is asked, is there any square dealing with Nature in her wilder moods—the storm, the avalanche, the floods, the earthquake, the volcano, the trackless waste of the desert, the savagery of the mountains, the terror of the jungle? Not through reading Wordsworth would one ever suspect that Nature is "red in tooth and claw." The green pastures and still waters of an earthly paradise are depicted with poetic charm; but scant is the reference to the valley of the shadow of death.

This criticism, not essentially new, has of late been expressed by Aldous Huxley in so drastic and challenging a way that it cannot be ignored. In a widely quoted essay, entitled *Wordsworth in the Tropics,* he argues that not only does the Poet misread and misinterpret the domi-

nant facts of the outer world, but he falsifies the findings
of our direct intuitions of Nature in her modes of being at
our very feet. The tenor of the essay can be judged from
its opening page:

> In the neighborhood of latitude fifty north and for the last
> hundred years or thereabouts, it has been an axiom that Nature
> is divine and morally uplifting. For good Wordsworthians—
> and most serious-minded people are now Wordsworthians,
> either by direct inspiration or at second hand—a walk in the
> country is the equivalent of going to church, a tour through
> Westmoreland is as good as a pilgrimage to Jerusalem. To com-
> mune with the fields and waters, the woodlands and the hills,
> is to commune, according to our modern and Northern ideas,
> with the visible manifestations of the "Wisdom and Spirit of
> the Universe."
>
> The Wordsworthian who exports this pantheistic worship of
> Nature to the tropics is liable to have his religious convictions
> somewhat rudely disturbed. Nature under a vertical sun, and
> nourished by the equatorial rains, is not at all like that chaste,
> mild deity who presides over the "gemutlichkeit," the pretti-
> ness, the cosy sublimities of the Lake District. The worst that
> Wordsworth's goddess ever did to him was to make him hear
>
> > "Low breathings coming after me and sounds
> > Of undistinguishable motion, steps
> > Almost as silent as the turf they trod";
>
> was to make him realize, in the shape of "a huge peak, black
> and huge," the existence of "unknown modes of being." He
> seems to have imagined that this was the worst Nature *could*
> do. A few weeks in Malaya or Borneo would have undeceived
> him. Wandering in the hothouse darkness of the jungle
> Wordsworth would not have felt so serenely certain of those
> "Presences of Nature," those "Souls of Lonely Places," which
> he was in the habit of worshipping on the shores of Winder-
> mere and Rydal.[16]

From these premises Mr. Huxley presents a series of
pictures "terrifying" and "profoundly sinister" from
Nature as *not* seen by the contemplative Poet of the
Lakes. He finds two principal defects. The first is Words-

---

[16] From *Do What You Will*, by Aldous Huxley, copyright 1928, 1929, by Doubleday, Doran & Co., Inc.

worth's concentration upon a country where Nature has been "enslaved to Man." The second is a "falsification of immediate experience," a wrong-headedness as to the deeper aspects of Nature even in her quiet modes. "For Nature, even in the temperate zone, is always alien and inhuman, and occasionally diabolic." The argument, as one would expect, is immensely clever and of challenging interest. It is a slashing attack upon the very citadel of the Wordsworth tradition. If Aldous Huxley is right then most of us are living in "the fools' paradise of a sentimental world."

To answer the Huxley objection effectively, especially in its philosophical assumptions, would require far more space than is possible here. But certain offsetting considerations and points of view rise quickly to the mind.

In the first place, as Lord Cecil has pointed out in his defense of Scott, every poet, like every painter, has his range. This range is determined by his temperament, the direction of his genius, the circumstances of his life, his power of imagination, and his philosophy of Nature and of human life. It is because these factors vary widely between poet and poet that we have the variety and richness of outlook that is so characteristic of English verse. We do not look to a poet like Cowper, with his shy disposition, his deeply religious nature, and the restriction of his experience to English parsonages and their contiguous fields and groves, for the contribution of a Byron, with his æsthetic sensibility, his play of wit, his wide experience and his voluptuous manner of life. We do not expect a *Jungle Book* from a Robert Bridges, or a *Testament of Beauty* from a Rudyard Kipling. And so with a Burns, a Wordsworth and a Tennyson; by running true to form we expect they will make the largest contribution to the apprehension of Nature as a whole. The geographic coverage of their views is not necessarily limited by the fact that they lived here or there. With Wordsworth, in view of the richness of his imagination and his doctrine of the whole of Nature pervading her separate parts, it is correct to say that the truer he was to his locality, the truer he would be to the deeper meanings of diverse conditions far removed. Certainly the unity of his message arises from his fidelity to those aspects of Nature which, through a life-long experience, had become a part of his being. On no other basis could his poetry have made its universal appeal.

In the second place, Wordsworth is not so lacking in the recognition of the calamitous and oppressive elements of Nature as Mr. Huxley contends. Even among the English Lakes there is a chance to study Nature in her sterner modes. Not every walk in that district "is the equivalent of going to church." Wordsworth has not a little to say of the violence of wind and rain and snow, of the storms that sweep in upon his mountain retreat from the Irish Sea. The fortitude and rugged virtues of his dales people he attributes in large measure to the fact that throughout their lives they were battling with adverse conditions of topography, climate and weather. Two of his poems (*Lucy Gray* and *George and Sarah Green*) relate to people of the dales who perished in winter storms close to their cottage doors.

In one place in *The Prelude* he speaks of the smooth life of the flock and the shepherd in the old time of the classic writers of Greece and Rome, and of the charm of their gentle pastoral scenes, in contrast with the far more invigorating life of his native regions:

> Yet, hail to you
> Moors, mountains, headlands, and ye hollow vales,
> Ye long deep channels for the Atlantic's voice,
> Powers of my native region! Ye that seize
> The heart with firmer grasp! Your snows and streams
> Ungovernable, and your terrifying winds,
> That howl so dismally for him who treads
> Companionless your awful solitudes![17]

[17] *Prelude*, VIII, 215-222.

Mr. Huxley needs to read his Wordsworth more carefully. He appears to be unaware of what the peaceful poet of the hills has to say about "the business of the elements." Yet it hardly seems possible he has overlooked such a poem as the *Elegiac Stanzas, Suggested by a Picture of Peele Castle in a Storm,* since this admittedly is one of the greatest Wordsworth ever wrote. In this sublime meditation the Poet contrasts the painting by Sir George Beaumont with the time when, for days during a summer vacation, he looked upon that same castle and sea in a season of perfect calm. He suggests the kind of picture, had he been an artist, he would have painted at that time:

> A Picture had it been of lasting ease,
> Elysian quiet, without toil or strife;
> No motion but the moving tide, a breeze,
> Or merely silent Nature's breathing life.

Then he relates how, as the result of bitter experience, he had been forced to consider the harsher side of life and to welcome it as tending to develop nobility of character. He now recognizes Beaumont's picture as true and right —a corrective of the dream of an earlier day. In the light of what came after he can even commend "This sea in anger and that dismal shore," "This rueful sky, this pageantry of fear," "The lightning, the fierce wind, and the trampling waves:"

> Farewell, farewell the heart that lives alone,
> Housed in a dream, at distance from the Kind!
> Such happiness, wherever it be known,
> Is to be pitied; for 'tis surely blind.
>
> But welcome fortitude, and patient cheer,
> And frequent sights of what is to be borne!
> Such sights, or worse, as are before me here.—
> Not without hope we suffer and we mourn.

Although *Peele Castle* is full of the sense of pain reflected in the external scene, it serves also to reveal how fully Wordsworth realized that the ultimate lesson of Nature must be a synthesis of storm and calm.

In another well-known poem, *Ruth,* the Poet pictures the very things in the tropics upon which Mr. Huxley descants so eloquently, and shows their effect upon a young English soldier who yielded to their seductive influences:

> The wind, the tempest roaring high,
> The tumult of a tropic sky,
> Might well be dangerous food
> For him, a Youth to whom was given
> So much of earth—so much of heaven,
> And such impetuous blood.

Clearly the range of Wordsworth's information was not as restricted as his experience. There is good reason for holding that, so far from overlooking the harsher aspects of the outer world, he at one time held these in the very front of his vision, and that, largely under the persuasions of his sister, he turned from these to Nature's softer measures as a truer indication of what lay at the heart of things. This is indicated in a passage which, from its location in the concluding book of *The Prelude,* would seem to express a carefully reasoned point of view. In lines addressed to Dorothy and referring to his former mood, he bears thankful witness to his change of view:

> I too exclusively esteemed *that* love,
> And sought *that* beauty, which, as Milton sings,
> Hath terror in it. Thou didst soften down
> This over-sternness; but for thee, dear Friend!
> My soul, too reckless of mild grace, had stood
> In her original self too confident,
> Retained too long a countenance severe;
> A rock with torrents roaring, with the clouds
> Familiar, and a favourite of the stars:
> But thou didst plant its crevices with flowers,
> Hang it with shrubs that twinkle in the breeze,
> And teach the little birds to build their nests
> And warble in its chambers.[18]

The question of the fundamental character of Nature

---

[18] *Prelude,* XIV, 244 ff.

—whether tender or harsh, or an unresolved disparity between the two—is involved in the closer question of the effect of Nature upon the character of Man. When Mr. Huxley deals with the Wordsworth reaction to Nature, his argument enters a realm where we all feel measurably at home. As a matter of fact, just what is the effect of Nature upon our nerves? Does she grate or does she soothe? And what, particularly, is the effect of Nature in those tropic regions from which Wordsworth so persistently stayed away? In many instances the people of the tropics are found to be more patient and gentle than those of the temperate zone. Nowhere is this more apparent than in those parts of Africa where the jungle reigns supreme. A recent book by Mr. Huxley's distinguished brother, Julian Huxley, the biologist, bears abundant testimony to the gentleness and joyousness of the natives in the central zone of the continent. Nothing pertaining to native characteristics impressed him more than their cheerfulness and gaiety even under trying conditions. He quotes General Smuts as declaring that the negroes are the only happy people in the world. In this connection one recalls that the Pigmies, who live in the perpetual gloom of the most impenetrable recesses of the Congo glades, according to Martin Johnson and other explorers, are superlatively of gentle and kindly disposition. I do not wish to labor the point, but I must maintain that any fair generalization as to Man's impression of Nature's inherent character would seem to rob Mr. Huxley's objection of much of its force.

On nearly every page of Mr. Huxley's brilliant attack one detects the anti-religious, anti-idealistic prejudice that characterizes so much of his writing. If Wordsworth's view is colored by the underlying optimism of his mind, the Huxley view may be as temperamentally pessimistic. One cannot easily imagine him as approving of any author who experiences an "ecstasy of joy," or who even indulges in a "cheerful faith." The slant of this thinking appears to his disadvantage when he inveighs against Words-worth as a convinced pantheist and on the same page classifies him as an orthodox Anglican. How both of these can be true at the same time the reader is left to figure out as best he can. It is evident enough, however, that so far as Mr. Huxley himself is concerned, he is neither pan-theist nor theist. But on either score the case must be al-lowed to rest not on any one's theology, certainly not on any one's prejudice, but on the facts of Nature's life in their bearing upon human character. To the mind of Huxley, the evidence points to a perpetual and relentless warfare against the tranquil and harmonious life. This is not a "Good Earth." To the mind of Wordsworth the evidence conveys the tale

> Of ebb and flow, and ever-during power;
> And central peace, subsisting at the heart
> Of endless agitation.[19]

As between the two views, Mr. Huxley is constrained to admit that "most serious-minded people" are now Words-worthians. Certainly his essay is not calculated to shatter the conviction that had the Poet been permitted to so-journ in the tropics, he would have been the same old Wordsworth who wrote *The Tables Turned, I Heard a Thousand Blended Notes,* and *The Kitten and the Fall-ing Leaves.*[20]

In all this we are to have in mind that it is not merely what Nature brings to Man, but what Man brings to Nature. As with education of all kinds, the process is reciprocal. When Wordsworth sings of Nature's power to lead from joy to joy, it is with reference to a congenial spirit:

> Knowing that Nature never did betray
> The heart that loved her.

---

[19] *Excursion,* IV, 1145-1147.

[20] For a critique of Aldous Huxley as "The last word in modernity," see *The Glory That Was Grub Street,* by St. John Adcock. In Mr. Huxley's universal anthology, published in 1933, only three poems and passages from Wordsworth are cited, and one of these by way of disapprobation. The last half at least of the title to this collec-tion—*Texts and Pretexts*—would appear to be justified.

Wordsworth's teaching is that the *seeing* of Nature is the resultant of the outer and inner processes of vision:

> The eye—it cannot choose but see;
> We cannot bid the ear be still;
> Our bodies feel, where'er they be,
> Against or with our will.

> Nor less I deem that there are Powers
> Which of themselves our minds impress;
> That we can feed this mind of ours
> In a wise passiveness.[21]

The expression "In a wise passiveness" is Wordsworthian to the core. It suggests, possibly, the reason for the marked difference we find between Wordsworth and certain other poets in the matter of the effect of Nature upon their inner lives.[22]

The right mental attitude being understood, four things, according to Wordsworth, are involved for all who would enter into the secret of the outer world: separation, solitude, meditation, memory. First, man must get away from

> the heavy and the weary weight
> Of all this unintelligible world.

He must find a way of escape from the tumult and traffic of city life, from the fret and fever of daily toil, and sojourn where Nature reigns supreme. The need is to secure what the Poet felicitously calls "spots of time," occasions "that with distinct preëminence retain a renovating virtue."[23] In a word, there must be a definite exposure to Mother Nature's soothing and elevating power.

But separation of place is not sufficient. There must also be periods of separation from one's kind. The mind must have a chance to live in a world of its own, untram-

---

[21] From *Expostulation and Reply*.

[22] In his *Life of Gladstone*, Viscount Morley comments upon Gladstone's fondness for both Shelley and Wordsworth arising from the fact that both poets possessed the quality of combining and connecting everywhere external nature with internal and unseen mind. But Gladstone recognized a wide difference in application, in that while nature fretted and irritated Shelley, it is the key to the peacefulness of Wordsworth. This is a distinction which Morley, as a deep student of the latter poet, seems to have taken peculiar satisfaction in bringing out. (Macmillan. Edition of 1905, Vol. I, p. 96.)

[23] *Prelude*, XII, 208.

meled by the proximity of other minds, the chance to speak to Nature face to face. Such was the experience of the young Wordsworth on the memorable walk around Esthwaite, where

> Gently did my soul
> Put off her veil, and, self-transmuted, stood
> Naked, as in the presence of her God.[24]

His poetry is full of like expressions, revealing the estimate he placed upon solitude as a requisite for communion of the more intimate kind. In one place he speaks of "the quiet and exalted thoughts of loneliness"; in another of "the self-sacrificing power of solitude." In the *Poet's Epitaph*, we have the familiar lines:

> The outward shows of sky and earth,
> Of hill and valley, he has viewed;
> And impulses of deeper birth
> Have come to him in solitude.

The classic passage, familiar and dear to many today, is the one in *The Prelude*, beginning:

> When from our better selves we have too long
> Been parted by the hurrying world, and droop,
> Sick of its business, of its pleasures tired,
> How gracious, how benign, is Solitude.[25]

But solitude meant more than abstraction, it was filled with the intensity of thought and feeling. As sung by Wordsworth, it lends itself to awareness, attention, expansion of mind. It is a *wise* passiveness that floods the soul. Hence his emphasis upon meditation in the presence of the natural scene. How else is one to sense "the calm that Nature breathes among the hills and groves?" How else have a feeling for the "Presence of Nature in the sky and on the earth," and for the "Souls of lonely places"? It is by the *contemplation* of beauty in its perfect dress that beauty has a chance to sink into the soul. The charac-

[24] *Prelude*, IV, 150-153.
[25] *Ibid.*, IV, 354-357.

teristic influences that radiate from natural objects and scenes demand a corresponding radiation from the centers of thought, feeling and will in the man who knows their fertilizing power. The recognition of the essential beauty of the universe, he tells us, "is a task light and easy to him who looks at the world in the spirit of love."[26]

And, finally, memory—the recalling of the scene, the impression, the mood, in subsequent days, the projection of the elevating experience into the din and toil of daily living. Here we find ourselves in a realm which Wordsworth may claim as peculiarly his own. It will be recalled that the *Tintern Abbey* poem begins with a description of the Poet's impressions upon revisiting the valley of the Wye after an absence of five years; then follows a tribute to what "these beauteous forms" had meant to him during the interval:

> These beauteous forms,
> Through a long absence, have not been to me
> As is a landscape to a blind man's eye;
> But oft, in lonely rooms, and 'mid the din
> Of towns and cities, I have owed to them,
> In hours of weariness, sensations sweet,
> Felt in the blood, and felt along the heart;
> And passing even into my purer mind,
> With tranquil restoration.

It will be recalled also that in the *Daffodils* poem it is the recollection of the scene that the Poet would impress upon our minds, as it was impressed upon his own, the happy moment, when

> They flash upon that inward eye
> Which is the bliss of solitude.

There are a number of other poems, notably *The Recluse,* which convey the same lesson of a perennial blessing arising from any association with Nature which allows the mind first to note and then absorb the essence

---

[26] Preface to *Lyrical Ballads,* 1800.

of the scene. Here is something for us to remember the next time we find ourselves in a lonely and a lovely spot.

There is another aspect of memory of which Wordsworth has not a little to say, and that is its power to glorify the scene of some past experience and spread over it a significance impossible of realization on the spot. Memory, to him, was far more than a recovery of the past. It was a re-collecting, a rebuilding of the experience in the light of a clearer and calmer mood. It is at this point that imagination is released and the scene takes on a higher significance. An emotional experience, mellowed by memory, passes easily from actuality either into romance or a deeper apprehension of its meaning. It was the latter trail that Wordsworth pursued, and always with the zest of an explorer. And here we find ourselves close to one of the secrets of Wordsworth's poetic power. His famous statement from the *Preface* will be recalled, that poetry "takes its origin from emotion recollected in tranquillity." This is usually misquoted by overlooking the words "takes its origin" and assuming that we have here a definition of poetry.

The message of Wordsworth arising from his conception of Nature as an educating and renewing power is just the message of the four things we have been considering —separation, solitude, meditation, recollection. They are desperately needed in our pleasure-chasing and jazz-infested world today. Possibly never has there been a time when they were needed more. Certainly the conditions that make for unrest and discontent were far less prevalent in the Poet's time than they are today.

Specifically, since ours is an age of work too often unrelieved by nobility of purpose or the temper of a quiet mind, when pace is reckoned as of far greater value than peace, we need the lesson of Wordsworth's attitude toward daily toil. Contrary to the popular impression, this looks not to withdrawal from the world, but to the capturing and the carrying over into the busy scene of the "calm that Nature breathes among the hills and groves." In no moment of his career, not even when disheartened and disillusioned by the failure of the French Revolution, was Wordsworth tempted to say with Emerson, "Good-bye! proud world, I'm going home." Rather would he be in the world as one who stood above its strife. This was the thought of Matthew Arnold, Wordsworth's great disciple, who must have had the older poet in mind when he wrote of *Quiet Work*:

> One lesson, Nature, let me learn of thee,
> One lesson which in every wind is blown,
> One lesson of two duties kept at one
> Though the loud world proclaim their enmity—
>
> Of toil unsever'd from tranquillity,
> Of labor, that in lasting fruit outgrows
> Far noisier schemes, accomplish'd in repose,
> Too great for haste, too high for rivalry.

Arnold's exhortation is needed today. And even more is there needed a warning against an unfeeling attitude in the presence of the harvest of beauty, joy and love which Nature brings to the quiet and spiritually receptive mind. It took a Wordsworth himself, and in one of his high moments of inspiration, to disclose the peril of a heedless age.

> The world is too much with us; late and soon,
> Getting and spending, we lay waste our powers;
> Little we see in Nature that is ours;
> We have given our hearts away, a sordid boon!
> This Sea that bares her bosom to the moon;
> The winds that will be howling at all hours,
> And are up-gathered now like sleeping flowers;
> For this, for everything, we are out of tune;
> It moves us not.—Great God! I'd rather be
> A Pagan suckled in a creed outworn;
> So might I, standing on this pleasant lea,
> Have glimpses that would make me less forlorn;
> Have sight of Proteus rising from the sea;
> Or hear old Triton blow his wreathed horn.

# CHAPTER VI

## "The Still Sad Music of Humanity"

THE eighth book of *The Prelude* has as its secondary
title "The Love of Nature Leading to Love of
Man." While containing fewer grand passages and quotable lines than certain other books, it is yet in a peculiar
sense the key-book of the poem, without which Wordsworth's major interest cannot be clearly understood. The
book begins with a lively description of the annual fair
held on a village green at the foot of Mount Helvellyn,
which served to bring together a throng of dalespeople,
with their cattle and wares, their chaffering over prices,
their exchange of gossip and their general sense of social
well-being. By means of admirably descriptive lines we
are made to visualize shepherds and tillers of the ground
assembled with their wives and little ones and the usual
admixture of itinerant hawkers and showmen—all in fes-
tive mood. As on a crowded stage in the theatre, certain
figures are brought into the foreground in order to give
accent to the pleasant scene. Thus we have the blind man
with his music, the old woman with her basket of notions,
the speech-maker and the mountebank, the rosy farmer-
lass peddling fruit, the old couple under the tree, and a
plentiful sprinkling of children exulting in their unwonted
freedom. Intermingling with the happy din, as an obbligato
in minor strain, we are made to hear the lowing of the
cattle and the bleating of the sheep. It is what the re-
porters like to call "a colorful scene," such a scene as
poets from the earliest time have loved to depict. What
gives it distinction in Wordsworth's hands is the fact that
"old Helvellyn" is looking on and all nature joins to
make this a service of love.

For all things serve them; them the morning light
Loves, as it glistens on the silent rocks;
And them the silent rocks, which now from high
Look down upon them; the reposing clouds;
The wild brooks prattling from invisible haunts;
And old Helvellyn, conscious of the stir
Which animates this day their calm abode.

Right here we have the turning point in the Wordsworth emphasis and point of view—the passing from the
love of Nature to the love of Man as the main motive and
region of his song. Essentially he was the poet of humanity. The reason why so many people speak of Wordsworth as exclusively or primarily the Poet of Nature is
because they do not read far enough. They are content
to remain in the Daffodils stage. Wordsworth's own testimony on the subject is explicit. In both *The Prelude* and
*Tintern-Abbey* he conducts us from Nature to Man by a
series of steps which to his mind were as distinct as the
stages in his scholastic education. He names his twenty-
second year as the turning point of interest. In the portion of *The Recluse* which he printed as an introduction
to *The Excursion* the objects of his concern are given in
this order:

On Man, on Nature, and on Human Life.

The order was intentional, and not a mere matter of
poetic convenience, since in the prose part of the same
introduction he states that his purpose was to deal with
"Man, Nature and Society." Clearly he aims at a balanced presentation of Man as an individual, and Man as
a social being, with Nature standing in between as that
from which both derive, and that to which both must be
wedded to the end of time. What Wordsworth has to say
as to the wonderful way in which the mind of man is
fitted to the external world, and the external world to the
mind of man, we must leave for later consideration. In
this chapter we shall deal with Wordsworth's conception
of Man in his varied characters and fellowships, against

the background of Nature as the molding influence of his career. Here is a theme worthy of the highest thought and the noblest expression in verse. And Wordsworth, be it noted, was content to have his poetic message judged by his success at this point.

We shall find that throughout *The Prelude,* and for the most part throughout his poetry as a whole, Wordsworth is more interested in men than in man. Philosophy there is, of course; but it is a philosophy arising from the observation of men and women like ourselves. The reason why some of us favor Wordsworth above all other poets is because of his burning interest in human lives; because he could approach the personality of a pedlar or a tramp as he would a shrine. We think of him as the Abraham Lincoln among the poets.

From among the characters of the village fair Wordsworth selects the shepherds as most worthy of attention. The argument of the eighth book may be said to center around the realistic life of Westmoreland shepherds as contrasted with the idyllic presentation in classic poetry and in the writings of Shakespeare and Spenser.[1] More than two hundred lines are devoted to this theme. In elevated strain he traces the course of his intimacy with these "freemen of nature" from early childhood to the time when they served to shape his innermost conception of the dignity and beauty of the human lot:

And shepherds were the men that pleased me first.

The picture of the shepherd in the springtime, as he leads his flock to the higher pastures among the hills is so fine that I must quote it in full, although it is of considerable length. It follows a passage in which the Poet dwells upon the loneliness and hazard of shepherd life during the winter months, when food must be carried

---

[1] See *The Theocritean Element in the Works of William Wordsworth,* by Prof. Leslie N. Broughton, of Cornell University. This author's contention is that in the best sense of the word Wordsworth is a *pastoral poet,* this in accordance with the standard of the Greek poet Theocritus, the undisputed master of pastoral poetry.

from the homestead up the craggy ways and dealt out to
the sheep on the frozen snow. But all that is changed
with the advancing season:

> And when the spring
> Looks out, and all the pastures dance with lambs,
> And when the flock, with warmer weather, climbs
> Higher and higher, him his office leads
> To watch their goings, whatsoever track
> The wanderers choose. For this he quits his home
> At day-spring, and no sooner doth the sun
> Begin to strike him with a fire-like heat,
> Than he lies down upon some shining rock,
> And breakfasts with his dog. When they have stolen,
> As is their wont, a pittance from strict time,
> For rest not needed or exchange of love,
> Then from his couch he starts; and now his feet
> Crush out a livelier fragrance from the flowers
> Of lowly thyme, by Nature's skill enwrought
> In the wild turf: the lingering dews of morn
> Smoke round him, as from hill to hill he hies,
> His staff protending like a hunter's spear,
> Or by its aid leaping from crag to crag,
> And o'er the brawling beds of unbridged streams.
> Philosophy, methinks, at Fancy's call,
> Might deign to follow him through what he does
> Or sees in his day's march; himself he feels,
> In those vast regions where his service lies,
> A freeman, wedded to his life of hope
> And hazard, and hard labour interchanges
> With that majestic indolence so dear
> To native man.[2]

To the boy Wordsworth the shepherd was a Lord of
Nature, and all common men were glorified in him:

> Thus was man
> Ennobled outwardly before my sight,
> And thus my heart was early introduced
> To an unconscious love and reverence
> Of human nature; hence the human form
> To me became an index of delight,
> Of grace and honour, power and worthiness.[3]

[2] *Prelude*, VIII, 229 ff.
[3] *Ibid.*, VIII, 274 ff.

He never ceased to rejoice that in those formative years his attention became fixed on the simplicity, the purity and the sturdiness of his fellow men, rather than upon "the weight of meanness," the "selfish cares," the "coarse manner," the "vulgar passions," that beat in "on all sides from the ordinary world." Here we find the basis for the buoyant optimism which characterized the Poet's later thinking. Here, too, we note his desire to give Nature all possible credit in the shaping of rustic character. He does not hesitate to speak of Nature's influence as

This sanctity of Nature given to man.

One of Wordsworth's most successful poems of the humanitarian sort, universally admired by literary men, is *Michael,* in which he portrayed the industry and the fortitude of shepherd life plus the domestic virtues as reflected in the occupations of the home. In a narrative of intensive, rather than dramatic power, harmonious in all its parts, we have the story of Michael, "stout of heart and strong of limb," his wife Isabel, "a woman of a stirring life," Luke, their comely child, and their two faithful dogs— and how they lived together in the cottage on the mountain side which, by reason of its position and the unfailing light in the window at night, became known as "The Evening Star"; of how Michael and this boy of his old age became bosom comrades in pleasure and toil; of how one day they started to build a fold for the sheep in a secluded vale, and had gathered a pile of stones, when the family became involved in debt and the ancestral land being imperilled, it was decided to send Luke to the city to earn the requisite money. There follows a description of what this separation meant to the aged pair; of their fears for Luke; of how Michael, the day before the departure, took the boy to the fold and bade him put the first stone in place as a sacramental act, a pledge of faithfulness and of a return some happy day to finish the wall; of how Luke was deeply moved; of how they both wept;

of how Luke went away and soon forgot all about the old couple, and falling into dissolute ways, ignominy and shame fell upon him and he was driven to seek a hiding-place beyond the seas; finally, of how Michael, bent and sad, would daily drag himself up the steep path, and, laboring all alone, attempt to complete the fold; but, as the neighbors remarked with a pitying shake of the head, how

> many and many a day he thither went,
> And never lifted up a single stone.

It took Matthew Arnold's keen poetic sense to discover the pathos and the beauty of that last line. "There is nothing subtle in it," he remarks, "no heightening, no study of poetic style, strictly so-called, at all; yet it is the expression of the highest and most truly expressive kind."

It is in this poem, notable for so many things, that we find the most explicit statement of the influence of Nature during the Poet's boyhood in the formation of his interest in his fellow men. In the introductory lines he speaks of how

> . . . the power
> Of Nature, by the gentle agency
> Of natural objects, led me on to feel
> For passions that were not my own, and think
> (At random and imperfectly indeed)
> On man, the heart of man, and human life.

It was with the poem *Michael* in mind .that Landor, in his fine tribute to Wordsworth, wrote these lines:

> There is a sheepfold he rais'd which my memory loves
> to revisit,
> Sheepfold whose wall shall endure when there is not a
> stone of the palace.

Alongside of *Michael* I would name *The Old Cumberland Beggar* and *Resolution and Independence* as poems calculated to reveal not only Wordsworth's interest in people from the humblest walks of life, but his conception

of the basic nobility that resides in the human heart. It
is difficult to choose between them. The picture of the old
beggar, a sort of neighborhood institution, who made his
stated round and whose gentle presence led of necessity to
acts of love, has become something of a classic:

> In the sun,
> Upon the second step of that small pile,
> Surrounded by those wild unpeopled hills,
> He sat, and ate his food in solitude:
> And ever, scattered from his palsied hand,
> That, still attempting to prevent the waste,
> Was baffled still, the crumbs in little showers
> Fell on the ground; and the small mountain birds,
> Not venturing yet to peck their destined meal,
> Approached within the length of half his staff.

Even better known are the lines in which the poet draws
the inference of human worth:

> 'Tis Nature's law
> That none, the meanest of created things,
> Of forms created the most vile and brute,
> The dullest or most noxious, should exist
> Divorced from good—a spirit and pulse of good,
> A life and soul, to every mode of being
> Inseparably linked. Then be assured
> That least of all can aught—that ever owned
> The heaven-regarding eye and front sublime
> Which man is born to—sink, howe'er depressed,
> So low as to be scorned without a sin.

Wordsworth's ideas on the subject of the relief and care
of the poor would scarcely pass muster with charity
workers today; but, in the case of a simple rural community such as he depicts, there is something to be said for
the more personal way of dealing with a character like the
Old Cumberland Beggar. Certainly the pure spirit of humanity has never been more effectively set forth.

Between the status of Michael with his cottage, his
field, his flock and his self-respecting toil, and that of the
beggar with his staff and his bag of crumbs, we have the

"Leech-gatherer" of the *Resolution and Independence* poem. Here the Poet has taken a leaf out of the book of his own experience. The poem, one of the most interesting Wordsworth ever wrote, cost him much labor, and it is clear the incident on which it is based made a deep impression. Yet the materials of the story are the simplest imaginable. On a rarely beautiful morning, following a storm, when all the air was filled with pleasant noise of waters, and all things that love the sun were out of doors, the Poet was walking across the moor, when his eye rested on the figure of an old man bent nearly double, at the edge of a pool into which he would peer eagerly while he stirred the muddy waters with a staff—"the oldest man he seemed that ever wore gray hairs." The Poet studied the weird figure for a moment and then, full of curiosity, accosted him and inquired what he was doing. In measured tones the old man explained that his occupation was gathering leeches, roaming from pool to pool from moor to moor, that he was old and poor and found the employment hazardous and wearisome; but that, by God's good help, he always found some place to lodge, and in this way could gain an honest maintenance, although, he added, when the Poet pressed the inquiry, leeches were growing extremely scarce:

> Once I could meet with them on every side;
> But they have dwindled long by slow decay;
> Yet still I persevere, and find them where I may.

Now it so happened, at the moment of their meeting, the Poet was indulging in a fit of the blues. The day was fine enough, but through the paradox of reaction, it served to remind him of how many miserable men there were in such a happy world, and of how many lives begin in sunshine only to end in gloom. He thought of his fellow poets as illustrations—Chatterton and Burns—and wondered about himself. And then appeared the Leech-gatherer! Here was a man who could face old age, hardship, biting poverty, disappointment of the extremest kind, and yet maintain a spirit of good cheer, fortitude and faith. The impression deepened as the conversation proceeded. The cheerfulness of the old man seemed to grow with the telling, and in the closing stanza Wordsworth reveals how profoundly he was moved by the nobility of the man's life:

> And soon with this he other matter blended,
> Cheerfully uttered, with demeanour kind,
> But stately in the main; and, when he ended,
> I could have laughed myself to scorn to find
> In that decrepit Man so firm a mind.
> "God," said I, "be my help and stay secure;
> I'll think of the Leech-gatherer on the lonely moor!"

Again we see memory becoming the promise of perennial cheer. It is the case of the Daffodils over again— only here it is the beauty of character taking the place of the beauty of flowers, and serving to dispel the mists of gloom. Throughout, the poem is in Wordsworth's best style, and some of its lines have been greatly admired, especially the characterization of the erratic genius of Chatterton:

> I thought of Chatterton, the marvellous Boy,
> The sleepless Soul that perished in his pride.

I would not risk losing the poem in the detail of analysis, but we shall miss its motive unless we realize that to Wordsworth the Leech-gatherer was not so much an individual as he was a type of the rugged virtues of plain folk found in many a spot, and nowhere more than among the valleys of his own lake country. To make this fact clear became one of the passions of his life. Just as it was his mission to show the poetry that lies hidden away in commonplace flowers and birds, so even more it was his mission to reveal the beauty in unsophisticated lives. The term "human values," so frequently found in the literature of social service today, has never had a better poetical expression than in his writings. On this account the social worker whose training has been primarily along technical lines may well familiarize himself with such poems as we have been considering, to which should be added *Humanity*. In the last analysis then, we are to think of Wordsworth as the poet who expressed the transcendent value of every human life.

It is impossible to speak of the many characters which crowd the pages of the narrative poems, and which emerge here and there in longer pieces like *The Prelude, The Excursion,* and *White Doe of Rylstone.* These are all needed to reveal what Wordsworth had in mind when on a certain occasion he described himself as "The attorney-general of Humanity," and which led him to speak of his poetry as "the well of homely life." Certainly one must read *The Brothers,* as reflecting the characteristic home life of the Lake District; and *The Farmer of Tilsbury Vale,* which pictures an agriculturist, driven from his farm and forced to live in London, who would wander up the Haymarket hill and thrusting his hands into a wagon, smell lovingly at the hay. Then there is *Simon Lee, The Old Huntsman,* who, in spite of some weak lines of characterization, is made to live before us in the pathos of helpless but not unthankful old age—the poem whose closing lines leave one in a thoughtful mood:

> I've heard of hearts unkind, kind deeds
> With coldness still returning;
> Alas! the gratitude of men
> Hath oftener left me mourning.

Here we have one of those profound human touches which commend Wordsworth to every lover of man.

Wordsworth is always on a high level of understanding when dealing with the sorrows of women, and one should not fail to familiarize himself with characters like Ruth, in the poem that bears her name; the unnamed *Sailor's Mother,* and the heroine of *The Affliction of Margaret.* The last of these is matchless as picturing the broodings of a mother over her only son, from whom no tidings have been received for seven weary years. One stanza is particularly admirable:

> My apprehensions come in crowds;
> I dread the rustling of the grass;
> The very shadows of the clouds
> Have power to shake me as they pass:
> I question things and do not find
> One that will answer to my mind;
> And all the world appears unkind.

The sheer force of motherhood, which appealed to Wordsworth under all conditions, took on a lofty significance when, through the exercise of imagination, he entered the realm of an experience like this. An illustration is found also in *The Force of Prayer,* which is one of the few poems dealing with humanity in the sphere of wealth and position. It portrays the grief of a widow of gentle birth whose only son, a lad of beauty and promise, met death by drowning. The poem *Maternal Grief* may also be mentioned in this connection.

Of quite a different character is the universally admired *Solitary Reaper,* where the perfection of artistry matches the perfection of characterization in the picturing of a lass of the Scottish Highlands reaping and singing to herself in a field. The poem is so famous that it must be quoted entire:

> Behold her, single in the field,
> Yon solitary Highland Lass!
> Reaping and singing by herself;
> Stop here, or gently pass!
> Alone she cuts and binds the grain,
> And sings a melancholy strain;
> O listen! for the Vale profound
> Is overflowing with the sound.
>
> No Nightingale did ever chaunt
> More welcome notes to weary bands
> Of travellers in some shady haunt,
> Among Arabian sands:

A voice so thrilling ne'er was heard
In spring-time from the Cuckoo-bird,
Breaking the silence of the seas
Among the farthest Hebrides.

Will no one tell me what she sings?—
Perhaps the plaintive numbers flow
For old, unhappy, far-off things,
And battles long ago:
Or is it some more humble lay,
Familiar matter of to-day?
Some natural sorrow, loss, or pain,
That has been, and may be again?

Whate'er the theme, the Maiden sang
As if her song could have no ending;
I saw her singing at her work,
And o'er the sickle bending;—
I listened, motionless and still;
And, as I mounted up the hill,
The music in my heart I bore,
Long after it was heard no more.

Aside from the delicacy of understanding and the imaginative reach of these lines, we must admire them as a well-nigh perfect example of the poetical simplicity for which Wordsworth pleaded in his early years and which must always be his chief distinction in the realm of lyrical verse. It is a masterpiece in miniature. Mr. Herbert Read goes so far as to say, he "would always send out *The Solitary Reaper* into the world of letters to represent the quintessence of English poetry."[4]

From the citations I have made—and they might be greatly extended—it is sufficiently plain that Wordsworth's major interest lay in Man rather than in Nature. And yet not Man in the daily round, the common task, so much as in the deeper aspects of his thought and life:

Their manners, their enjoyments and pursuits,
Their passions and their feelings; chiefly those
Essential and eternal in the heart.[5]

---

[4] Quoted by C. H. Herford in his *Wordsworth*, 1930.
[5] *Excursion*, I, 341-343.

It is this deeper look that explains Wordsworth's strong emphasis upon the element of hardship and sorrow in the human lot. List the characters that crowd his stage and you will find that, with rare exceptions, they are taken from the ranks of the poor and the distressed. He reveals an extraordinary fondness for old men, orphans, pedlars, vagrants, broken down farmers, deserted mothers and wives—people not only from the humblest but from the hardest walks in life. The poet of joy in the natural world becomes the poet of sorrow in the world of man. It was "the still *sad* music of humanity" which he heard. Even in the case of the reaper-lass, it is a melancholy strain that she sings. And yet—and here we have a lesson for our day—this music does not make us sad, the reason being that so often it carries the undertone of hope and cheer. The joy of Nature is the joy of that which is constant, the joy of an eternal blessedness breaking through in sunshine and song and in the on-goings of the cosmic scene. The characteristic joy of Man is the joy of achievement, and of triumph in the moral realm.

The quotation from *Tintern Abbey* which I have used as a title to this chapter should be taken in connection with the lines that follow, which for the purpose in view we may well underscore:

> For I have learned
> To look on nature, not as in the hour
> Of thoughtless youth; but hearing oftentimes
> The still sad music of humanity,
> *Nor harsh nor grating, though of ample power*
> *To chasten and subdue.*

Man accepting toil and deprivation in the spirit of "The Happy Warrior," resolved to turn life's hardship to good account, is the "main region" of this poet's song. In each character delineation he is dealing with

> The passions *that build up* our human soul.

And so we find it was the element of heroism in the daily

life of the dalespeople that awoke his poetic admiration. To him they were "nature's noblemen." Even of his boyhood he could say:

> The face of every neighbor whom I met
> Was like a volume to me.[6]

Back of all was the poet's sense of the dignity of the individual—of personality as the "primary and victorious element in the universe." Wordsworth's dalesman is as far removed from the "Man with the Hoe," as he is from the "Man on Horseback." In all the eight volumes of the complete works, not a character is portrayed who does not help us to recognize

> A grandeur in the beatings of the heart.

It is when we turn from Wordsworth's consideration of the character of individual men to his discussion of the social problems of his age that the quality of his humanitarianism becomes doubly apparent. This is a sphere in which as poet and prophet he has rarely received his dues. And the reason is that few of his readers, few even (I suspect) of his critics, have the patience to reach the books of *The Excursion,* where these problems are presented. For those whose perseverance carries to that point the reward is great. They will discover that to this contemplative thinker of the hills belongs the honor of being the first writer of prominence to discern the dangers lurking in the factory system, as indeed in the whole movement which, after a century of social mal-adjustment, has landed us in what, by common consent, we call "the machine age." This is an aspect of the Wordsworth message on which an entire chapter might well be written. The barest summary must here suffice.

After repeated readings of *The Excursion,* the impression I gain is of an extremely well balanced consideration of the industrial system as the Poet saw it working out in

---

[6] *Prelude,* IV, 67-68.

the early period of its growth. His attitude throughout reveals poise, good sense and the love of fair play. Above all, it reveals that the virtue of *humanity*, which is something more than either sympathy or understanding, lay at the basis of all his thinking.

The matter is presented in the eighth and ninth books of *The Excursion*, especially the eighth. The four characters who engage in the conversation are the "Wanderer" (a retired pedlar of the old school, full of idealism and wisdom, and conversant with social conditions throughout the north of England), the "Solitary" (sceptically inclined, pessimistic, disillusioned by the failure of the French Revolution, undoubtedly representing, in a measure, the attitude of the youthful Wordsworth), the Pastor (rector of the Grasmere Parish, whose knowledge of social conditions, while more restricted, was more intimate than that of the "Wanderer"), and the Poet himself. It is, however, the "Wanderer" who does most of the talking. Wordsworth's method is to bring out the gains and losses of the factory system, then taking on new importance through the introduction of steam as a motive power. The "Wanderer" begins by speaking of the changes wrought in the once beautiful countryside through the growth of cities, the fruitage of "an inventive age," dwelling especially upon the loss of romantic interest. Such innovations appear to him as an "outrage done to Nature."

Yet even here the Poet admits the benefit of abundant work and of good roads which have taken the place of the old-time "foot-path faintly marked, the horse-track wild." These changes he characterizes as "a new and unforeseen creation," which has arisen "from out the labours of a peaceful land." There follows a dark picture of the springing up of one of the new industrial centers with the accompanying curse of smoke and dirt, suggestive of all the squalid misery of its slums:

> From the germ
> Of some poor hamlet, rapidly produced
> Here a huge town, continuous and compact,
> Hiding the face of earth for leagues—and there,
> Where not a habitation stood before,
> Abodes of men irregularly massed
> Like trees in forests,—spread through spacious tracts,
> O'er which the smoke of unremitting fires
> Hangs permanent, and plentiful as wreaths
> Of vapour glittering in the morning sun.[7]

As a compensating consideration there is presented the thought of the growth of commerce and the spread of the arts and materials of civilization into distant parts of the earth—England becoming a world-power, as the gift of the age of invention. Not for a moment does the Poet forget the benefits which have come with mechanical devices. They are indeed "improvements." They are admirable in themselves. It is against an "ill-regulated and excessive application" that he inveighs:

> . . . yet do I exult,
> Casting reserve away, exult to see
> An intellectual mastery exercised
> O'er the blind elements; a purpose given,
> A perseverance fed; almost a soul
> Imparted—to brute matter. I rejoice,
> Measuring the force of those gigantic powers
> That, by the thinking mind, have been compelled
> To serve the will of feeble-bodied Man.
> For with the sense of admiration blends
> The animating hope that time may come
> When, strengthened, yet not dazzled, by the might
> Of this dominion over nature gained,
> Men of all lands shall exercise the same
> In due proportion to their country's need;
> Learning, though late, that all true glory rests,
> All praise, all safety, and all happiness,
> Upon the moral law.

Specifically, the Poet laments the fouling of streams,

---

[7] The quotations in this chapter relating to social problems, except as otherwise noted, are from the eighth book of *The Excursion*, but not in every case in the Wordsworth order.

the turning of night into day, the exploitation of child-hood, the lessening of Man's dignity and his sense of free-dom, the tendency to make of him a mere tool, and the impairment of the moral sense. Here is his picture of the periodic shifting of gangs at the summons of the factory bell:

> And at the appointed hour a bell is heard,
> Of harsher import than the curfew-knoll
> That spake the Norman Conqueror's stern behest—
> A local summons to unceasing toil!
> Disgorged are now the ministers of day;
> And, as they issue from the illumined pile,
> A fresh band meets them, at the crowded door—
> And in the courts—
>
> . . . . . . . . . . . .
>
>         Men, maidens, youths,
> Mother and little children, boys and girls,
> Enter, and each the wonted task resumes
> Within this temple, where is offered up
> To Gain, the master-idol of the realm,
> Perpetual sacrifice.

Does literature contain a more severe indictment of child-labor than the following:

>        The boy, where'er he turns,
> Is still a prisoner; when the wind is up
> Among the clouds, and roars through the ancient woods;
> Or when the sun is shining in the east,
> Quiet and calm. Behold him—in the school
> Of his attainments? no; but with the air
> Fanning his temples under heaven's blue arch.
> His raiment, whitened o'er with cottonflakes,
> Or locks of wool, announces whence he comes.
> Creeping his gait and cowering, his lip pale,
> His respiration quick and audible;
> And scarcely could you fancy that a gleam
> Could break from out those languid eyes, or a blush
> Mantle upon his cheek.

In another place Wordsworth speaks of child-labor in terms of

> A Little-one, subjected to the arts
> Of modern ingenuity, and made
> The senseless member of a vast machine,
> Serving as doth a spindle or a wheel.[8]

These lines were written at a time when it was not unusual for children to be taken at five and six years of age and thrust into a mill to work twelve hours a day.

And it was for the mothers that Wordsworth felt almost as deeply as he did for the children:

> Can the mother thrive
> By the destruction of her innocent sons
> In whom a premature necessity
> Blocks out the forms of nature, preconsumes
> The reason, famishes the heart, shuts up
> The infant Being in itself, and makes
> Its very spring a season of decay!

It was Wordsworth's view—abundantly justified by the event—that society as a whole is bound to suffer from the oppression of a single class:

> Our life is turned
> Out of her course, wherever man is made
> An offering, or a sacrifice, a tool
> Or implement, a passive thing employed
> As a brute mean, without acknowledgment
> Of common right or interest in the end;
> Used or abused, as selfishness may prompt.[9]

To name the final and most serious indictment of the industrial movement, there is a passage, over-long for quotation, in which the Poet dwells upon the decadence of "the old domestic morals of the land," especially in the rural districts, recording the "lamentable change" of the preceding years and forecasting an even greater defection in the years to come.

Remember all this was written in 1814 or the preceding years, decades before the people of England became sufficiently aroused to make possible the Parliamentary acts

---

[8] *Excursion*, IX, 157 ff.
[9] *Ibid.*, IX, 113 ff.

which served to lessen but not to banish the evils against which he complained with such bitterness of soul. Southey, as Poet Laureate, attracted attention by his *Colloquies on Society,* in which he inveighed (not over-wisely) against the oppression of the artisan class; but Wordsworth anticipated him by sixteen years. In 1833 Carlyle wrote, "Our age is mechanical," and it was then accounted an astute and original generalization. Yet Wordsworth said the same in 1814. Large credit belongs to Robert Owen, the manufacturer, a contemporary of Wordsworth, for the humanity and the vision not only to discern the signs of the time, but also to put into practice an impressive array of reform measures, so far as his own properties were concerned. To him belongs the honor of leading in the direction of a voluntary and self-denying movement for a juster and more kindly treatment of the factory employee. But Owen's measures, so commendable on the score of humanitarian intent, failed by reason of his rabid socialism and his strongly anti-religious creed. And a similar judgment may be passed upon the work of John Thelwall, with whom as a member of the Godwin circle, Wordsworth came into contact in the years following upon his return from France. Thelwall, with Wordsworth, believed the poor of England were being oppressed, and in one of his poems, long since forgotten, he wrote trenchantly on the subject. His poetry, however, was of so poor a quality, and his reputation as a professional agitator was such, that his endeavors resulted in more harm than good.

Wordsworth revealed his hard-headed wisdom by avoiding mistakes like these. Unlike Rousseau, whom he followed in so many ways, he did not seek to do away with existing institutions, but rather to have them informed with the spirit of humanity and common sense. He never indulged in undiscriminating denunciation of manufacturers for conditions over which they could have only limited control. On the other hand, there is no glorification of the poor, as though they alone among the people of earth are worthy of consideration and praise. Wordsworth was no socialist. On the contrary, although he repudiated the assumptions of aristocracy, he was as thorough-going an individualist as the age produced. The ideal society, as he viewed it, was one of freedom conjoined with even-handed justice, of opportunity for all. More possibly than any writer of his time, he lamented the unequal distribution of the good things of life. The fault, and hence the remedy, lay with Man himself. This is brought out in the ninth book of *The Excursion*, in a noble passage from which space allows that I quote only the opening and the closing lines:

> Alas! what differs more than man from man!
> And whence that difference? Whence but from himself?
> For see the universal Race endowed
> With the same upright form! The sun is fixed,
> And the infinite magnificence of heaven
> Fixed, within reach of every human eye;
> The sleepless ocean murmurs for all ears;
> The vernal field infuses fresh delight
> Into all hearts.
>
> . . . . . . . . . . . .
>
>                   The smoke ascends
> To heaven as lightly from the cottage-hearth
> As from the haughtiest palace. He, whose soul
> Ponders this true equality, may walk
> The fields of earth with gratitude and hope;
> Yet, in that meditation, will he find
> Motive to sadder grief, as we have found;
> Lamenting ancient virtues overthrown,
> And for the injustice grieving, that hath made
> So wide a difference between man and man.

It is on the strength of sentiments like these that Miss Vida D. Scudder, in her *The Life of the Spirit in the Modern English Poets*, pays tribute to the greatness of Wordsworth as "The High Priest of the new democracy."[10]

---

[10]Chapter on *Wordsworth and the New Democracy*. See also *The Social Philosophy of Wordsworth*, in *Social Studies in English Literature*, by Prof. Laura J. Wylie, of Vassar College, a work of profound scholarship.

In no respect did the Poet reveal his social sanity to better advantage than by refraining from the suggestion of remedial measures of a legislative or economic character looking to the relief of the poor. These he was content to leave to the judgment of those whose practical experience was greater than his own.[11] He would not make the mistake into which Southey fell so miserably in later years. Enough for the Poet of Man to point to Man's noble stature and his deplorable estate. The nearest approach to a remedial suggestion was his advocacy, in the closing book of *The Excursion,* of a system of universal education supported by the State, resulting not only in the spread of economic justice but also in the enrichment of social life, the inculcation of morals and the establishment of religion. Under the stimulus of such a program Wordsworth forecasts an age of plenty and peace for England and the world. It is a commentary upon his prophetic quality of mind that not until 1878, or sixty-four years after the publication of *The Excursion,* did his dream of universal education for the people of England become a reality. And if, in that land, as in others, the results have fallen short of expectations, and "the still sad music of humanity" continues to resound, who shall say the Prophet of the Lakes did not lift up a mighty voice?

What value has that voice for us today? This at least: it summons us to a full-fledged faith in the intrinsic worth of the individual man, and that without regard to race, nationality, or social condition. To quote an expression of Dr. Harry Emerson Fosdick, it challenges us to "take up the cudgels for personality as the most valuable thing in the universe"; and it does this at a time when the insignificance of personality is being preached by a materialistic science and practiced by a socialistic state. There are those who think that upon this issue will hinge the

---

[11] Such a one was the Earl of Shaftesbury, who, only after fourteen long and bitter years of agitation, succeeded in carrying through Parliament the Ten-hour Factory Bill for the relief of Lancashire operatives. In connection with the French Revolution Wordsworth had had his fill of the idea that society can be redeemed by legislation. This is a lesson which many in both Europe and America have yet to learn.

future of Christian civilization. The doctrine, of course, is nothing new. It was the ideal of Rousseau, of Crabbe, of Burns and of many others. But Wordsworth's message has a quality of its own, in that, like the Bible writers, he saw all these men *in God*. He alone among the poets of the time dared to speak of "the godhead which is ours." It was through the human personality that the divine personality was revealed and that the meaning of creation was made known. It is to this spiritually apprehended conception of Man that the world needs to turn at the present time.

Especially is this true in respect to the bearing of the industrial system upon intellectual and æsthetic appreciation. On every side we hear thoughtful men discussing the problem of maintaining the higher values of personality in a mechanical age. What effect is our technological development to have upon the culture of the masses? How are we to prevent the day laborer from becoming little better than a slave, or what is far worse, little better than a machine? By common consent, the crux of the problem lies in the wise use of leisure. In Wordsworth's day the machine left little time for leisure. In ours it leaves little aptitude for the extraordinary amount of leisure it has brought within the reach of the laboring man. The situation is exactly reversed. Yet is the Wordsworth solution as pertinent today as it was in 1814—education, directed to such a well-rounded scheme of living that the wage-earner no less than the employer shall share in the good things of life. The hope of the situation would appear to lie in a system of popular education directed to the sense of the high values of personality, in the physical, the intellectual, the spiritual, and the social realms; and together with this, the teaching of the technique of such an enjoyment of Nature, art, music, recreation, as shall offset the deadening influence of a purely mechanical pursuit. Nothing can be more timely than Wordsworth's emphasis upon an education which, framed

on Nature's balanced plan, leads to both the simple and
the abundant life. It was with a rare prescience that in the
passage of *The Excursion* relating to popular education,
the Poet expressed, at the close, the ideal of a culture
sufficiently broad and deep to be a guarantee against the
brutalizing effects of the mechanical civilization which
seemed to him to impend:

> so that none,
> However destitute, be left to droop
> By timely culture unsustained; or run
> Into wild disorder; or be forced
> To drudge through a weary life without the help
> Of intellectual implements and tools;
> A savage horde among the civilized,
> A servile band among the lordly free![12]

Having drawn so largely upon *The Excursion* for evidence of Wordsworth's breadth of humanitarian interest,
I am minded to add a word in behalf of this poem on
general grounds, and to indicate its significance in the
total estimate of the Poet's work. This, I am aware, from
the standpoint of the critics, will not be a popular thing
to do, since for generations *The Excursion* has been a pet
target for abuse. Jeffrey set the style when, in the year of
publication, he began his review in the *Edinburgh Quarterly* with the scornful observation—"This will never do"
—possibly the most damaging comment ever handed out
by a reviewer. Although the injustice of the Jeffrey dictum
is generally recognized today, the idea he released has
proved to be one of the hardy perennials of criticism.
Complaint is made that the poem is too long, too dull,
too pious, and too preachy. On the artistic side, it is held
that the discourses are artificial, not to say impossible,
and that throughout there is a sad lack of the dramatic
element. Some critic—Swinburne, I think—has suggested
that the tameness of the material may be judged from
the fact that the narrative begins with two old gentlemen

---

[12] *Excursion*, IX, 303-310.

conversing in front of a tumble-down farmhouse, and ends with afternoon tea in the parsonage.[13]

There are defects enough in *The Excursion,* whether considered as a poem or a treatise, as any open-minded reader must allow. It cannot be said to make exciting reading. Beyond question there is over much of exposition, and the religious message could have been conveyed to better effect, at least for our age, by the occasional use of indirection. Undoubtedly the poem carries a good deal of excess baggage in the way of onesided discussion. Yet I have never felt that the lack of the dramatic element was a defect. The poem makes no pretense in that direction. It undertakes to record the conversations of a group of serious men on serious questions of the day—the sort of thing that is frequently attempted in college debate and even in the broadcasting by radio of divergent views upon public events. Why not accept it at that, and be thankful there is any dramatic element at all—that the participants, while discoursing so sagely, at least move from place to place? That is more than can be said of the Book of Job. And such places! The descriptions of scenery should be recompense enough. Here is the Lake country spread before our view in an entrancing way. Take for example the description of the cloud effects in the mountains, following a storm:

> Glory beyond all glory ever seen
> By waking sense or by the dreaming soul—

as given at the close of the second book. It is a scene to be treasured in one's heart and recurred to again and again.

Moreover, scattered through the nine books, a sufficient number of noble passages may be found to make their reading a rewarding experience quite apart from the

---

[13]This is not strictly true, since after the tea-party there was a row across the lake, a picnic on the island, and finally the climbing of a hill from which an extended view was had, and where the *Pastor* pronounced an eloquent, if rather extended, blessing as the sun sank gloriously in the west.

import of the poem as a whole. One never knows when he will meet with lines like these:

> The primal duties shine aloft—like stars;
> The charities that soothe, and heal, and bless,
> Are scattered at the Feet of Man—like flowers.[14]

It is in *The Excursion* that we find the famous passage about the child applying to his ear the convolutions of a shell and hearing the murmurings of the sea—the passage which, as we have seen, James T. Fields knew by heart and one day repeated in the presence of the Poet. Admittedly the poem is contemplative rather than dramatic. But to rule it out on that score is to pronounce judgment on ourselves. Coleridge once expressed the opinion that if the first book of *The Excursion* had been published separately under the title *The Ruined Cottage*, it would have been rated as one of the famous poems in our language. Similarly Landor spoke with delight of "the series of enchanting idyls into which *The Excursion* would subdivide." Charles Lamb, writing of *The Excursion* as a whole, pronounced it the noblest conversational poem he had ever read. Van Wyck Brooks, in his penetrating *Life of Emerson*, records that the Sage of Concord had read Wordsworth's *Excursion* in the days when it was ridiculed by the *Edinburgh Review*, and found it "a revelation." To Keats it was "one of the wonders of the age." The French critic Taine, in his monumental *History of English Literature*, rates *The Excursion* extremely high, comparing its lines to "the grand and monotonous music of the organ, which in the eventide, at the close of the service, rolls slowly in the twilight of arches and pillars." Viscount Morley, in writing to a friend, once spoke of his delight in re-reading *The Excursion*, and made this comment: "The last half of Book IV is among the finest things in great poetry. It is real religion. Some saint,

---

[14]Book IX, 238-240.

who knows how to write, might do worse than try his hand at putting the doctrine of it in a prose reverie."[15]

So there are critics and critics. Possibly no poem in the language is better calculated to draw the line between those who view poetry primarily as the expression of beauty and those who view it primarily as the expression of truth. By the latter *The Excursion* will always be reckoned among the great poems of the world. Better than anything that fell from Wordsworth's pen, it exemplifies

Wisdom married to immortal verse.[16]

[15] From *Recollections*, by John, Viscount Morley. Macmillan Co., 1917.
[16] *The Excursion*, VII, 536.

# CHAPTER VII

# "The Child Is Father of the Man"

THERE was one class of people for whom Wordsworth felt a deeper interest than he did for pedlars
and shepherds. I refer to his affection—amounting to a
passion—for children. Although he wrote no poems ex-
pressly for children, he is for many *the* children's poet. It
was a true instinct that led educators to print pieces like
*Alice Fell, Lucy Gray* and *Goody Blake* in the school
readers of the olden time. And it is even more significant
that the earliest of the scores of Wordsworth anthologies
were made for educational use. Even today it cannot be
said that Stevenson, Field, Milne and the other acknowl-
edged poets of childhood have crowded old Wordsworth
off the stage. Nor does the case rest solely, nor even primarily, on the compositions—twenty in number—brought
together by the Poet in the section of his works entitled
*Poems Referring to the Period of Childhood.* Some of
these are very fine; some not particularly fine. Rather it is
a matter of life-time record, embracing poems both grave
and gay; as conspicuous in *The Prelude* and *The Excursion* as in short pieces like *The Pet Lamb* and *We Are
Seven* which come more easily to the mind. Most impressive of all, it shines in Wordsworth's masterpiece,
*Intimations of Immortality from Recollections of Early
Childhood,* which, by common consent, we now speak of
as *The Ode.* That this devotion was to be a lifelong affair
is indicated in the little poem which the Poet placed at the
head of the group referring to childhood, whose closing
lines he chose as the text for the great *Ode,* and whose
most familiar line I have placed at the head of this
chapter:

138

# THE CHILD IS FATHER OF THE MAN

> My heart leaps up when I behold
> A rainbow in the sky:
> So was it when my life began;
> So is it now I am a man;
> So be it when I shall grow old,
> Or let me die!
> The Child is father of the Man;
> And I could wish my days to be
> Bound each to each by natural piety.

The biographers, one and all, speak of Wordsworth's deep affection for his own children, of whom, not counting his French daughter, there were five. There is abundant evidence of this in his poems. Three of these relate to Dorothy, his second child, generally known as Dora, to distinguish her from the Poet's sister. Although Dora became his favorite, the poems she inspired are philosophical rather than personal in tone. The one entitled *My Infant Daughter, Dora, on the day when she was one month old,* has to do with mother-love and the characteristics of infancy, the babe being compared, playfully, with the moon, whose placid round had marked the first span of her life. As such the poem is one of considerable beauty. If the reader is repelled by the formality of the address, "Wild Offspring of infirm humanity," there is compensation in such lines as:

> . . . or shall those smiles be called
> Feelers of love, put forth as if to explore
> This untried world, and to prepare thy way
> Through a strait passage intricate and dim?
> Such are they; and the same are tokens, signs,
> Which, when the appointed season hath arrived,
> Joy, as her holiest language, shall adopt;
> And Reason's godlike Power be proud to own.

The prophecy was fulfilled, and Dora became a rarely happy child, as the reference in *The Kitten and Falling Leaves* makes pleasantly clear. This is a poem praised or blamed according to the reader's taste and point of view. Taine, in his *History of English Literature,* pronounced the poem "childish and almost foolish." Lafcadio Hearn, in his somewhat dogmatic yet always interesting lectures to Japanese students, on the English poets, devotes several pages to the poem and bestows upon it high praise, noting the happy coupling of Dora and the kitten as a playful pair. Hearn is more nearly right, in spite of the poem being over-long and a bit preachy at the end.

Still another Dora poem is entitled *The Longest Day*, being written when, having reached the age of thirteen, she might be supposed to be impressed by the solemnity of the passage of time—but wasn't. It contains a pleasant picture of the youthful Dora romping on the lawn at Rydal Mount, but otherwise is not important.

The poem which above all others reflects the tenderness of the Poet's heart toward children has to do with his second daughter, Catherine, an unusually attractive and original bit of humanity, whose death during the absence of both parents on a walking-tour, brought a crushing blow upon the home. The poem is in sonnet form:

> Surprised by joy—impatient as the Wind
> I turned to share the transport—Oh! with whom
> But Thee, deep buried in the silent tomb,
> That spot which no vicissitude can find?
> Love, faithful love, recalled thee to my mind—
> But how could I forget thee? Through what power,
> Even for the least division of an hour,
> Have I been so beguiled as to be blind
> To my most grievous loss!—That thought's return
> Was the worst pang that sorrow ever bore,
> Save one, one only, when I stood forlorn,
> Knowing my heart's best treasure was no more;
> That neither present time, nor years unborn
> Could to my sight that heavenly face restore.

On the ground of intimacy and affection we may almost count Coleridge's eldest child, Hartley, as a member of the Wordsworth household. The poem *To H. C.—Six Years Old*, composed in 1802, exquisitely conceived and elaborated, reveals not only an affection but an understanding of the child's nature, not unmingled with concern, which few parents could equal. The boy Hartley, like his father, was a genius, but, also, like his father, a genius of unstable equilibrium. To any one acquainted with the pathetic outcome of the elf-like personality that inspired Wordsworth's poem, these are lines which become almost uncanny in their prophetic suggestion.[1] Here is a poet whose observation of children was not of the casual kind; it partook of the same quality of intimacy, penetration and reflection that characterized his study of Nature in her more subtle moods. The poem should be read entire, but I venture to quote only the closing part:

> O blessèd vision! happy child!
> Thou art so exquisitely wild,
> I think of thee with many fears
> For what may be thy lot in future years.
>
> I thought of times when pain might be thy guest,
> Lord of thy house and hospitality;
> And Grief, uneasy lover! never rest
> But when she sate within the touch of thee.
> O too industrious folly!
> O vain and causeless melancholy!
> Nature will either end thee quite;
> Or, lengthening out thy season of delight,
> Preserve for thee, by individual right,
> A young lamb's heart among the full-grown flocks.
> What hast thou to do with sorrow,
> Or the injuries of to-morrow?
> Thou art a dew-drop, which the morn brings forth,
> Ill fitted to sustain unkindly shocks,
> Or to be trailed along the soiling earth;

---

[1] It will be recalled that Hartley Coleridge, after his father's death, settled at Grasmere in order to be near the Wordsworths, who bestowed upon him the tenderest attention. Although a scholar of rare attainment, he was an utter failure as a teacher. As a poet he had exquisite taste and felicity and some of his sonnets are as fine as anything of the kind in English. He inherited his father's lack of will power and inconstancy in work, and from his college days at Oxford was the victim of intemperance. During his last years he spent much of his time in the taverns of the neighborhood. Everywhere he endeared himself by reason of his democratic, whimsical ways, and among the dalesmen to the day of his death, in 1849, he was universally known as "Little Hartley." At the time of his death one of his peasant neighbors was heard to remark: "Li'le Hartley was the cliverist man in England as some say, and did a deal to help Mr. Wudsworth with his potry and all."

> A gem that glitters while it lives,
> And no forewarning gives;
> But, at the touch of wrong, without a strife
> Slips in a moment out of life.

Swinburne, so often bitter in his criticism of Wordsworth, speaks of the Hartley Coleridge poem as "that incomparable little masterpiece whose irregularity has a charm of its own."

We know now that the "six year's darling," so accurately set forth in the seventh stanza of the *Immortality Ode,* was none other than this same Hartley Coleridge; and Professor Harper has made the interesting suggestion that the poem *To H. C.* was originally a part of *The Ode.* He points out that the metre is similar, that there are coincidences of time and place, and that the poem fits in naturally between the seventh and eighth stanzas. If this was the case—and the argument is a persuasive one —we have an added reason for admiring *The Ode* in its characterization of child-life, on the ground that this arose from an intimate and understanding experience with actual boys and girls. Does the literature of childhood, psychological or otherwise, give us a better picture than this in the seventh stanza of *The Ode:*

> Behold the Child among his new-born blisses,
> A six years' Darling of a pigmy size!
> See, where 'mid work of his own hand he lies,
> Fretted by sallies of his mother's kisses,
> With light upon him from his father's eyes!
> See, at his feet, some little plan or chart,
> Some fragment from his dream of human life,
> Shaped by himself with newly-learned art;
>     A wedding or a festival,
>     A mourning or a funeral;
>     And this hath now his heart,
>     And unto this he frames his song:
>     Then will he fit his tongue
> To dialogues of business, love, or strife;
>     But it will not be long
>     Ere this be thrown aside,

> And with new joy and pride
> The little Actor cons another part;
> Filling from time to time his "humorous stage"
> With all the Persons, down to palsied Age,
> That Life brings with her in her equipage;
> As if his whole vocation
> Were endless imitation.

In *Anecdote for Fathers* Wordsworth narrates an experience with a five-year-old boy, whom he calls Edward, that had been entrusted to the Poet and his sister for education during their stay at Racedown in 1795. The poem is noteworthy as affording the earliest indication of the Poet's psychological interest in childhood. He and Edward were out for a walk on a rarely beautiful day. They were having a grand time together, and in their chatter, with home full in view, they recalled the fun they had had a year before at Kilve, a seaside resort; and the Poet idly asked the small boy which he preferred— Kilve or home. Edward promptly replied "Kilve." This was unexpected, and the Poet demanded the reason. Of course the boy could give no reason; he had spoken from impulse and remained silent. Then, as the Poet proceeded to argue the matter and to press for an answer, the boy hung his head in shame. Once more came the demand, and upon this Edward looked up and, catching sight of a glittering weather-cock on the roof of the house, unlocked his tongue and blurted out:

> At Kilve there was no weather-cock;
> And that's the reason why—

In other words, being forced to give a reason against his will, he proceeded to invent one. The lesson, of course, which the Poet is good enough to leave to our own intelligence, is the danger of encouraging children to lie through failure to recognize the limitations of their minds. The child of five can think of but one thing at a time. Of that one thing his thought is of the instinctive rather than of the reasoning kind. Moreover, when par-

ents seek to crowd children in their mental processes, they
only make them ashamed. The poem has been ridiculed
on the ground of its over-explicitness (one of Wordsworth's early faults):

> And three times to the child I said,
> "Why, Edward, tell me why?"

But it is true to life, its psychology is sound and important, and the nature-descriptions are in the Poet's
happiest vein. The closing stanza is a favorite one with
teachers:

> O dearest, dearest boy! my heart
> For better lore would seldom yearn,
> Could I but teach the hundredth part
> Of what from thee I learn.

The so-called "Lucy Poems," five in number, universally admired for their exquisite simplicity and tenderness,
are usually considered in connection with Wordsworth's
emphasis upon education by Nature, or as affording biographical material revealing the significance of a boyhood
love-affair. But they are of value also as a study in childhood traits, and all the more so in view of the insight of
a deep, if immature affection reflected in so many of the
lines. I agree with those who hold that there was a Lucy,
although of course this was not her real name, that the
child was not a purely ideal creation. Although this matter has been much discussed, we must not run the risk of
losing the charm of these lovely pieces by over much
curiosity as to what lies hidden between the lines. We
have to do with so delicate a thing as the love of a high-
minded, sensitive boy for a beautiful girl, abruptly ended
by her death. The underlying theme is love and sorrow in
a world of childhood joy. A rarer and more beautiful
theme it would be difficult to name. That Wordsworth
has handled it in a perfect way is sufficient evidence that
something more than imagination was at work. Undoubtedly there *was* a Lucy; and, after making allowance for

the sublimations of memory and the glorifying touches of imagination, a careful reading of the poems will reveal the manner of child she was, as well as the circumstances in which she grew up. She lived in a cottage, located on a hill among the mountains, overlooking an orchard and a green field. It was a secluded and beautiful spot. She knew how to use a spinning-wheel, but spent most of her time in play and in roaming the fields and woods. She sought out the secret places of Nature, the obscure little brooks, and she was fond of gazing at the stars at night. As for her characteristics, it appears that she was beautiful, tall and well developed, graceful and airy, athletic, industrious, possessing a sportive wildness, yet contemplative at times, in love with Nature, rich in emotion, full of æsthetic sensibility. Hidden away in her mountain retreat—presumably the valley known as Dovedale, lying to the west of Brotherswater—Lucy was the boy-Wordsworth's own discovery, and (in the judgment at least of poetry lovers) he did not make a more important discovery in his early years. Here is child-psychology and a good deal more. The Lucy Poems belong at the side of those dealing with the Poet's own children and the one referring to Hartley Coleridge, as uncovering the deeper springs of his understanding of the-child-mind-and-heart. They enabled him to mark the high spots of childhood-apprehension with a good deal of accuracy.

To none of the Lucy Poems did Wordsworth affix a title. But the first lines are: "Strange fits of passion have I known," "She dwelt among the untrodden ways," "I travelled among unknown men," "A slumber did my spirit seal," "Three years she grew in sun and shower." Among these I select the last for quotation, on the ground of the beauty of its thought and diction, its comprehensiveness, and because, in addition to its charming characterizations, it pictures in sharp yet graceful outlines the educational value of an out-door life. Sometimes the poem is called *Nature's Lady*, but more often *Education by Nature.*

The fifth stanza should be noted for the adaptation of
the sound of the words to the idea presented, that of the
music of a running brook, what the rhetoricians call
onomatopoëia. This stanza is commended to readers who
are under the impression that Wordsworth lacks utterly
the singing quality.

> Three years she grew in sun and shower,
> Then Nature said, "A lovelier flower
> On earth was never sown;
> This Child I to myself will take;
> She shall be mine, and I will make
> A Lady of my own.

> "Myself will to my darling be
> Both law and impulse: and with me
> The Girl, in rock and plain,
> In earth and heaven, in glade and bower,
> Shall feel an overseeing power
> To kindle or restrain.

> "She shall be sportive as the fawn
> That wild with glee across the lawn
> Or up the mountain springs;
> And hers shall be the breathing balm,
> And hers the silence and the calm
> Of mute insensate things.

> "The floating clouds their state shall lend
> To her; for her the willow bend;
> Nor shall she fail to see
> Even in the motions of the Storm
> Grace that shall mould the Maiden's form
> By silent sympathy.

> "The stars of midnight shall be dear
> To her; and she shall lean her ear
> In many a secret place
> Where rivulets dance their wayward round,
> And beauty born of murmuring sound
> Shall pass into her face.

> "And vital feelings of delight
> Shall rear her form to stately height,
> Her virgin bosom swell;

Such thoughts to Lucy I will give
While she and I together live
Here in this happy dell."

Thus Nature spake—The work was done—
How soon my Lucy's race was run!
She died, and left to me
This heath, this calm, and quiet scene;
The memory of what has been,
And never more will be.[2]

Lucy was a cottage-child; that is, she came from the home of one of those peasant farmers or shepherds whose virtues Wordsworth celebrates in so many different ways. They were a sturdy, independent, God-fearing lot. As a rule they were not tenant farmers; but for generations had owned the land upon which they lived and toiled. As such they were known in the North Country as "Statesmen." Their traditions were those of English freemen. Their home-life was such as Burns celebrated in *The Cotter's Saturday Night*. It is easy to see why their children made so congenial a theme for a poet who specialized on "Man, on Nature and on Human Life."

There are a number of other poems relating to cottage children, each having some special beauty of characterization. Some of these—worthy of careful reading—are: *We Are Seven, Idle Shepherd Boys, Lucy Gray, To a Highland Girl*. Then there are two poems relating to children of the poorer class: *Alice Fell*, and *Beggars*. All of these, as also the Lucy Poems, were written between 1798 and 1803, in the period of Wordsworth's highest

[2]The theory of Fausset, set forth in his *The Lost Leader*, 1933, that Lucy was a composite of Annette and Dorothy, is rather far-fetched. Wordsworth's characterization of his Lucy as a child of nature might apply to Dorothy but not to Annette, who was city bred. Similarly the lines,
And she I cherished turned her wheel
Beside an English fire,
leave no place for a maid of France. Annette is completely out of the picture as drawn by Wordsworth. The fact that four of the five Lucy poems refer to her early death and are elegiac in tone Fausset explains by the supposition that what the poet had in mind was the death of his love for Annette! Aside from troublesome details like these, the spontaneity and entire naturalness of the poems, their directness and obvious sincerity are inconsistent with the devious mindedness which Fausset attributes to the Poet. The consideration of the Fausset theory as to the cause of the loss of power in Wordsworth, which is the main thesis of the book, will come up for consideration in a later chapter, the tenth.

inspiration. This is important as indicating the prominence of childhood in the thinking of those creative years.

It is not necessary to comment upon these poems separately, nor to quote extensively from them. But, attention should be called to Lucy Gray (not to be confused with the Lucy of the love-poems) as telling in matchless diction one of the most pathetic stories in literature—"the tragedy of a young and beautiful life lost within close proximity to those who could have saved it and would cheerfully have given their own lives to save it." The tale is set before us in such unadorned simplicity, so devoid is it of all the trappings and tricks of emotional narration, that its beauty is easily overlooked. That an effect like this could be produced by the use of small, straight and common words will indicate to the thoughtful reader the perfection of art. On this account some critic—Mr. J. H. Fowler, I think—has held that *Lucy Gray* is the ultimate test of a reader's capacity to appreciate Wordsworth's most characteristic verse. If, because of the bareness of its diction, he can find nothing to praise in *Lucy Gray,* he may be dismissed as a hopeless case. This may be a bit strong. But if we add the other "Lucy Poems," we may say with confidence that they are Wordsworth in his purest and most exacting vein.

The poem *To a Highland Girl* relates to a maiden of fourteen whom the Poet and his sister discovered in their tour of Scotland in 1803, and who is pictured against a background of rocks and trees, a waterfall, a lake, and a cabin home. It is usually associated with *The Solitary Reaper* and *Stepping Westward,* the fruitage of the same tour, and as such it fairly cries out for quotation in full. I refer to it here because of its characterization of childhood at its ripest moment of innocence and of beauty, all unconscious of itself, and especially because it conveys the idea of a human life becoming the truest interpretation of a natural scene. The vision of such a child in such a place, the Poet pleads, is the treasure of a lifetime, and we are

not surprised to have the poem close on the familiar note
of memory as the mind's great reward:

> Now thanks to Heaven! that of its grace
> Hath led me to this lonely place.
> Joy have I had; and going hence
> I bear away my recompense.
> In spots like these it is we prize
> Our Memory, feel that she hath eyes:
> Then, why should I be loth to stir?
> I feel this place was made for her;
> To give new pleasure like the past,
> Continued long as life shall last.
> Nor am I loth, though pleased at heart,
> Sweet Highland Girl! from thee to part;
> For I, methinks, till I grow old,
> As fair before me shall behold,
> As I do now, the cabin small,
> The lake, the bay, the waterfall;
> And Thee, the Spirit of them all!

To *We Are Seven* I shall have occasion to refer when
we deal more particularly with the *Imitations Ode*.

In the first two books of Wordsworth's great autobiographical poem we have his incomparable description
of his own childhood days. These books are unique for
the gift of recapturing the scenes of childhood, and a pleasure quite impossible to describe awaits the man who will
take the time even to run through their eleven hundred
lines. A single hour of leisurely reading would make this
a treasurable possession for all time. As a study in child
psychology these opening books of *The Prelude* are as
significant as anything Wordsworth ever wrote.

Both books bear the same title, *Childhood and School
Time*. Their scope may be gathered from their sub-titles:
Childhood's promise (Cockermouth, 1770-78), School
life (Hawkshead, 1778-87), Early awe of Nature, Weird
hauntings, A favored child, The skater's vision, The
season's ministry, Cottage life, Indoor pastimes, Eager-
ness of boyhood, Desire of calmer joys, Influence of fair
surroundings, Rides to historic ruins, Music and waters

and evening sky, Nature sought for her own sake, The babe moved by love, The babe already a poet, Early morning walks, The creative soul.[3]

The life spread before us is that of a normal, healthy, intensely vital childhood, in which sports and pastimes seem to have occupied the leading place. The Hawkshead Free Grammar School must have been a remarkable institution, unique even in those days of untrammeled educational theory. One can scarcely imagine a private school today suffering the boys to roam the woods and mountains unattended in the way Wordsworth describes. I have listed the following activities alluded to or set before us by the Poet: mountain climbing, bird nesting, snaring woodcocks, trout fishing, swimming, rowing, boat racing, skating, kite flying, horseback riding, picnicing, excursions to historic spots, early morning strolls with his dog. There were, of course, the usual games that boys will play out of school hours, and for which the long twilight of that northern country afforded protracted opportunity, although there is no mention of cricket. Of such a life the Poet could say, "We ran a boisterous course." As for indoor pastimes there is a delightful passage where he speaks of playing tit-tat-two on their slates, and of games of loo and whist played with an old and grimy pack of cards, whose fantastic kings, queens and knaves afforded him material for whimsical allusion. One wonders when those Hawkshead boys did their studying. Apparently there was no distinction between "inside" and "outside" activities. All were "inside" so far as educational theory was concerned, and Esthwaite, Windermere and Old Man might be considered members of the faculty. We learn from certain other poems, such as *Matthew, The Two April Mornings, The Fountain*, that Wordsworth's relations with his teacher were of the most intimate sort.

---

[3] These sub-titles, for the most part, I have taken from the *Temple Classics* edition of *The Prelude*, J. M. Dent and Sons. This is an excellent pocket edition.

The teacher's name was William Taylor, but in the poems he is called Matthew:

> We talked with open heart, and tongue,
> Affectionate and true,
> A pair of friends, though I was young,
> And Matthew seventy-two.[4]

There is something about these school poems that tugs at one's heart.

In these same books of *The Prelude* Wordsworth traces the progress of his mind from an early sense of awe to a love of Nature for her own sake, and he seems even in those boyhood-days to have recognized the sobering and refining influence of fair surroundings. Parallel to this he experienced a steady quickening of conscience under the sense of Nature's purity and peace. In spite of an emphasis upon sports which would delight a prep-school boy of today, it is essentially a spiritual autobiography that we have in his account of his early educational career. The passages that bring this out most clearly are those relating to the snaring of birds, the stolen boat, the skating experience and the early morning walk. The stately passage beginning "Wisdom and Spirit of the universe" may also be included; and, although it is found in the fifth book of *The Prelude,* the superb lines beginning "There was a boy," to which I have referred in a previous chapter, have a place also at this point. The detached poem *Nutting* deals with a Hawkshead experience and is rich in spiritual suggestion. In fact nearly all we have considered under Wordsworth's theory of education by Nature and his philosophy of Being are shadowed forth in these tales of his own juvenile activities and processes of thought.

---

[4] The Matthew of the poems in actual life was far from being an old man, since he died at the age of thirty-two in the midst of his pupils. In the poem *Matthew,* which Wordsworth wrote as an epitaph and which was placed on the wall of the schoolroom opposite the teacher's name, the poet pays tribute to this man in terms somewhat closer to reality. Trevelyan, in his *History of England* (p. 522, note) refers his readers to *The Prelude,* Books I-II, for a description of an eighteenth century Grammar School at its best.

An impressive list of child-characteristics might be drawn up on the basis of the poems dealing directly with child-life. All the familiar traits would be there: innocence, trustfulness, teachability, vitality, playfulness, fickleness of mood, mischievousness, love of noise, spontaneity, self-assertion, imagination. But the keenness of his observation is evidenced better by traits which the eye of the ordinary parent and teacher does not detect. For instance, the fact that the typical child finds its richest enjoyment in the presence of Nature. Think back on your own childhood and consider if this is not true. Here is the early awakening of the æsthetic sense. Here, also, is the awakening of the moral sense—Nature's joy and anger, Nature's eternal No—the "vague hauntings," which "impressed upon all forms the characters of danger or desire." Then there is the sense of mystery reflected in the day-dreams of the normal child. We are not to forget that it was in childhood that the Poet felt "the Presence of Nature in the sky," "the visions of the hills," and the "Souls of lonely places."[5]

Above all, were what we may call the *prophetic* qualities of childhood, the attributes which Wordsworth had in mind when he said, "The child is father of the man." The line has become proverbial in its popularity and significance. Its psychology pervades the Poet's work, especially that of the earlier years. Nothing appealed to him more than to trace the subtler appreciations of adult life to the deep-rooted instincts of childhood. Thus in the first book of *The Prelude* we have a passage which, curiously enough, follows immediately upon the one in which he deals with indoor games:

> I have felt,
> Not seldom even in that tempestous time,
> Those hallowed and pure motions of the sense
> Which seem, in their simplicity, to own

---

[5] A thorough study of this subject will be found in *English Childhood—Wordsworth's Treatment of Childhood in the Light of English Poetry from Prior to Crabbe*, by A. Charles Babenroth, Ph.D., Columbia University Press, 1922. The final chapter, containing a summary of the Wordsworth point of view, I have found of special value.

> An intellectual charm; that calm delight
> Which, if I err not, surely must belong
> To those first-born affinities that fit
> Our new existence to existing things,
> And, in our dawn of being, constitute
> The bond of union between life and joy.[6]

It accords with this that Wordsworth set great store by the sense-impressions of childhood, even those occurring in moments of "vulgar joy." Nothing that passes into the deep reservoir of the subconscious mind can be lost:

>          . . . even then I felt
> Gleams like the flashing of a shield;—the earth
> And common face of Nature spake to me
> Rememberable things: . . .
> Albeit lifeless then, and doomed to sleep
> Until maturer seasons called them forth
> To impregnate and to elevate the mind.[7]

Similarly, Wordsworth loved to explore the gropings of the child mind toward the glories of the future life, either in this world or the world to come. This is a theme he develops in connection with his discussion of the place of books in the education of the child, especially books of imagination. The passage is too long for quotation, but it contains these noteworthy lines:

> Dumb yearnings, hidden appetites, are ours,
> And they *must* have their food. Our childhood sits,
> Our simple childhood, sits upon a throne
> That hath more power than all the elements.[8]

In connection with this, one should read the exquisite sonnet composed at Calais in 1802, beginning:

> It is a beauteous evening, calm and free,
> The holy time is quiet as a Nun
> Breathless with adoration . . .

to which I have alluded in another chapter as expressing

[6] *Prelude*, I, 549-558.
[7] *Ibid.*, I, 585-596.
[8] *Ibid.*, V, 506-509.

the sentiment of Being in the mighty deep. The reference in the closing lines to the child walking by his side on the beach at Calais was none other than his own French daughter, Caroline, at this time nine years of age:

> Dear Child! Dear Girl! that walkest with me here,
> If thou appear untouched by solemn thought,
> Thy nature is not therefore less divine:
> Thou liest in Abraham's bosom all the year;
> And worshipp'st at the Temple's inner shrine,
> God being with thee when we know it not.

In one section of *The Prelude* Wordsworth does not hesitate to carry his theory of childhood impression as far back as the beginnings of infancy. He speaks of the early days,

> In which, a Babe, by intercourse of touch
> I held mute dialogues with my Mother's heart,

and characterizes "this infant sensibility" as "the great birthright of our being."[9]

In all this Wordsworth is surprisingly modern. I am unable to say how closely his views agree with Freud and the other ultras of psychology who emphasize the subconscious as the dominant factor in human thought and behavior; but they certainly look in that direction. So modernistic a person as Herbert Read, in traversing the experiences of his own childhood, has actualized the Wordsworth idea in an interesting and challenging way:

> The echoes of my life which I find in my early childhood are too many to be dismissed as vain coincidences; but it is perhaps my conscious life which is the echo, the only real experiences in life being those lived with a virgin sensibility—so that we only hear a tone once, only see a color once, see, hear, touch, taste, and smell everything but once, the first time. All life is an echo of our first sensations, and we build up our consciousness, our whole mental life, by variations and combinations of these elementary sensations.[10]

---

[9]*Prelude*, II, 267-268.
[10]*The Innocent Eye*, London, 1933, Faber and Faber.

# THE CHILD IS FATHER OF THE MAN

In the well-known and, at the time of publication (1798), much ridiculed poem, *We Are Seven,* Wordsworth was bold enough to suggest that an eight-year-old child possesses (or may possess) a sure instinct of immortality. The story scarcely needs to be recalled, how the Poet met the little cottage girl whose wild beauty attracted him, and how he argued with her as to the number of her sisters and brothers and found himself worsted in the argument. She informed him she had six brothers and sisters, so that there were seven in all, although two of them had died ("went away"). The Poet argued there could be in that case only five. But the little girl stood her ground and related how she was accustomed to play around their graves in the churchyard, and at times to eat her supper there and "sing a song to them." So the Poet, wondering at it all, left her in possession of the field:

> "But they are dead; those two are dead!
> Their spirits are in heaven!"
> 'Twas throwing words away; for still
> The little Maid would have her will,
> And said, "Nay, we are seven!"

There are those who hold that the purpose of the poem is to teach the impossibility of a child as young as this realizing the fact of death, and that there is no such thing as an innate child-sense of a life beyond the grave.[11] There is a sense, of course, in which this is true, as the opening stanza suggests:

> A simple child,
> That lightly draws its breath,
> And feels its life in every limb,
> What should it know of death?

But this is not the indwelling idea of the poem. In my opinion Wordsworth intended to convey exactly the opposite idea—the fact that, while the child cannot realize

---

[11] So Harper (in his Introduction to *Poems by Wordsworth*), and Hearn.

all that is involved in death, she knows that it does not exist so far as spiritual separation is concerned; that, in spite of all appearances, those who die and whose bodies lie in the grave, actually live on, and we may rejoice in the thought of communion with them. In other words, Wordsworth believed in and sought to express a naïve sense of immortality on the part of an eight-year-old child. This would seem to be the obvious meaning of the poem, although, for a wonder, the Poet leaves us to draw our own conclusions. Thus the question of the opening stanza is to be answered by saying, "The child, simple as it is, can and does know the most important thing of all about death."[12] This view is supported by the eighth stanza of *The Ode*, in which the child's instinct of immortality is explicitly taught:

> Thou, whose exterior semblance doth belie
>     Thy Soul's immensity;
> Thou best Philosopher, who yet does keep
> Thy heritage, thou Eye among the blind,
> That, deaf and silent, read'st the eternal deep,
> Haunted forever by the eternal mind,—
>     Mighty Prophet! Seer blest!
>     On whom those truths do rest,
> Which we are toiling all our lives to find,
> In darkness lost, the darkness of the grave;
> Thou, over whom thy Immortality
> Broods like the Day, a Master o'er a Slave,
> A Presence which is not to be put by;
>     (To whom the grave
> Is but a lonely bed without the sense or sight
>     Of day or the warm light,
> A place of thought where we in waiting lie;)
> Thou little Child, yet glorious in the might
> Of heaven-born freedom on thy being's height,
> Why with such earnest pains dost thou provoke
> The years to bring the inevitable yoke,
> Thus blindly with thy blessedness at strife?
> Full soon thy Soul shall have her earthly freight,
> And custom lie upon thee with a weight,
> Heavy as frost, and deep almost as life!

---

[12] Prof. Sneath carries the idea of the poem somewhat farther than this, maintaining that it teaches that "To the child immortality is an ever-present reality."

In writing *We Are Seven* the Poet evidently had more than his conversation with the cottage child in view, since he quotes its first stanza in the note attached to *The Ode,* remarking, "Nothing was more difficult for me in childhood than to admit the notion of death as a state applicable to my own being." It seems clear, then that Wordsworth held rather firmly to the view of a child-instinct or intuition of immortality. Whether or not he was justified in holding such a view is another matter.

In *The Ode* we find Wordsworth arguing for a childhood instinct of immortality reaching not forward, as in *We Are Seven,* but backward to a preëxistent state.

The doctrine of preëxistence is as old as the religion of Egypt and the philosophy of the Hindu sages. It is widely prevalent in the Far East today, where it is usually associated with belief in the transmigration of souls (metempsychosis). It was a part of the early Pythagorean philosophy of the Greeks, and is reflected in the writings of Plato, who taught, or at least implied, that the intuitive ideas of space, time, cause, substance, sight, God, are learned in a previous state of being, and that human knowledge is only recollection of some other world.[13] Origen and several of the early church theologians approved of the idea as a corollary to existence after death. The same conception appears in the "angel infant" idea of the Welsh poet and mystic, Henry Vaughan (1622-1692), especially in his *Retreate.* (It is known that Wordsworth had a copy of Vaughan in his library.) Shelley, in his *Prometheus Unbound,* as a recent writer has pointed out, "traces the course of the soul back through manhood, youth, and infancy to the 'diviner day' which it lost by birth and can only regain by death."[14] But so profound has been the impression of Wordsworth's *Ode* that to the majority of educated people the mention of preëxistence at once calls his poem to mind.

[13] See the *Meno* and the *Phaedo.*

[14] George Sampson, in the *Times Literary Supplement* (London) Oct. 20, 1932.

It is to be noted that Wordsworth finds the "intimations" not in recollections of knowledge, or of any of the
spiritual states of preëxistent being, but in the vividness
and intimacy of the child's enjoyment of Nature, as contrasted with the soberer appreciation of adult years:

> There was a time when meadow, grove, and stream,
> The earth, and every common sight,
> To me did seem
> Apparelled in celestial light,
> The glory and the freshness of a dream.
> It is not now as it hath been of yore;—
> Turn wheresoe'er I may,
> By night or day,
> The things which I have seen I now can see no more.
>
> The Rainbow comes and goes,
> And lovely is the Rose,
> The Moon doth with delight
> Look round her when the heavens are bare,
> Waters on a starry night
> Are beautiful and fair;
> The sunshine is a glorious birth;
> But yet I know, where'er I go,
> That there hath past away a glory from the earth.

The problem of a receding splendor, propounded in
these opening stanzas, is developed in beautiful and wist-
ful detail in the two that follow, but is left unsolved, the
fourth stanza closing with the haunting inquiry:

> Whither is fled the visionary gleam?
> Where is it now, the glory and the dream?

Wordsworth spent two years in finding an appropriate
answer to that question, and they were among the most
fruitful years of his life. In his prefatory note he merely
mentions a gap of at least that time between the writing
of the first four stanzas in 1803 and the finishing of the
poem in 1806. Herford calls attention to the fact that
during the interval Wordsworth was writing the account
of his own recovery of imagination in the later books of
*The Prelude,* and in that recovery the memory of his own

childhood had played an important part, leading to a sense of awe as he contemplated the meaning of the instincts of childhood in the development of his maturer powers. It may be added that during this same period, having married Mary Hutchinson, his first child, John, was born. These facts are important as serving to unify the teachings as to childhood which we have found scattered so widely through the poems. In my desk copy I have marked twelve places, other than *The Ode*, where the idea of preëxistence is referred to or suggested as a possibility, these covering a period of thirty-nine years—1798-1837. Certainly we may say that Wordsworth's answer to his own question, the one that emerged in 1806, marks the highest level of his insight and poetical expression:

> Our birth is but a sleep and a forgetting:
> The Soul that rises with us, our life's Star,
> > Hath had elsewhere its setting,
> > > And cometh from afar:
> > Not in entire forgetfulness,
> > And not in utter nakedness,
> But trailing clouds of glory do we come
> > From God, who is our home:
> Heaven lies about us in our infancy!
> Shades of the prison-house begin to close
> > Upon the growing Boy,
> But He beholds the light, and whence it flows,
> > He sees it in his joy;
> The Youth, who daily farther from the east
> > Must travel, still is Nature's Priest,
> > And by the vision splendid
> > Is on his way attended;
> At length the Man perceives it die away,
> And fade into the light of common day.

It is not my intention to trace the full argument of this matchless ode, from the Poet's development of the idea of the child's vanishing dream, through his reflection upon "Thy Soul's immensity," and the compensating experiences arising from the sweet memories of childhood days and the fruitage of the years "that bring the philosophic mind," to the comfort of those closing lines:

> To me the meanest flower that blows can give
> Thoughts that do often lie too deep for tears.

Nor it is necessary. As Wordsworth remarked in his note dictated to his friend, Miss Fenwick, "To the attentive and competent reader the whole sufficiently explains itself." The poem has so completely taken possession of the highest place in Wordsworth's poetry that a knowledge of its structure may reasonably be assumed. We have to do with what Emerson characterized as "the high-water-mark which the intellect has reached in this age." Almost every line repays thoughtful attention. A line like "Our birth is but a sleep and a forgetting" has the firmness and finality and something of the sonority of Shakespeare.[15]

But it would not be fair to leave the impression that Wordsworth intended to commit himself to the doctrine here set forth in such an intriguing way. *The Ode* is to be taken as poetry and not as formal exposition. Late in life the Poet took pains to disown any such intention. In the prefatory note he says:

> To that dream-like vividness and splendour, which invests objects of sight in childhood, every one, I believe, if he would look back, could bear testimony, and I need not dwell upon it here; but having in the poem regarded it as a presumptive evidence of a prior state of existence, I think it is right to protest against a conclusion, which has given pain to some good and pious persons, that I meant to inculcate such a belief. It is far too shadowy a notion to be recommended to faith as more than an element in our instincts of immortality. But let us bear in mind, though the idea is not advanced in Revelation, there is nothing there to contradict it, and the Fall of Man presents an analogy in its favor.

This statement has been criticized as not truly reflect-

---

[15] For the study of the *Ode*, as indeed of many other poems, I commend the notes of J. H. Fowler in his editing of the *Fourth Book of Palgrave's Golden Treasury of Song and Lyrics*, Macmillan, 1922.

ing the Wordsworth of 1803-6, since in those days he had little if any faith in "Revelation," and certainly did not believe in the "Fall of Man." But if our argument in Chapter IV, to the effect that Wordsworth's conversion to orthodox, or essentially orthodox Christianity, was prior to 1798, has weight, then the above references to the views he held in 1806 are not inappropriate.

Coleridge held *The Ode* in high regard, and in view of his intimacy with the Wordsworth household throughout the period of composition, the comments upon its doctrinal basis found in his *Biographia Literaria* are of peculiar value:

> The ode was intended for such readers only as had been accustomed to watch the ebb and flow of their inmost nature, to venture at times into the twilight realms of consciousness, and to feel a deep interest in modes of inmost being, to which they know that the attributes of time and space are inapplicable and alien, but which yet cannot be conveyed, save in symbols of time and space. For such readers the sense is sufficiently plain, and they will be as little disposed to charge Mr. Wordsworth with believing the Platonic interpretation of the words, as I am to believing that Plato himself ever meant or taught it.

For the majority of us, even if we are unable to qualify under the Coleridge description, *The Ode* stands preëminent among modern writings for its teaching that the soul is derived from God, for its appeal for the recovery of early childhood's appreciation of the outer world, and for its glorification of the high instincts of the heart:

> Which, be they what they may,
> Are yet the fountain-light of all our day,
> Are yet a master-light of all our seeing.

The message of Wordsworth to our time, arising from his poems relating to childhood, is a message of reassurance. These poems of one hundred and more years ago encourage us to think that in our measures of reform, we at least are moving in the right direction. There is no question where Wordsworth would stand today in the matter of child-labor. His poems constitute a Bill of Rights for the children of the poor. There is no question where he would stand today in respect to the prime importance of the early years of education, the necessity, above all considerations of expense, of exposing the children of each community to the highest influences which the intellectual, the æsthetic and the religious culture of the age affords. The time has come when the author of *The Prelude* should be recognized by the side of Rousseau and Froebel as a pioneer in those educational theories and processes which derive from Nature as the Mother and Master of us all. In no small degree we owe it to him that once more the child is "in the midst," not merely as an object of affection, but as an object of profound study and reverent concern. We owe it to him that the fact that Man's greatness never shines in so divine a light as in the simplicity of childhood days has been expressed in immortal verse. It is the inculcation of this truth, even more than the faithful depiction of childhood scenes, that assigns to Wordsworth the place of preëminence among the poets who deal with child life and thought.

> Oh! mystery of man, from what a depth
> Proceed thy honours. I am lost, but see
> In simple childhood something of the base
> On which thy greatness stands.[16]

---

[16]*Prelude*, XII, 272-4.

# CHAPTER VIII

## "We Must Be Free or Die"

It is not to be thought of that the Flood
Of British freedom, which, to the open sea
Of the world's praise, from dark antiquity
Hath flowed, "with pomp of waters, unwithstood,"
Roused though it be full often to a mood
Which spurns the check of salutary bands,
That this most famous Stream in bogs and sands
Should perish; and to evil and to good
Be lost forever. In our halls is hung
Armoury of the invincible Knights of old:
We must be free or die, who speak the tongue
That Shakspeare spake; the faith and morals hold
Which Milton held.—In everything we are sprung
Of Earth's first blood, have titles manifold.

READERS of that delightful book *The Letters of Walter Hines Page* will recall Mr. Page's devotion to Wordsworth and how he came to depend upon the soothing and steadying quality of the patriotic poems during the distracting days of the World War. Imagine, then, his delight in discovering that Sir Edward Grey was also a lifelong lover of the same poet. Who can say what diplomacy owes to this congeniality of interest? There is at least a suggestion in that amusing incident when a roomful of secretaries was kept waiting several hours in great suspense over the forced retention of American ships, while Mr. Page and Viscount Grey were supposed to be closeted over the problem. "At last," says his biographer, "when his care worn and distracted subordinates were almost prepared to go in search of their chief, the ambassador walked jauntily in, smiling and apparently carefree. What had happened? What was to be done about the detained ships? 'What ships?' asked

Page, and then suddenly he remembered. 'Oh, yes, those'
—that was all right; Sir Edward had at once promised
to release them; it had all been settled in a few minutes.
'Then why were you so long?' The truth came out that
Sir Edward and Page had quickly turned from inter-
cepted cargoes to the more congenial subject of Wordsworth and other poets, and the rest of the afternoon
had been consumed in discussing this really important
business."[1]

In keeping with this incident is the report that morning
after morning, during the War, as Britain's Secretary of
Foreign Affairs walked from his home to his office in
Downing Street, he would repeat softly to himself such
of Wordsworth's poems as were calculated to steady his
thought as he faced the stupendous decisions of the day.
On one occasion, of which Mr. Page speaks, the Viscount
asked him as to his opinion of the war poems and remarked that he regarded them as "the best of all war
poems," because, he added, "they don't glorify war, but
have to do with its philosophy." It was at this time that
he called the ambassador's attention to a little volume
of these war pieces selected from Wordsworth by Mr.
Acland, a friend of his, and promised to send him a copy.[2]

The fact that it was to the contemplative singer of the
Lakes that the people of England turned during the dark
days of the war is of immense significance—significant
alike for Wordsworth and the people of England. It uncovers one of those underlying affinities which go so far
to explain national character and destiny, a fact that will
become even more evident when we consider poems like
the *Ode to Duty* and *The Happy Warrior*.

There is evidence that the Wordsworth influence increased throughout the period of the war. In 1917 appeared *The Statesmanship of Wordsworth*, by Professor

---

[1] *Letters of Walter Hines Page*, Houghton Mifflin Co., Vol. II, p. 104.

[2] *The Patriotic Poetry of William Wordsworth*. A Selection (with Introduction
and Notes) by Right Hon. Arthur H. D. Acland, Oxford, 1915. The book is dedicated
to Edward Grey.

Dicey of Oxford, which even more than the Acland selections, served to center attention upon Wordsworth as the leading patriot-poet of the realm. Dicey's essay urges that Wordsworth's eminence as a Poet of Nature should not be allowed to obscure his genius as an interpreter of English thought and aspiration during the perilous period of the Napoleonic campaigns. Tracing the development of the Poet's ideas during the Revolutionary and post-Revolutionary era, he maintains that more than any other writer of the period Wordsworth expressed the inner and spiritual life of the country. For this reason, under the strain of recent war experiences, he found his countrymen turning to Wordsworth for strength. "England," he remarks, "today stands in the same position in which she stood from 1803 to 1815; she is now, as then, engaged in a sacred war against armed and despotic Imperialism."[8]

And it appears that in other struggles than that of 1914-1918 men have turned to the philosopher-poet of the North for the inspiring and steadying word. A few summers ago, browsing in an old book-shop of an English provincial town, I ran across a thin little volume, of which I had not known, entitled *Poems Dedicated to National Independence and Liberty,* with an introduction by Stopford Brooke. The title-page stated that it was a republication of poems selected from Wordsworth on behalf of Crete. The reprint was in 1897, when, by reason of a concert of the Powers, England might easily have pursued the policy of checking the national aspirations of the Cretans, in favor of maintaining the tyranny of the Turks. The *Independence and Liberty Sonnets* of Wordsworth were a factor in holding England to her traditional policy of sympathy for a people struggling for their rights.

How are we to reconcile all this with Wordsworth's advocacy of aloofness and solitude as the ideal way? How reconcile a life devoted to "Nature's calm," with

---

[8] *Statesmanship of Wordsworth,* by A. V. Dicey, Oxford, Clarendon Press.

one concerned so largely with the hatred and strife of a warring world? To the mind of the Poet there was no conflict of ideals. The seclusion he sought was not seclusion for its own sake, but seclusion for the world's sake. Always his eye was upon the moving scene of the world's wider horizon. At least it came to be so. There was a time, following hard upon the disillusionment incident to the failure of the French Revolution, when the Poet, still a youth, sought for nothing so much as to escape from the pressure of the multitudinous life of the world, and to become a "Recluse" in very fact. But this soon passed, and after a few years Grasmere became his watch-tower from which with eager eye he scanned the battlefields of Europe. In spite of his detachment and the infrequency of the mails, it is doubtful if any man in England followed more keenly the events which began with Napoleon's assumption of the title of First Consul of France and ended with his becoming the dictator of the larger part of Europe. Here was something more than a youthful mood. It was the central thrust of his poetic career, so that with a good conscience he could picture himself as living

> In a still retreat
> Sheltered, but not to social duties lost.[3]

Wordsworth was no "literary monk."

Consistent with this changed point of view is the fact that in 1803, when England was threatened by invasion, Wordsworth went so far as to enlist in a voluntary military company that was being formed in the neighboring village of Ambleside. One does not readily picture Shelley or the author of *The Lost Leader* exerting himself to that extent.

A Wordsworth far removed from the popular tradition emerges at this point—a Wordsworth whose primary interest confessedly was not in poetry but in public

---

[3] From *The Recluse.*

events. Late in life the Poet remarked to an American visitor, Rev. Orville Dewey, that "although he was known to the world only as a poet, he had given twelve hours thought to the conditions and prospects of society for one to poetry." While this undoubtedly was the case between the years 1800 and 1815, we are to remember that but for the poetry of this same period we should have little or none of the fruitage of his broodings over "the conditions and prospects of society."

It is to be recognized of course that the Wordsworth of the patriotic sonnets is not the Wordsworth of the early period of the Revolution, the period set before us so compellingly in the sixth, ninth, tenth and eleventh books of *The Prelude*. It is a Wordsworth whose republicanism has been sobered by the excesses in France and the overshadowing figure of Bonaparte—a Wordsworth whose admiration for France has given place to a passionate devotion to England. The marking event for this change is the visit of the Poet and his sister Dorothy to France in July 1802, during a time of peace, for the purpose of conferring with Annette Vallon as to the contemplated marriage of the Poet to Mary Hutchinson. It was during their sojourn at Calais that the news came of the granting to Napoleon of the Consulship for life. A series of sonnets, written at Calais, or at Dover on the return journey, bear witness to the awakening of the new patriotism in the Poet's soul. Of these sonnets two were written on the very day, August 7, when the news was received, and when the strength of his reaction led him to speak of the people of France as "Ye men of prostrate mind," and to characterize their leaders as "to slavery prone." In a sonnet written twelve days later, on Napoleon's birthday, when festivals were being held throughout France, he recalls the festival he had witnessed at Calais in 1790 when France was "standing on the top of golden hours." In the light of the intervening years he has come to discount heavily the promise of the earlier day:

> The senselessness of joy was then sublime!

and we find him regarding the future with mingled feelings of dismay and hope:

> Happy is he, who, caring not for Pope,
> Consul, or King, can sound himself to know
> The destiny of Man, and live in hope.

To so sensitive and high-strung a spirit as Wordsworth a change like this could not come without profound significance. If it brought disappointment it brought also one of the master-inspirations of his career.

Wordsworth has been sharply criticized for the change in political view which followed upon his renunciation of France in favor of England. Browning's *Lost Leader* and Shelley's derogatory sonnet are reflections of a controversy which has continued down to the present day. A volume has been written on the alleged "apostasy" of Wordsworth.[*] Having become a confirmed Tory in middle life, the Poet, it is maintained by the critics, grew ashamed of his early views, and in his revision of *The Prelude* undertook to tone down the radical opinions of his youth, especially those referring to his revolutionary ardors in France. Fortunately, since the publication of the *variorum* edition of *The Prelude* by de Selincourt in 1926, we find the means of "checking up" on charges of this nature. Here we have, printed side by side on opposite pages, the work as it originally came from the pen of Wordsworth in 1805 and the work as it was given to the public after the Poet's death in 1850, and after it had been subjected to a process of lifelong revision. As an aid to this fascinating study in poetical evolution, the editor has provided copious notes relating to the five extant and widely differ-

---

[*] *An Examination of the Charge of Apostasy against Wordsworth*, by William Hale White, 1898.

ing manuscripts which were placed in his hands, together with an illuminating introductory essay.

And what does the comparative version reveal as to the Poet's change of front? The detractors will obtain small comfort from Professor de Selincourt's comparison of texts. In the matter of abandonment of liberal views he clears the field by a single lucid statement, reminding us that in the year 1804, Wordsworth "was already heart and soul with his own country in her struggle with Napoleon, convinced that the cause of liberty depended upon her ultimate triumph." There *are* evidences of a toning down of opinions as the true nature of the Revolution was unrolled to view and the hopes he had entertained previously to 1801 proved abortive. His love for England grew as his confidence in France faded away. Naturally *The Prelude* was altered to correspond with the exalted patriotism of the sonnets to which allusion has been made. But in the essential ideals of human aspiration and liberty Wordsworth stood his ground. He left practically untouched Book IX, in which he describes his conversion to the cause of France, and reserved the more drastic changes for passages relating to the objectionable features of the Revolution. The passage in Book X, referring to the September massacres of 1792, in which, it will be recalled a thousand royalists and nonjuring priests were slain by the mob, was left unchanged except for verbal improvements, and may well be read today as an indication of the Poet's prophetic mood as foreboding events began to appear.

Professor de Selincourt calls attention to the convincing way in which Wordsworth met the charge of apostasy when he wrote to a friend: "You have been deluded by places and persons, while I have stuck to principles. I abandoned France and her rulers when they abandoned liberty, gave themselves up to tyranny and endeavored to enslave the world." This is true enough, as any historically minded person should be quick to discern. Unfortunately Wordsworth did not content himself with substituting England for France as the nation of his affections and as the best hope of the world. In an England delivered from the menace of Napoleon we find a Wordsworth whose patriotism took color from the extremest Toryism of the day, even to the point of opposing the reform measures of 1830 and subsequent years, which looked to the broadening of the suffrage and the emancipation of Roman Catholics and Jews. This inconsistency has given offense to many. Whether or not it can be resolved, or the extent to which it can be resolved, depends upon one's fairness of mind and ability to balance between considerations of larger and smaller importance. Dean Church in his discriminating essay remarks: "The changes in his fundamental principles, in his thought of man and his duties, were not great; the change in his application of them and in his judgment of the man, the parties, the institutions, the measures by which they were to be guarded and carried out, was great indeed."[5] With this Swinburne is in agreement. In the essay from which I have had occasion to quote at several points, he says: "As the poet of high-minded loyalty to his native land, Wordsworth stands alone, above all compeers and successors." And again: "Royalist and conservative as he appeared, he never really ceased, while his power of song was unimpaired, to be in the deepest and most liberal sense a republican; a citizen to whom the common weal—the common good of all . . . was the one thing worthy of any man's and all men's entire devotion."[6] The case against Wordsworth has been materially strengthened by the position taken by Professor Harper in his well-known biography. It may be said to be the main thesis of this author that there were *two* Wordsworths—Wordsworth the ardent Republican, and Wordsworth the timid Tory— and that there is no reconciling of the two except on the

---

[5] *Dante and Other Essays*, 1889, p. 199.
[6] *Miscellanies*, 1886.

ground of a moral decline, the gradual settling upon him
of a spirit of timorousness and hesitation, which accounts
not only for his political defection, but also for his
waning poetic inspiration.[7] Professor Harper's carefully
elaborated and well defended position has not gone without challenge. Both in England and America there have
been protesting reviews by those well qualified to speak,
notably by Professor George Herbert Palmer, of Harvard University, and Miss Edith C. Batho, of University
College, London.[8]

The issue is so involved in the rapidly changing conditions of the European world, that the onlooker today may
be pardoned for steering a middle course. My own feeling
is that, while the inconsistency cannot be wholly resolved,
it cannot be said to constitute anything in the nature of a
moral lapse or apostasy, and that in the light of the
superb contribution of Wordsworth to the cause of freedom during the Napoleonic Wars, the fact of his timidity
in later years may well be allowed to drop out of sight.

In considering the large body of Wordsworth's patriotic verse, we find the poems falling naturally into three
groups, according as they deal with his love of England;
his condemnation of France and Napoleon; his devotion
to liberty for all mankind. For the most part the patriotic
utterances may be found in the section of the complete
works to which Wordsworth gave the name *Poems Dedi-*

---

[7] In the biography by Harper see especially Chapter XXIII, *Retreat and Surrender.*
[8] See article by Palmer in *Harvard Theological Review*, Jan. 1917. For a vigorous
protesting British opinion, see *Quarterly Review*, July 1916, article by John Bailey.
For a balanced discussion of the whole issue, see *Wordsworth Since 1916*, by Prof.
R. A. Rice, in *Smith College Studies in Modern Languages*, Jan. 1924. In Miss
Batho's *The Later Wordsworth*, 1933, however, the subject is reopened as the result
of a painstaking examination of the contention that in later life there was a marked
decay of Wordsworth's faculties, accompanied by a loss of the generous feelings of his
youth and the conversion to a timid orthodoxy in both political and ecclesiastical
affairs. Miss Batho maintains that in youth Wordsworth was less radical than has
been supposed, and in old age he was far from being a rabid and unreasoning Tory.
In his later political views she holds that the Poet, judged by the historical outcome,
was more often right than wrong, and always was able to defend himself on well
reasoned grounds. In religion, Miss Batho presents evidence to show that the Poet
was no more conservative in his old age than he was in his early youth, and that the
period of doubt has been given an exaggerated importance. She admits no essential
decay of poetical power, attributing the lack of creative verse in middle life and old
age to a disease of the eyes from which the poet suffered. Miss Batho's championship
is of the most vigorous sort. She undertakes to prove too much, especially as to the
change in political views, but her book is one of vast research and should be welcomed
as a corrective.

*cated to National Independence and Liberty,* seventy-four in all. Only a few of these can be mentioned even by name, and still fewer can be quoted. Yet, possibly no poems of Wordsworth are likely to appeal more forcefully to the thoughtful mind of today.

On the evening of the day when, at Calais, Wordsworth received the news of Napoleon's assumption of the dictatorship, the day on which he wrote those scathing lines beginning "Is it a reed that's shaken by the wind," he looked across the Channel and in the purple twilight beheld the dusky outlines of the coast of England and overhead the shining of the evening star. A sonnet that will live as long as English speech was the result:

> Fair Star of evening, Splendour of the west,
> Star of my Country!—on the horizon's brink
> Thou hangest, stooping, as might seem, to sink
> On England's bosom; yet well pleased to rest,
> Meanwhile, and be to her a glorious crest
> Conspicuous to the Nations. Thou, I think,
> Shouldst be my Country's emblem; and shouldst wink,
> Bright Star! with laughter on her banners, drest
> In thy fresh beauty. There! that dusky spot
> Beneath thee, that is England; there she lies.
> Blessings be on you both! one hope, one lot,
> One life, one glory!—I, with many a fear
> For my dear Country, many heartfelt sighs,
> Among men who do not love her, linger here.

As so often happens, Wordsworth's realization of his love for his native land came to him on a foreign shore. There had been a similar experience three years before when he and Dorothy and Coleridge were spending the winter in Germany, and he had written the little poem beginning:

> I travelled among unknown men,
>   In lands beyond the sea;
> Nor, England! did I know till then
>   What love I bore to thee.

Mr. Acland calls attention to the fact that about fifteen

months after *Fair Star of Evening* was composed, Napoleon, like Wordsworth, was scanning the horizon across the Channel, and catching a glimpse of England, he wrote to Consul Cambacères: "I saw the coast of England from the heights of Ambleteuse as distinctly as one can see the Calvary from the Tuileries. I was able to distinguish the houses and even objects moving. It is merely a ditch that will be crossed when we are bold enough to undertake the enterprise."

Upon the return journey the Poet and his sister tarried at Dover, and, upon looking back at France, he was inspired to write the sonnet beginning "Here, on our native soil, we breathe once more," closing with the lines:

> Thou art free,
> My country! and 'tis joy enough and pride
> For one hour's perfect bliss, to tread the grass
> Of England once again, and hear and see,
> With such a dear Companion at my side.

Parallel to the awakening affection for his imperiled country, was the sense of confidence in the solid worth of her men and institutions. This is expressed in the noble sonnet which I have placed at the head of this chapter— *It is not to be thought of,* and in the rousing lines addressed *To the Men of Kent*—as those likely to bear the brunt of the expected invasion—

> Vanguard of Liberty, ye men of Kent.

In the same sonnet he expresses his confidence in England's citizenry as a whole:

> In Britain is one breath;
> We all are with you now from shore to shore;—
> Ye men of Kent, 'tis victory or death!

But the patriotic sonnets by no means reflect unqualified praise of native land. Many of them—and they are among the best he ever wrote—express sorrow and dismay over what appeared to him England's moral decline.

While Pitt and Nelson were appealing for men, Wordsworth was appealing for a revival of the ancient virtues. He was far more concerned over England's "trespasses" and "offences" than he was over her lack of man-power and financial resource. The Wordsworth sonnets which bear upon the faults of his countrymen are the finest possible illustration of that saving grace of self-criticism which characterizes the Anglo-Saxon people the world over, and which is so painfully lacking in the nations of the Far East, not to mention some nearer at hand. Not only did England's Poet say these searching things, but England—the real England—was glad he said them. Wordsworth became their Isaiah, their Hosea. They knew that his chastisements were just, that they came from a heart of love. Certainly one has no difficulty in detecting the prophetic note in the famous *Milton Sonnet,* written in 1802, immediately after England declared war on France:

> Milton! thou shouldst be living at this hour:
> England hath need of thee: she is a fen
> Of stagnant waters: altar, sword, and pen,
> Fireside, the heroic wealth of hall and bower,
> Have forfeited their ancient English dower
> Of inward happiness. We are selfish men;
> Oh! raise us up, return to us again;
> And give us manners, virtue, freedom, power.
> Thy soul was like a Star, and dwelt apart;
> Thou hadst a voice whose sound was like the sea:
> Pure as the naked heavens, majestic, free,
> So didst thou travel on life's common way,
> In cheerful godliness; and yet thy heart
> The lowliest duties on herself did lay.

In the almost equally noble sonnet beginning "O Friend! I know not which way I must look," the Poet becomes more specific in his accusations. He charges his countrymen with possessing a menial mind, with a love of vain show, with the idolatry of wealth—"The wealthiest man among us is the best." He grieved that forces like these were sapping the strength of the old English order.

This sonnet contains a line that has become proverbial in our speech—"Plain living and high thinking are no more." The best known of all the sonnets, *The world is too much with us,* carries the same indictment, inspired by a mood of fear lest England's morale should be unequal to the strain which had already proved too much for Italy, Austria, Switzerland and Germany. In several of the sonnets of criticism, especially those written in 1802 and 1803, there is a violence of feeling and expression which seems exaggerated. Apparently Wordsworth came to recognize this fact, and in a way he made apology in a sonnet published in the *Morning Post* in September 1803, which begins with the words "When I have borne in memory what has tamed Great Nations," and in which he confesses the unworthiness of the fears he had felt, and pleads that, having spoken out of affection, he should not be blamed:

> Of those unfilial fears I am ashamed.
> For dearly must we prize thee; we who find
> In thee a bulwark for the cause of men;
> And I by my affection was beguiled:
> What wonder if a Poet now and then,
> Among the many movements of his mind,
> Felt for thee as a lover or a child!

In the sonnet of 1803:

> England! the time is come when thou shouldst wean
> Thy heart from its emasculating food,

we have what amounts to a balancing of the account of praise and blame. In these lines, in spite of her "trespasses," which are many, England stands forth as the sole hope of the world:

> Therefore the wise pray for thee, though the freight
> Of thy offences be a heavy weight:
> Oh grief that Earth's best hopes rest all with Thee!

That the final verdict was one of high appreciation for the people and the institutions of England is indicated in passages scattered through his longer poems. Thus in the eleventh book of *The Prelude,* in addressing Coleridge, who was sojourning in Malta for his health, he expressed his regret that he was gone

> From this last spot of earth, where Freedom now
> Stands single in her only sanctuary.

Similarly, in *The Excursion,* he speaks of England as

> the blessèd Isle,
> Truth's consecrated residence, the seat
> Impregnable of Liberty and Peace.[9]

When once he had changed his mind, Wordsworth's condemnation of France was deep and unrestrained. This is expressed not only in "Is it a reed that's shaken by the wind," in which he speaks of Frenchmen as "Ye men of prostrate mind," but even more unsparingly in "Great men have been among us," a sonnet in which, after singing the praise of England's mighty men of the past, like Sidney, Vane and Milton, he contrasts what appears to him France's poverty in nobility of this description:

> France, 'tis strange,
> Hath brought forth no such souls as we had then.
> Perpetual emptiness! unceasing change!
> No single volume paramount, no code,
> No master spirit, no determined road;
> But equally a want of books and men!

Yet he never lost sight of the mightiness of France for evil and for good. Old affections were stirred when he recalled her pleasant scenes, and the industry of her rural population:

> But 'tis a chosen soil, where sun and breeze
> Shed gentle favours: rural works are there,
> And ordinary business, without care;
> Spot rich in all things that can soothe and please!

In the sonnet *Inland, within a hollow vale, I stood,* we find the Poet, in a somewhat tempered indignation, tak-

---

[9] *Excursion,* VIII, 145-7.

ing a second look at France across the Channel, reminding his countrymen that only by virtue and wisdom can they expect to prevail over such a power, and reminding France that

> One decree
> Spake laws to them, and said that by the soul
> Only, the Nations shall be great and free.

For Napoleon, Wordsworth had only reprobation and scorn. He was "That Adventurer," "The enemy of liberty," the "Tyrant." Scarcely any language was too strong. In October 1803 he wrote:

> When, looking on the present face of things,
> I see one man, of men the meanest too!
> Raised up to sway the world, to do, undo,
> With mighty nations for his underlings.

He wonders if the man ever had a tender mood. Thinking upon such leadership in human affairs he is even tempted to question Providence:

> Nothing is left which I can venerate;
> So that a doubt almost within me springs
> Of Providence, such emptiness at length
> Seems at the heart of all things.

The sonnets traverse the leading events of the Napoleonic wars, and one may almost trace the progress of the struggle in their resounding lines. It was in 1802 he wrote the particularly fine sonnet *On the Extinction of the Venetian Republic* (the event having occurred in 1797), which begins with the line,

> Once did She hold the gorgeous East in fee.

A year later the invasion of republican Switzerland stirred Wordsworth to write one of the most perfect things that ever fell from his pen, the sonnet entitled: *Thought of a Briton on the Subjugation of Switzerland,* and beginning with the lines:

> Two voices are there; one is of the sea,
> One of the mountains; each a mighty Voice.

At the time Napoleon was assembling his army at **Bou-logne** just across the Channel, with the known purpose of invading England, Wordsworth and his sister were traveling in Scotland. Coming to Killicranky, where in 1689 the attack of the English was repulsed by the Scottish Highlanders under Dundee with terrific loss of life, and where Dundee himself was killed, Wordsworth wrote that tremendous thing: *In the Pass of Killicranky, an Invasion Being Expected, October 1803,* with its closing appeal:

> O for a single hour of that Dundee,
> Who on that day the word of onset gave!
> Like conquest would the Men of England see;
> And her Foes find a like inglorious grave.

After the defeat of the Prussians at Jena in 1806, which resulted in the crushing of the power of Prussia, England's sole remaining ally on the Continent, Wordsworth gave forth the sonnet beginning:

> Another year!—another deadly blow!
> Another mighty Empire overthrown!
> And We are left, or shall be left, alone;
> The last that dare to struggle with the Foe.

The campaign in Spain in 1807-8 brought forth Wordsworth's greatest prose work—*The Tract on the Convention of Cintra,* in which, with rare eloquence, he argues that "Napoleon's tyranny is founded on his utter rejection of the restraints of morality," and in which he condemns the Spanish settlement—following an English victory—as false strategy and a betrayal of the sacred cause of liberty in which England had joined hands with Portugal and Spain. Several of the sonnets reflected the same point of view. It is clear that he regarded the war as a direct contest between the principles of evil and good.

It was his faith in the ultimate triumph of the good that sustained him to the very end.

Following the defeat of Austria, for the fourth time, at Wagram in 1809, when patriotism was at a low ebb, Wordsworth wrote the sonnet beginning "The martial courage of a day is vain," in which he pleaded for fortitude and hope and in which he expressed his scorn at the pusillanimity of Austria in the bestowing of the Princess Marie Louise upon Napoleon in marriage.

It was at the very height of Napoleon's success that Wordsworth foretold his doom. This he did in two sonnets, written in 1809, contrasting the French Adventurer with Gustavus IV of Sweden. Both of these are as noble in conception as they are in expression. The characterization of the Swedish King, who was forced to abdicate after the loss of Finland to Russia, has not been borne out by the verdict of history, which holds that either he was hopelessly incompetent or insane. But the characterization and forecast in respect to Napoleon is a remarkable piece of work. Unfortunately Wordsworth did not publish these sonnets until 1815. The one referring to Napoleon starts with the lines:

> Look now on that Adventurer who hath paid
> His vows to Fortune—

and ends:

> And, if old judgments keep their sacred course,
> Him from that height shall Heaven precipitate
> By violent and ignominious death.

The *Poems Dedicated to National Independence and Liberty* close with four pieces—two sonnets and two odes —in celebration of the victory at Waterloo. The best known of these—*The Thanksgiving Ode*, written on the morning of January 18, 1816, the day set apart for general thanksgiving, while containing some good lines, is scarcely worthy of the Poet or of the occasion. The ode entitled *1815*, written apparently a little later, is the more vigorous of the two, but abounds in exultation delivered in a pompous, non-Wordsworthian vein.

In order to evaluate Wordsworth's influence as the Poet of Patriotism during the Napoleonic wars, we need to have in mind the low state of public morale during much of this period. As many people in England during the dark days of 1916 and 1917 despaired of winning the war against Germany, so in 1807-1812 many despaired of winning the war against France. Even so great a statesman as William Pitt was unable to cast out the demon of fear. The historian Green relates that after the battle of Austerlitz, where Napoleon crushed the combined armies of Austria and Russia, Pitt remarked to his friends, "Roll up that map," pointing to a map of Europe which hung on the wall; "it will not be needed these ten years." When, on January 23, 1806, he lay dying, those who bent over him caught a faint murmuring from his lips—"My country! How I leave my country!"[10] This was the time when the mighty Jeffrey, of the *Edinburgh Review,* who had made sport of Wordsworth for his childish verse, was predicting the ruin of all who dared oppose the Corsican. He and his associates "ridiculed the romantic hopes of the English nation; the fate of Spain, they declared in 1810, was decided; it would be cruel, they said, to foment petty insurrections; France had conquered Europe."[11] Indeed it may be said that after the death of Fox, the leaders of the Whig Party, then in control, despairing of a successful issue to the war, were for a bargained peace ("Peace without victory")—their interest being primarily in the maintenance of England's economic prestige and success. Against this policy of what we today would call defeatism Wordsworth fought valiantly and successfully for twelve long years. And in this connection it is worth recalling that while the Poet of the English Lakes was rallying his countrymen to resist the French invasion

[10] *Short History of the English People,* p. 822.
[11] *Southey,* by Edward Dowden (English Men of Letters Series), p. 150.

at every point and in every possible way, the German Goethe was fawning upon the conqueror of his native land.

Throughout these critical years Wordsworth was ably supported by Coleridge, Southey and Sir Walter Scott, who not so much by their publications as by their correspondence and public address threw their influence in favor of national steadfastness and hope. Recalling the frequent goings and comings between Grasmere and Keswick—only eighteen miles apart—Coleridge's daughter wrote: "How gravely and earnestly used Samuel Taylor Coleridge and William Wordsworth and my uncle Southey to discuss the affairs of the nation as if it all came home to their business and bosoms, as if it were their private concern! Men do not canvass these matters now-a-days, I think, quite in the same tone."

England has yet to acknowledge in a suitable way what she owes to her poets in the time of the most terrible ordeal of her history. It is, however, a large compensation that, as by a deeply rooted instinct, it was to the solitary thinker of the Lakes she turned during the ordeal of the World War.

Incidentally, it is worth noting that Wordsworth's extensive use of the sonnet in connection with his patriotic appeal, resulted in the rehabilitation of this poetical form. In the years following Shakespeare and Milton the sonnet had been neglected almost to the point of extinction. With Wordsworth it blossomed into new life and became again the best vehicle of the prophetic note. In his well-known *Scorn Not the Sonnet* Wordsworth paid tribute to Milton's superb use of this form by saying:

> in his hand
> The Thing became a trumpet; whence he blew
> Soul-animating strains—alas, too few!

Equally of Wordsworth it may be said the thing became a trumpet in his hand. Nowhere does "the steady swell and climax of the Wordsworth sonnet," which has been so much praised, appear to better advantage than in the Patriotic Series. Of this entire body of verse Dicey well says: "They are the finest war songs ever composed by a patriot to stir up the valour and the nobility of his country; they might be termed the psalms of England, and like the Psalter they combine penitence for past errors with confidence in final victory based on the belief in the ultimate triumph of righteousness. They contain not a word which is mean, ignoble, or savage."[12] In 1837, in connection with a tour in Italy, he wrote a sonnet on being shown the favorite seat of Dante at Florence, in the closing lines of which he ventured, for the moment, to identify himself with the poet who lived and died in exile rather than acknowledge the rule of a tyrannous state:

> But in his breast the mighty Poet bore
> A Patriot's heart, warm with undying fire,
> Bold with the thought, in reverence I sate down,
> And, for a moment, filled that empty Throne.

Wordsworth's devotion to Liberty for all mankind is manifested in several of the poems which touch upon England's mission and place in the world, but far more in those which deal directly with other states. The international outlook reflected in his early love for France did not fade in later years. Not even in respect to the ultimate destiny of France. An examination of the seventy-four *Independence and Liberty* poems reveals that, apart from England and France, he dealt with nine different lands, and in each case by means of a separate composition. The list is impressive: Venetian Republic, Switzerland (seven poems), Greece (two), Austria (two), Sweden (three), Spain (twelve), Germany (three), Russia (three), Haiti. Where else in poetry have we such a sequence as this?

The outstanding impression is Wordsworth's unswerving faith in liberty as something instinctive in the human

---

[12] *Op. cit.*, p. 84.

breast. Because he is dealing with the issue of the Napoleonic wars, England and Switzerland are singled out as the best examples—"Two voices are there—each a mighty voice"; "We must be free or die." But the same unquenchable fire he finds in Toussaint L'Ouverture, the pure-blooded African patriot of Santo Domingo, who, after capitulating to the forces of Napoleon and being pardoned, by an act of perfidy was arrested and sent to France, where he remained a prisoner until his death. There is a sonnet, not of special poetic merit, but revealing a fine intensity of belief, dealing with a well-to-do Negress, who, in the wave of intolerance which swept over France, had been expelled from the country, and whom he had met as a fellow passenger on a vessel from Calais. This woman, with her down-cast looks and pride of personality, became a symbol of her injured race:

> Yet still her eyes retained their tropic fire,
> That, burning independent of the mind,
> Joined with the lustre of her rich attire
> To mock the Outcast—O ye Heavens be kind!
> And feel, thou Earth, for this afflicted race.

A kindred impression is that of a convinced and passionate belief in nationality as an instrument for the realization of humanity on the larger scale. Wordsworth has yet to receive the acclaim he deserves as the Prophet of Nationalism as we are beginning to understand that term today. He anticipated Mazzini by more than twenty years, by teaching that nationalism means "a great deal more than the mere admiration of patriotism." Says Dicey:

Ever since the days of Marathon and Thermopylæ, and indeed from a much earlier date, there have existed plenty of men and women able to admire the bravery of heroes dying in defense of their own native land. But modern Nationalists have done much more than teach that patriotism is a virtue. They have spread far and wide the political creed that every State, at any rate in Europe, ought, if possible, to be inhabited by citizens who were, or felt themselves to be, one nation, and that no nation should be governed by any foreign power. . . . Whence it follows that every independent nation should support, and if necessary be prepared to defend, the independence of any other nation.[13]

By virtue of this broader view Dicey does not hesitate to pronounce Wordsworth "the greatest European patriot of his day."

But this strongly democratic ideal must not be separated from Wordsworth's insistence upon the moral and spiritual qualities as essential to nationality. His teaching was that the progress of society in any state depends upon certain constants of ethical principle, such as freedom, justice, toleration, good faith, neighborliness, good will, without which there can be no assurance of permanence. The essential article of Wordsworth's political faith was that spiritual values ought to be supreme in national life:

> There is a bondage worse, far worse, to bear
> Than his who breathes, by roof, and floor, and wall,
> Pent in, a Tyrant's solitary Thrall:
> 'Tis he who walks about in the open air,
> One of a Nation who, henceforth, must wear
> Their fetters in their souls—

Were Wordsworth with us today, beyond question he would be pointing out that in a country like China, the struggle for democracy and freedom is handicapped less by the aggression of outsiders than by the lack of the moral and spiritual resources necessary to cope with a situation of such magnitude. Similarly, he would have nothing but scorn for "the lethal falsehoods" of much of the talk to which we have to listen in our political campaigns. No more scathing indictment of hypocrisy in high places has ever been put into poetry than those lines from *The Excursion:*

---

[13] *Op. cit.*, p. 81.

And Heaven is weary of the hollow words
Which States and Kingdoms utter when they talk
Of truth and justice.[14]

It is scarcely necessary to add the impression, gained from reading the patriotic poems, that Wordsworth was an intense believer in internationalism. He was indeed "a patriot of the world." Aside from an occasional lapse in respect to France, he was singularly free from the hating element which characterizes the patriotism of many. Instinctively he became interested in the multitudinous life of mankind. His internationalism, aroused by the wrongs of oppressed peoples, came to include every aspect of their life. As a result, belief in a commonwealth of internationality became a major article in his political creed. We find nothing in him of the rampant type of nationalism which has arisen in the wake of the World War. The chauvinism and supernationalism of our day would have impressed the author of *The Happy Warrior* as an ugly thing, a demon of bigotry to be cast out. Nor do we find a trace of the Jingoism of our pre-war period, when Kipling, Roosevelt and Cecil Rhodes were the heroes of the Anglo-Saxon world.

Wordsworth's moral ideals pervade the war poetry, and even more that too little known and rarely read prose-piece *Tract on the Convention of Cintra of 1809.* The statesmanship of Wordsworth might be allowed to rest on that pamphlet alone. The full title was as follows: "Concerning the relations of Great Britain, Spain and Portugal, to each other, and to the common enemy, at this crisis; and specifically as affected by the Convention of Cintra; the whole brought to the test of *those principles by which alone the independence and freedom of nations can be preserved or recovered.*"[15] Of this tract Professor Harper remarks: "His style is as heroic as his theme. It has a volume and weight unequalled even by

[14] *Excursion*, V, 379 ff.
[15] The italics are my own.

Burke, and matched only by Milton. Every sentence is like a gun of huge caliber. The detonation stuns and bewilders." Professor Harper pronounces this "the last great example of a Miltonic tract." Alfred Cobban, in his book on Edmund Burke, speaks of Wordsworth's *Convention of Cintra* as "forming the most sympathetic statement of what was to be the first-fruits in political thinking of the new outlook—the theory of nationality."[16]

The message of Wordsworth's patriotism is obvious enough, since all the principles of nationality which have been named are pertinent today. Have they ever been more so? But aside from this, from out those experiences of more than one hundred years ago, he speaks a word of cheer for all who hold to the fundamentals of political well-being, as opposed to those who pin their faith to the nostrums of an opportunist age. His message at this point is as to the *sin of pessimism* and the *duty of hope.* Two of the greater sonnets relate to this theme. One was composed in 1811, when the career of Napoleon was drawing to an end, and may be taken as the Poet's justification of his unfaltering faith in the cause of righteousness and good will; the other, relating to Toussaint L'Ouverture, was composed in 1802, when the struggle had barely begun and may be taken as one of those prophecies of the ultimate triumph of the good, which have buoyed the faith of reformers in all ages of the world, and which come with peculiar inspiration in a day like our own. Together these sonnets present the inner essence of Wordsworth's political creed:

> Here pause: the poet claims at least this praise,
> That virtuous Liberty hath been the scope
> Of his pure song, which did not shrink from hope
> In the worst moment of these evil days;

---

[16]*Edmund Burke and the Revolt Against the Eighteenth Century*, by Alfred Cobban, of University of Durham, London, 1929, p. 137. For an admirable analysis of the *Cintra* pamphlet and an exposition of its timeless significance as an argument for a moral and mystical basis of nationalism, see *Political Ideas of the English Romanticists*, by Brinton, Oxford Press, 1926, pp. 56 ff. For a notably thorough and readable account of the composition and publication of *Cintra*, see monograph by Prof. John Edwin Wells, of the Connecticut College for Women, in *Studies in Philology*, Jan. 1921, University of North Carolina.

# WE MUST BE FREE OR DIE

From hope, the paramount *duty* that Heaven lays,
For its own honour, on man's suffering heart.
Never may from our souls one truth depart—
That an accursed thing it is to gaze
On prosperous tyrants with a dazzled eye;
Nor—touched with due abhorrence of their guilt
For whose dire ends tears flow, and blood is spilt,
And justice labours in extremity—
Forget thy weakness, upon which is built,
O wretched man, the throne of tyranny!

# TO TOUSSAINT L'OUVERTURE

Toussaint, the most unhappy man of men!
Whether the whistling Rustic tend his plough
Within thy hearing, or thy head be now
Pillowed in some deep dungeon's earless den;—
O miserable Chieftain! where and when
Wilt thou find patience! Yet die not; do thou
Wear rather in thy bonds a cheerful brow;
Though fallen thyself, never to rise again,
Live, and take comfort. Thou hast left behind
Powers that will work for thee; air, earth, and skies;
There's not a breathing of the common wind
That will forget thee; thou has great allies;
Thy friends are exultations, agonies,
And love, and man's unconquerable mind.

# CHAPTER IX

# "Stern Daughter of the Voice of God"

**B**Y A well sustained popular verdict the three finest poems of Wordsworth are *Lines Composed a Few Miles Above Tintern Abbey*, the *Immortality Ode*, and the *Ode to Duty*. The two odes, with some fifty other pieces, appeared in the diminutive volumes of 1807— reckoned today among the great treasures of literature. Yet the review of these volumes by Francis Jeffrey was of a blighting character. Of the *Ode to Duty*, the best he could say was that it is a poem "in which the lofty vein is very unsuccessfully attempted." The famous lines:

> Thou dost preserve the stars from wrong;
> And the most ancient heavens, through Thee,
> are fresh and strong,

he dismissed as "utterly without meaning." As for the *Immortality Ode*, the editor of the *Edinburgh Review* did not consider it worthy of the slightest mention. In the *Annual Review and History of Literature* for 1807 there was a long article dealing with Wordsworth's "Two Volumes of 1807," in which the editor alluded to the *Ode to Duty* as "a meanly written piece, with some good thoughts." Such was the trend of contemporary criticism. Eighty years later we find James Russell Lowell, at the time American ambassador to Great Britain, characterising the same poem as "The incomparable Ode." His praise is expressed in such terms as these: "the *Ode to Duty*, in which he speaks to us out of an ampler ether than in any other of his poems, and which may safely 'challenge insolent Greece and haughty Rome' for a comparison in kind or degree." Mr. Lowell was addressing the Wordsworth Society, which was composed of such notables as Robert Browning, John Ruskin, Matthew Arnold, Stopford Brooke, Aubrey De Vere, the Archbishop of Canterbury, Lord Chief Justice Coleridge, Lord Selborne, James Bryce and Professor William Knight, and which met once a year in recognition of the supreme place Wordsworth had come to occupy among the poets of his time. Similarly Swinburne, who would not have been welcomed in the Wordsworth Society group, recorded in his *Miscellanies,* "I should place on the one hand the *Ode to Duty,* and on the other hand the *Song at the Feast of Brougham Castle,* as instances of decisive and perfect success." President Strong, in his *Theology of the English Poets,* characterized the "Duty Ode" as the "most noble and complete of Wordsworth's poems"; he praised it as having "a flavor of antique grandeur which reminds us of the best work of Milton." For a more recent appraisal, we have so critical a writer as Professor Herford commending the ode for "its noble and flawless art."

Since in this ode we have the quintessence of Wordsworth's message in the realm of morals and the moral sense, its seven stanzas should be the familiar possession of all who would appreciate the Poet in the profounder reaches of his art.

## ODE TO DUTY

*"Jam non consilio bonus, sed more eò perductus, ut non tantum rectè facere possim, sed nisi rectè facere non possim."*

Stern Daughter of the Voice of God!
O Duty! if that name thou love
Who art a light to guide, a rod
To check the erring, and reprove;
Thou, who are victory and law
When empty terrors overawe;
From vain temptations dost set free;
And calm'st the weary strife of frail humanity!

189

There are who ask not if thine eye
Be on them; who, in <u>love</u> and <u>truth</u>,
Where <u>no misgiving</u> is, rely
Upon the genial sense of youth:
Glad Hearts! without reproach or blot;
<u>Who do thy work, and know it not</u>:
Oh! if through confidence misplaced
They fail, thy saving arms, dread Power!
    around them cast.

Serene will be our days and bright,
And happy will our nature be,
When love is an unerring light,
And joy its own security.
And they a blissful course may hold
Even now, who, not <u>unwisely bold</u>,
Live in the spirit of this creed;
Yet seek thy firm support, according to their need.

I, loving freedom, and untried;
No sport of every random gust,
Yet being to myself a guide,
Too blindly have reposed my trust:
And oft, when in my heart was heard
Thy timely mandate, I deferred
The task, in smoother walks to stray;
But thee I now would serve more strictly, if I may.

Through no disturbance of my soul,
Or strong compunction in me wrought,
I supplicate for thy control;
But in the quietness of thought:
Me this <u>unchartered freedom</u> tires;
I feel the weight of chance-desires:
My hopes no more must change their name,
I long for a repose that ever is the same.

Stern Lawgiver! yet thou dost wear
The Godhead's most benignant grace;
Nor know we anything so fair
As is the smile upon thy face:
Flowers laugh before thee on their beds
And fragrance in thy footing treads;
Thou dost preserve the stars from wrong;
And the most ancient heavens, through Thee,
    are fresh and strong.

90

lines is sufficiently clear. There is little need of a commentary. For the general reader the use of the eight-line stanza, the regularity of the versification, and the employment of rhyme are a welcome aid, both in respect to meaning and poetic impression. On this account the *Ode to Duty* has attained a greater popularity than has the one on Immortality. A further consideration in its favor is the fact that it bears more closely upon the problems of daily thought and experience. In every sense it is a human document. Considering it as such, certain impressions arise from *The Ode* taken as a whole which may be worthy of attention.

First and foremost, is the feeling of gratitude, not unmingled with surprise, that an ascription to duty like this should come, not from a teacher of ethics or a preacher, but from a *poet*. We have not, as a rule, thought of poets in that connection—certainly not the romantic poets. We are more accustomed to think of poets as moral problems than as moral guides. In an age which numbered among its stars a Burns, a Byron, a Shelley, and a Coleridge, it is worthy of note that the noblest poem on the moral life found in the literature of any land came from the pen of a Wordsworth. Explain it as we may, the fact is there. When a poet of the first rank turns moralist, the world is bound to take notice. And the world certainly has taken notice—never more than during the past ten years.

The next impression one receives is that in this ode the doing of duty is made glorious. The hard, forbidding thing contained in that uncompromising Anglo-Saxon monosyllable—the thing we associate with taxes and debts, the thing which is *due,* what one does not wish to do but is morally bound to do, or as likely, to refrain from doing—the whole stern concept of *the ought*—the Poet in these lines makes a thing of radiance and of joy. This he accomplishes by the magic of personification. It is no mere abstraction whose praises the Poet chants. Not *it* but *she.* As philosopher he might content himself with a discussion of ethics. As poet he holds converse with the "Daughter of the Voice of God." Duty, to him, is the Goddess of Joy—austere at the beginning but gleaming on us with tender graces at the end:

> Stern Lawgiver! yet thou dost wear
> The Godhead's most benignant grace;
> Nor know we anything so fair
> As is the smile upon thy face.

Before all else *The Ode* teaches the transmutation of duty into joy. It is the one thing that gives both dignity and beauty to life.

Furthermore, duty here is conjoined with religion—made, in fact, the head and center of the ethically conceived religious life. The opening line "Stern Daughter of the Voice of God," as interpreted by De Quincey, who undoubtedly received the explanation from the Poet himself, is a Hebrew expression—"The daughter of a voice," he comments, "meant an echo, the original sound viewed as the Mother, and the reverberation, or secondary sound, as the Daughter." In other words, the Poet would have us feel that when we find ourselves under the compulsion of the right, we are undergoing a distinctly religious experience; we are listening to an echo of the Divine Will. This is the religious consciousness in its most intimate approach, corresponding to the "Thy will be done" of the Lord's Prayer. In another place Wordsworth speaks of conscience

As God's most intimate Presence in the soul,
And his most perfect image in the world.[1]

Incidentally, it is worth noting that there is no suggestion of pantheism in this ode. Quite the opposite. God and the Soul are separate entities; the one calls, the other listens; the one commands, the other obeys. And since the *Ode to Duty* was composed in 1804, a year before *The Prelude* in its original form, we have here additional evidence that the Poet could not have meant to convey a pantheistic impression at that time.[2] Nor is there here any such vague conception of duty as satisfied Matthew Arnold when he coined the phrase "Something not ourselves that makes for righteousness." Arnold's ethical sense (reflecting for the most part his religious upbringing) was sound and good. Righteousness is indeed the basis of the world-order. What he lacked was the recognition of the principle of righteousness as proceeding from the personality of an all-holy Will. To Wordsworth, more than to any teacher of his day, it was given to see the light of the knowledge of the glory of God in the face of Duty.

It follows logically that duty is made a constituent of the inner nature of Man. The Moral Sense, by which we distinguish between the Right and the Wrong, is to be classed with the perception of the True, the Perfect, and the Good as a mode of being which belongs to Man as such. It is the sense of duty imposing laws that links Man indissolubly with the Eternal. This the Poet clearly recognizes in the second stanza, where he pays tribute to "Glad hearts" who follow the right as by the instinct of the inner life, "who do thy work, and know it not." For those, like himself, who must struggle upward toward the right, he finds the evidence in the fact (third stanza) of the underlying correspondence of the life of rectitude and the life of joy. As between the two schools of ethicists today

---

[1] *Excursion*, IV, 226-227.

[2] I accept the earlier date for the composition of the *Ode to Duty* (1804, instead of 1805), as established, beyond reasonable doubt, by *Prof. E. H. Hartsell*, of the University of North Carolina. See *Times Literary Supplement* (London), May 30, 1935.

—the absolutists, who believe in fixed and universal standards of right, and the relativists, who consider ethics a matter of climatic influence, of protective custom and of the social code, the compulsion of the "mores,"—there can be no question that Wordsworth stands squarely with the former. Throughout *The Ode* duty is regarded as having objective and universal validity.

In view of the moral sag which followed the World War, the special message which *The Ode* carries to our age is likely to be found at this point. When, in certain of our universities, the students are taught that conscience is nothing more than the voice of custom operating within; when, as a result of our educational processes, the minds of the young are filled with physical facts at the expense of the knowledge of moral principles; when ethical philandering furnishes the *leit motif* of many a "best seller," on the theory that in sexual matters and matters of bodily appetite generally, a man is free to concoct his own code of morals; when the repudiation of debts and of treaties has become a commonplace in international relations; when among the disclosures of the financial depression we must reckon the shockingly low level of business ethics as practiced by prominent banks and corporations to which multitudes have entrusted their savings; when self-indulgence is found gnawing at the root of nearly everything that the moral sense enjoins, so that, viewing the trend of events, a leading writer can speak of this as "a *de*moralized age"; there is bound to be a fresh interest in the poet with whom the sense of obligation derives from

> the law supreme
> Of that Intelligence which governs all.[3]

Surely there is nothing more important for our generation to know than that the foundation of the universe

---

[3] An interesting comparison might be made with Clough's poem on *Duty*, in which he develops the idea of moral obligation resting solely upon custom, and maintains that this is "pure nonentity of duty." In the *Life and Letters of Clough* (p. 321) we find a definite recognition of the Wordsworth view: "To have attained a law, to exercise a lordship by right divine over passions and desires—this is Wordsworth's preëminence."

is laid in moral law. Undoubtedly the most original and brilliant conception of *The Ode* is that of the sixth stanza, where duty is given a cosmic significance. The lines which the prosaic stupidity (not to say malice) of Jeffrey found empty of meaning, we recognize today as of supreme beauty and worth:

> Flowers laugh before thee on their beds
> And fragrance in thy footing treads;
> Thou dost preserve the stars from wrong;
> And the most ancient heavens, through Thee,
>     are fresh and strong.

This is thoroughly Wordsworthian, since it brings Nature and Man into the concord of one harmonious rule. What physical law is to Nature, the moral law is to Man. It is in his consciousness of the Right that Man finds himself allied to the undeviating uniformities of natural law. It is interesting to note that the trend of science today is to confirm this conception of the Poet. While the theory of relativity has modified many of our ideas of matter and energy, space and time, which once seemed fundamental, it leaves us a universe where obedience to law is still the principle by which life proceeds and things subsist. Nothing exists in isolation. Least of all the souls of men. Everywhere is the interdependence of finite intelligence and the totality of Nature. It follows that freedom is to be found not in the assertion of self but in identification with the grander harmonies of the universe. Not by rebelling, but by belonging, true freedom is attained. As Professor Gingerich remarks in explaining the closing stanzas of *The Ode,* "With a complete self-surrender, which requires the exercise of a unique imaginative energy, the poet draws the very Godhead that keeps the most ancient heavens fresh and strong to the humble function of living within himself and becoming to him a permanent guide. He realizes heaven, in the instant, here on earth."[4]

---

[4] *Essays in the Romantic Poets*, by Solomon Francis Gingerich, Ph.D., of the University of Michigan, Macmillan Co., 1929, p. 153.

At the same time, it cannot be said that Wordsworth places duty squarely on the Christian basis. *The Ode* moves in the sphere of Greek and Hebrew thought more than in that of the New Testament. Following the Stoics, the Poet associates duty with the good and appropriate life, the life of virtue, the life of achievement and success. With the Stoics, too, Wordsworth conceived the nature of the good to be determined by and to be realized in a cosmical law, or universal reason. He differed from the Stoics by refusing their pantheistic view of necessity. In his choice between evil and good Man is a free moral agent. His manner of achieving is determined by himself, in coöperation with a beneficent Deity. The good life is not prescribed; it is presented. Freedom is necessary for ethics.

The conception is Hebrew, and at the same time Christian, in that it recognizes a revealed will of God, a divine law laid upon Man, to which the structure of his higher nature responds. Duty thus becomes a matter of spiritual insight and of obedience. A closer adherence to the Hebrew-Christian ideal would have recognized that the intuition of the right, majestic and morally compelling as it is, can only become dynamic in the highest sense when reënforced by the love that inspires obedience to law. This principle, foreshadowed in the Old Testament—"O how love I thy law!"—becomes resplendent in the New. "Love," according to St. Paul, is "the fulfilling of the law." The way to do the moralities is to transfuse them with a holy affection. More explicitly, Jesus taught that to love God supremely and one's neighbor in equal measure with one's self, constitutes the totality of moral obligation. Wordsworth approximates the Christian view in the second and third stanzas where he rejoices that there are persons (it is thought that he had his sister Dorothy in mind) who "in love and truth," that is through an inner law of unconscious rectitude, meet the full requirements of duty. But this, he urges, is an insecure position; it is liable to become a "confidence misplaced." In some far-off ideal world love may become "an unerring light" and "joy its own security"; but it was not there that he anchored the hope of a virtuous life. In the final stanza he comes somewhat closer to the Christian idea, where, under the form of a prayer, he pleads for the insight of a divinely implanted humility and the guiding grace of the sacrificial life:

> Give unto me, made lowly wise,
> The spirit of self-sacrifice.

Wordsworth's failure to recognize love as the highest moral law is surprising in view of his insistence in *The Prelude, To My Sister,* and other poems upon the principle of love as pervading Nature and as underlying her power over the human spirit. Similarly in a noteworthy passage of *The Prelude* (XIV, 162-187) he stresses love as essential to the well-being and freedom of the soul. The *Ode to Duty* would have gained from a clear recognition of this principle in the moral realm.

The poem *Character of the Happy Warrior,* much quoted by teachers and editors (occasionally, too, by politicians in their expansive moments), is to be associated with the *Ode to Duty* as the description of the man who, under the varying and trying circumstances of life, especially those of public life, "makes his moral being his prime care." Here Duty is presented not in the abstract but as incarnate in frail human flesh. The two poems were written only a year apart and in all the later editions they are printed side by side. The person characterized as the Happy Warrior is known to be, in the main, a composite of two sailors of heroic build, Lord Nelson ("England expects every man to do his duty"), and the Poet's brother John, a sea captain who went down with his ship, "dying as he had lived in the very place and point where his duty stationed him." The poem reaches its climax in lines more suggestive of the New Testament idea of the heroic life than any found in *The Ode:*

> But who, if he be called upon to face
> Some awful moment to which Heaven has joined
> Great issues, good or bad for human kind,
> Is happy as a Lover; and attired
> With sudden brightness, like a Man inspired.

The final impression one is likely to receive from a careful reading of the *Ode to Duty* is as to its autobiographical significance. We find not a little of the story of Wordsworth's struggle for character adumbrated in these lines. The fourth, fifth and seventh stanzas are purely personal, and in the light of our present knowledge, they may be regarded as conveying a hint of the battle between the higher and lower impulses of his nature during that crucial year in France. The Poet appears to have regarded this as an experience of early defeat followed by a hardly won but tenaciously held victory. It was the age-old issue of personal liberty, of unregulated self—especially in the realm of "chance desires"—*versus* the "mandate" of Duty as the "Daughter of the Voice of God." In view of the bearing of the poem upon the Poet's moral career, it is to be noted that these lines picture a youth less passionate than determined:

> I, loving freedom, and untried;
> No sport of every random gust,
> Yet being to myself a guide,
> Too blindly have reposed my trust.

His fault, as he came to conceive it in after life, was less that of sensual uncontrol than of love of pure independence. It was a case of the ungovernable disposition of youth—the "living-my-own-life" idea of our day, and of blindness in respect to the "Footpath to Peace." He pictures himself as reaching the point where he could say, "Me this unchartered freedom tires." The achievement of victory was not sudden; his blindness was not removed at a stroke. It came rather as the result of a gradual process of disillusionment in respect to the life of self-indulgence, and of orientation in the realm of moral law:

> Through no disturbance of my soul,
> Or strong compunction in me wrought,
> I supplicate for thy control;
> But in the quietness of thought.

There is, however, a suggestion of a definite point in his career when the Poet came to recognize that he had passed from darkness into light, from the dissatisfaction of the life of selfish freedom to the rest and peace of a life controlled from on high. This may not be conveyed by the word *"now"* in the last line of stanza four ("But thee I *now* would serve more strictly if I may"), but it seems more than likely from the employment of so definite a time-term as "hour" in the prayer of dedication with which the poem ends:

> I myself commend
> Unto thy guidance, *from this hour;*
> Oh, let my weakness have an end!

As to just when that hour may have struck in the Poet's career, one of course can only surmise. But possibly it is more than a pleasing fancy when I entertain the thought that it was none other than the hour when, in the autumn of 1795, having withdrawn from the free-thinking and free-living Godwinian circle in London, as he had previously escaped from the brutal ardors of revolutionary France, he settled down with the pure and spontaneously dutiful Dorothy at Racedown in the south of England. To consider that the reference is to the hour of writing, 1804, after two happy years of married life with Mary Hutchinson at Grasmere, and after nine years of association with Dorothy at Racedown, Alfoxden and Grasmere, would be to rob the poem of its most intensive autobiographic expression. However, I would have no quarrel with any one who maintained that the Poet seeks only to indicate that, by a process of moral awakening, at a certain point in his career he knew he had passed from a state of selfish freedom to a state of joyous bondage to the higher control. To one who is interested in the moral aspects of Wordsworth's career, the closing line of the *Ode to Duty* carries a meaning of large personal significance:

And in the light of truth thy *Bondman* let me live!

And of almost equal importance is the Latin motto which Wordsworth attached to the poem in old age and which may be taken as the Poet's verdict upon his own life. It has been translated as follows: "What urges me on is not so much good counsel as habit; so that my condition is not that I am able to do right, but rather that I am unable to do wrong."

## NOTE

An interesting parallel might be drawn between Wordsworth's idea of duty and the "categorical imperative" of the philosopher Kant, and, correspondingly, between the Wordsworth Ode and Kant's noble Apostrophe to Duty, found in his *Critique of Practical Reason*. In both there is a personification of duty as a divine compulsion in the soul. Both are defective in the failure to recognize the Law of Love as of greater potency than the Law of Right intellectually apprehended. Kant's Apostrophe is as follows:

"Duty! thou great, sublime name! Thou dost not insinuate thyself by offering the pleasing and the popular, but thou commandest obedience. To move the will thou dost not threaten and terrify, but simply settest forth a law, which of itself finds entrance into the soul; which even though disobeyed wins approval and reverence; before which the passions are silent even though they work secretly against it. What origin is worthy of thee, and where is the root of thy noble pedigree, which proudly disowns all relationships with passions, and descent from which is the indispensable condition of that worth which alone man can of himself confer on himself? It can be nothing less than that which lifts man above himself so far as he belongs to the world of sense, and unites him to an order of things that subjects to itself the entire world of sense, as well as the existence of man so far as it is empirically determined in time. It is nothing less than personality; that is, freedom from and independence of all the mechanism of nature; and this implies that man himself, considered as belonging to the world of sense, is subjected to his own personality so far as he belongs to the rational system. No wonder then that man, belonging to both worlds, must regard his own being, in connection with this higher system, with reverence, and its laws with the highest veneration.[5]

[5] Quoted by Dr. Samuel Harris in *The Philosophical Basis of Theism*, p. 379.

# CHAPTER X

# "Oh, Let My Weakness Have an End"

FROM what is said in the preceding chapter, it will be inferred that I have no sympathy with the recent school of criticism (if it may be so dignified) which holds that Wordsworth's life, taken as a whole, must be considered an ethical failure; that he who essayed to be a moralist on so bold a scale and who for so long has been revered as such, was, no less than certain other poets of the time, in reality *a moral problem*. By what we must consider an extraordinary series of discoveries, followed by a penetrating and at times merciless criticism, this issue has come to the front and must be faced by all who would understand the true Wordsworth and receive his message in their hearts. In recent years not less than eleven books have been written on the subject. As for articles and reviews, they may be numbered by the score. Nor can it be said that this indicates a mere prurient curiosity, or a propensity of the "realistic" school of biographical writing which takes pleasure in the tearing down of the reputations of our great men of the past. In nearly every instance the interest of the writer has been in the bearing of Wordsworth's inner life (now possibly better understood) upon the message of his verse. So far as motive is concerned, the discussion has been conducted on a high level, and it bids fair to become a landmark in literary criticism. Fortunately we have reached the time when shocked surprise has given way to a desire to know the facts as facts and a willingness to fit these into a new conception of Wordsworth, both as poet and man.

The issue was precipitated by the disclosures of Professor Harper in regard to Wordsworth's sojourn in France in 1791-2. These were given to the public in his two-volume life of the Poet issued in 1916—a work of not only painstaking scholarship but of such absorbing human quality that, more than any publication we can name, it accounts for the growing interest of our time. In 1921 Professor Harper supplemented the biography by a small volume entitled *Wordsworth's French Daughter,* in which he records the outcome of his later researches in France. In 1929 he published a revised edition of the life, in one volume, in which he included not only the results of his own investigations but also those of Professor Legouis of Paris, whom he had stirred up to undertake research among official records at Orleans, Blois and Paris. As a result of his study of certain poems and letters—more by their omissions than by any positive trace—Professor Harper had become convinced that while he was in France Wordsworth's nature "had received a blow from which he never wholly recovered and whose causes had not been made known to the world." Having reached this conclusion as a result of a subtle piece of higher criticism, he was constrained to follow the clue for the sake of any light that might be thrown upon the Poet's mental processes and work. Obtaining the permission of the Wordsworth family, he proceeded to examine certain manuscripts in the British Museum, and there he found a collection of letters from Dorothy Wordsworth to her friend Mrs. Clarkson, the wife of the well-known abolitionist, in which she referred repeatedly to her brother's daughter Caroline, who had been born out of wedlock, of a French mother, Marie Annette Vallon, by name. It became evident that the circumstance was known by the Wordsworth family and certain intimate friends and that before the Poet's marriage to Mary Hutchinson, and for many years after, by means of letters and occasional visits, friendly relations were sustained between the Wordsworths in England and Marie Annette Vallon and her daughter in France.

With the revelations of Harper and Legouis before us,

supplemented by certain details discovered later by Miss Edith J. Morley and Miss E. Batho in the diaries and correspondence of Wordsworth's intimate friend Henry Crabb Robinson,[1] we are able to reach a fairly accurate understanding of this regrettable episode in the Poet's life. Wordsworth, it will be recalled, upon graduation from Cambridge in the autumn of 1791, took up his residence in France, where he became an ardent supporter of the Revolution, then in its early stages. Establishing himself at Orleans, he engaged in the study of the French language, with Marie Annette Vallon as his teacher. The daughter of a surgeon of Blois, she was of good family, and quite naturally the associations of study led to a friendship which ripened into love. We have no means of knowing whether marriage was contemplated. In all probability it was, so far as the young people were concerned, although there is a good deal of reason for supposing that Annette's brothers were opposed, as most certainly were the Wordsworth relatives the moment the situation was divulged. Before judging the young couple too harshly we are to recall that this was eighteenth century France; that the times were both loose and chaotic; that liberal views as to instinct and natural right were undermining both political and social conventions; that, owing to the Revolution, many governmental regulations, including those of marriage, were in abeyance or in a state of flux; that an international marriage would have presented special difficulties; that Wordsworth, a youth of twenty-one, was away from home and country, and burning with the new passions of the time, and that having entered no profession, he was without means of support beyond the small allowance provided by his uncles. It is to be noted that the pure-souled Dorothy, when informed by her brother, was able to understand, and, while undoubtedly condemning his affair with Annette,

---

[1] See *The Later Wordsworth*, by Edith C. Batho, Appendix C, *The Settlement on Caroline Baudouin.*

that she stood by him and her with friendly help and advice.

A child was born at Orleans December 15, 1792, while Wordsworth was in Paris, on his way to England for the purpose of publishing his two poems, *The Evening Walk* and *Descriptive Sketches,* hoping to obtain some money thereby, and in order to reach an agreement with his uncles, who, disapproving of his republican views, and possibly fearing for his life (he was on the point of offering himself as a leader of the Girondins), were seeking to force him home by the stoppage of his allowance. By his written instructions the child was given his name, being baptized as Anne Caroline (Wordsworth), he being represented by a proxy. The official record, unearthed by Harper, discloses that he was set down by the Vicar as *(sic)* "Williams Wordswodsth, anglais."

It was while the Poet was detained in England that war was declared, and thereafter for nine years, 1793-1802, or until the Peace of Amiens, a return to France was extremely difficult, and for him as a Girondist sympathizer it could be undertaken only at the peril of his life. Professor Harper has established the fact, or at least the strong probability, that, notwithstanding the peril, Wordsworth, for the sake of rejoining Annette, in the autumn of 1793, during the Reign of Terror, did journey as far as Paris, but, so far as the evidence goes, did not reach Blois, where Annette was residing with her child. The next time he met Annette was in 1802, at Calais, where, aided by Dorothy, he arranged a settlement looking to his marriage a few months later to Mary Hutchinson.

The story has grown with the telling, and too easily certain of the critics have assumed as proven facts what can only be a matter of conjecture. When it comes to the bearing of the episode upon the Poet's character and work, one may choose between widely variant interpretations, although there is a consensus to the effect that the experience left an unforgettable scar and is reflected in several of the earlier poems, notably: *Vaudracour and Julia* and *Guilt and Sorrow*. *The Prelude,* which deals intimately with the Poet's career, three of the books being devoted exclusively to his residence in France, is conspicuously lacking in any reference to the affair with Annette.

Regarding the matter broadly, the varying views may be listed under five heads. First, is the opinion of Professor Garrod,[2] Professor Legouis, and undoubtedly of many others, that, in spite of all the difficulties and the long delay, Wordsworth should have married Annette. As a modification of this view, the opinion has been expressed that he might and should have married her secretly before the birth of the child. Second, while possibly justified in the course he followed, the Poet should not have concealed the facts from the public. Third, the view of Herbert Read, that the affair was sordid from beginning to end, and the end was far down on the horizon of the Poet's life. In fact, Wordsworth never stood four-square with his conscience and the world, the upshot being that the one-time revered "Sage of Rydal Mount," in the light of modern disclosures, must be set down as a very ordinary human so far as master-motives are concerned. Mr. Read does not hesitate to speak of the "manifest hypocrisy" of *Laodamia* and other poems.[3] Fourth, the view of Fausset,[4] that while we must recognize that Wordsworth's life as a whole was a failure, the reason was spiritual rather than moral, in that he failed to reconcile the conflicting claims of the natural and the spiritual man, at every critical point suffering the deadening effect of compromise dictated by prudence, the result being an unfulfilled genius, steadily declining in power, and an essentially inharmonious career. Fifth, the view that Wordsworth, recognizing the gravity of his offense, ac-

---

[2] *Wordsworth—Lectures and Essays,* 1923, pp. 71, 72.
[3] *Wordsworth,* pp. 96, 97, 218.
[4] *The Lost Leader,* by Hugh I. A. Fausset, Harcourt, Brace & Co., New York, 1933.

cepted the responsibilities involved, seeking at every point to do the honorable thing, even to claiming Annette as his wife and Caroline as his child, until circumstances made it clear that such a course would be wise neither for Annette nor for himself. Going a step farther, there are those, like myself, who hold that, as a result of the experience, the Poet underwent a process of spiritual transformation, from which he emerged a purified and ennobled soul, this fact being reflected in the *Ode to Duty* and in the impression of sincerity and purity of mind one receives from his poetry as a whole.

Obviously it will be impossible in a single chapter to discuss these widely varying points of view in anything like an exhaustive way. Nor should it be necessary, since one's instinctive reaction to the general impression of the Poet's work is, after all, the safest guide. On the main question as to whether or not the Poet's life, taken in its entirety, registers a moral failure, I would rather trust the opinion of an open-minded yet sympathetic general-reader than all the historical investigations and psychological probings of the experts in literary research. In the final estimate Wordsworth must (and does) speak for himself. What I shall attempt is a brief comment upon some of the more flagrant of the above opinions.

The main issue, of course, is as to whether the young poet should have squarely faced the obligations arising from his moral lapse and have met them by marrying the mother of his child. The bare statement of the case would certainly call for an answer in the affirmative. But the case was not as simple as at first appears. In addition to the difficulties in the way of marriage that have been suggested above, we come upon an array of incompatibilities that might well stagger the most lion-hearted of lovers. William was English, Annette was French, and the two countries were at war. William was an ardent Republican, Annette and her brothers were ardent Royalists, even to the point of engaging in plots against the government.

William was a Protestant, Annette a Catholic. William was twenty-one, Annette was twenty-five. Whatever the young couple may have felt as to possessing little or much in common, the families on both sides appear to have entertained no doubt on the subject. Only by a miracle could such an ill-assorted match be a success. Annette settled in an English village as the wife of a patriot-poet was as impossible as William located in France during the Napoleonic wars. Moreover, the elements of incompatibility increased with the years, and, as is apparent from Dorothy's letters written from Calais in 1802, during the long interval a change had come over Annette no less than over William, so that it was by mutual consent and on an entirely friendly basis that the relationship was brought to an end.[5]

Opinions formed one hundred and forty years after such occurrences will of course differ at certain points, but, assuming that a clandestine marriage was out of the question (Annette being a conscientious Catholic), and that Wordsworth was in no wise responsible for the subsequent delay, there would appear to be sufficient justification of the course followed to warrant the belief that the decision was reached in a wise and honorable way. The alternative view, of a course of lifelong hypocrisy, makes too heavy a strain upon the reader's instinctive reactions to the Poet's life and work as a whole to secure more than passing attention. Wordsworth simply was not that kind of a man.

And right here it may well be taken into consideration that, argue the question as we may on the grounds of justice and honor, one must face the situation that had

---

[5]There can be little doubt that both before and after the Calais visit, Wordsworth either provided an annuity for the care of Caroline, or from time to time sent her such sums as he could spare. Since the publication of the books by Harper and Legouis, we have learned that upon the marriage of Caroline to Mr. Baudouin in 1816, the poet, in lieu of a dowry, agreed to send her thirty pounds a year. This he continued until 1835, when, in view of the uncertainty of his income in old age, he made a final settlement of four hundred pounds. In all he paid Caroline about one thousand pounds, which may be considered a fairly large sum for a man of his means. These interesting facts were drawn from unpublished portions of the Diary of Henry Crabb Robinson and are now given to the world by Edith C. Batho, of the University College of London, in the work already referred to.

Wordsworth married Annette, in all probability the world would not possess the poet Wordsworth today. Either he would have lived without the stimulus of his association with Coleridge, which meant so much for him in later years, as well as the incalculably fine influence of Dorothy, to whom he accredited his poetical awakening, and thus have fallen short of true greatness, or, as is far more likely, along with other republicans who were opposed to Robespierre and the Jacobin régime, he would have paid the price of his devotion on the guillotine in Paris.[6]

The objection that the Poet was at fault in not giving publicity to his moral defection in France has been made in an editorial of a prominent American newspaper, in referring to the discovery in the Harvard University Library of an unpublished poem by Shelley on the Celandine, in which he makes sarcastic reference to Wordsworth's defection to a timid and compromising conservatism after his sojourn in France. The editorial remarks: "It is easier for modern liberals to forgive Wordsworth's natural reversion to conservatism than his lifelong concealment of his loose love in the days of his enthusiasm for revolutionary France." No justification can be found for such an indictment. What, one may ask, would this writer have had the Poet do under the unfortunate conditions that arose in connection with his moral lapse? Should he, in imitation of King David, have written a poem on the subject? And if so what good would it have done? Or should he, following the favorite pastime of educated Englishmen, have written a letter to the *Times?* We have seen that he informed his sister Dorothy, and he asked her to inform his uncles. We know that Dorothy

---

[6] After I had written the above, I received a letter from a gentleman in England who is in the best possible position to understand the circumstances and also the probabilities of the Annette incident, and while in no way condoning the wrong that was done, he emphasizes the fact that Wordsworth was a lonely country-bred lad of twenty-one, in a foreign land, at a time of relaxation of all moral standards, with no parental influences behind him, wholly unused to feminine society, save that of the utterly different Dorothy. Annette, on the other hand, some four years older, was evidently possessed of a strong individuality. Under the circumstances it was juxtaposition rather than affinity that brought the romance to a crisis. My correspondent closes with the remark, "In fact the war of 1793 was an unmixed blessing for English literature."

told Mrs. Clarkson. We know that Crabb Robinson and several other friends were informed of the incident, and that just before Wordsworth's marriage to Mary Hutchinson, with the knowledge of the latter, and of the entire circle, Dorothy and her brother met Annette at Calais and arranged some sort of settlement. We know that Wordsworth insisted upon the child bearing his name, thus giving her the standing of legitimacy, according to French usage, and that in 1815 she was married to a M. Baudouin as Caroline Wordsworth; also that Dorothy, together with Wordsworth's friend Robinson, and Sara Hutchinson (sister of Mrs. Wordsworth) planned to attend the wedding, carrying presents, but were prevented by the Waterloo campaign. And, if this is not enough, it has been brought to light that the Wordsworths and four of their friends were in France in 1820 and visited back and forth with the French family, including Caroline, her husband, and her mother. Any one who will acquaint himself with all the facts will be convinced that the Poet informed everybody who had a right to know, and, I think, will agree with Professor Harper when he says: "It must be inferred that Wordsworth being a just, merciful and brave man, admitted his fault freely and endeavored to shield with his name, the innocent child of his wrong-doing. Not only once, but twice, and the second time at the risk of losing a reputation for peculiar correctness of conduct, did he publicly acknowledge Caroline as his daughter."[7]

With all this the position taken by Mr. Read is in sharp conflict. In maintaining that the Poet's attitude was one of studied duplicity (although not without evidence of struggle), he occupies the extreme left among the critics of the past few years. His conclusions are reached in the main by the processes of psycho-analysis, just now so popular with the writers of biography. Perhaps it is sufficient to point out that fact. But, in addition, we have

---

[7] *Wordsworth's French Daughter*, p. 39.

to do with a criticism impregnated with the Freudian theory of sex as the determining element in human behavior. Under the stress of this idea the Annette incident becomes the key to the Poet's disposition and to pretty much everything he said and did in subsequent years. Mr. Read goes so far as to attribute the change in Wordsworth's political views in respect to the French Revolution and the cause of republicanism to the cooling of his passion for Annette. Wordsworth lost his love for Annette. Annette was French. Ergo: Wordsworth lost his love for France. "We grow," says this author, "to hate the object of a dead passion; . . . we translate that hatred to the things associated with the dead passion. In this manner Wordsworth gradually renounced the cause of France and then the cause of the Revolution, and finally the cause of humanity." Such is the explanation offered of how one of the mightiest intellects of his time saw fit to abandon the political ardors of his youth. It is far more likely that the opposite was true, and that Wordsworth's growing distrust of France accentuated his lessening regard for the girl of France. From Mr. Read one would suppose Wordsworth was the only person who changed his mind about the French Revolution, whereas, the same reversion of opinion was experienced by the large majority of liberals in both England and America. Mr. Read's book contains much that is original and profound; his defense of philosophical poetry as "felt thought" is admirable, and might be given a wider application.[8] Incidentally, Mr. Read rates Wordsworth extremely high on the artistic side, assigning to him a place only a little lower than Milton. But the Freudian bias and the one-sidedness of the resulting argument are so apparent that the book is not likely to shake the faith of the traditionally reverent reader of Wordsworth, or to impress those who, with open mind, are seeking a clearer

---

[8]This is quite in accord with Wordsworth's own idea expressed in the lines:
. . . he whose soul hath risen
Up to the height of feeling intellect.—*Prelude*, XIV, 225.

understanding of *The Prelude* and the *Ode to Duty* and the other poems in which the Poet uncovers the processes of his heart and mind.

And very much the same comment may be made upon the opinions of Mr. Fausset in his *Lost Leader*. The approach is from a different angle, being that of an inquiry into the bearing of what the author considers the Poet's gradually formed habit of "playing safe" upon his character and work as a whole. If the Read book may be said to emphasize the sensual as an element of weakness, in the Fausset book we have the spiritual stressed in a similar vein. Yet the outcome is practically the same, in that we have presented to us a poet whose life in no large sense was a moral success. Mr. Fausset makes bold to adopt as his title the epithet for which the poet Browning in later life practically apologized, but in so doing he shifts the charge of apostasy from the sphere of politics to that of private living. Of the Fausset book, too, it may be allowed that the scholarship is painstaking and, along predetermined lines, profound. There is, however, a heavy drawing upon the imagination in respect to the processes of the Poet's inner life, an over-strained ingenuity in reading between the lines of poems which hitherto have been considered clear, and far too much of the pernicious process of bending poetic facts to suit the exigencies of a poetic theory. The argument by which the Lucy of the early love-poems is made a composite of Dorothy and Annette, and to which allusion has already been made, may be cited as a case in point.

The idea that Wordsworth was a man of drab and gloomy existence, given to brooding over an unhappy past, the victim of an unsuccessful struggle between the higher and the lower in his nature, forever seeking peace and not finding it, is totally and absurdly wrong. If the poetry of this man reflects anything of personal character, it is the picture of an essentially pure and placid soul. That there were seasons of unsettlement, of sorrow and strife, is apparent enough; but he rose above them in a magnificent way, and from out a hard-won victory he radiated the message of courage and cheer which has endeared him to multitudes of struggling souls who, like himself, "too blindly have reposed their trust." Miss Edith Morley in her selections from the remains of Henry Crabb Robinson, quotes an entry in which Wordsworth remarked to his friend: "But no one has completely understood me—not even Coleridge. He is not happy enough. I am myself one of the happiest of men. . . ."[9] Possibly Coleridge is not the only critic who has lacked the insight of a truly happy life.

In this connection it may be appropriate to mention the bizarre attitude of Bertrand Russell, as set forth in an article in a prominent American magazine, entitled *The Harm That Good Men Do.*[10] In his defense of those the world considers "bad men" as the ones who actually bring about the progress of civilization, Russell cites the change in Wordsworth's views after his sojourn in France. These are his words: "In his youth he sympathized with the French Revolution, went to France, wrote good poetry, and had a natural daughter. At this period he was a 'bad' man. Then he became 'good,' abandoned his daughter, adopted correct principles, and wrote bad poetry." Bertrand Russell is nothing if not brilliant. The trouble with his thesis as applied to Wordsworth is that it is seriously out of joint with the facts. The early poems that Wordsworth wrote in France, or in what might be called the French period, were *An Evening Walk* and *Descriptive Sketches,* both inferior, as compared with his later work, although prophetic of what was to come. It was not until 1795, three years after his French experience, when he took up his residence in the south of England and came under the influence of Dorothy and of Coleridge, that his

---

[9] *Blake, Coleridge, Wordsworth and Lamb,* 1932, p. 49. In keeping with this suggestion is an entry in one of Coleridge's Note Books which reads as follows: "The sea, the sea, and the breeze, have their influences on me. . . . I feel a pleasure upon me. . . . But oh! I am never happy, never deeply gladdened."

[10] *Harper's Magazine,* Oct. 1926.

great work began. It was during those years in which he succeeded in freeing his system of what Russell calls his badness that he became one of the voices of the age. Mr. Russell should have known that the great decade ushered in by the publication jointly by Wordsworth and Coleridge of the *Lyrical Ballads* in 1798 belongs wholly to the time when Wordsworth had turned "good." I will not be so ungracious as to suggest that so distinguished a writer as Bertrand Russell would descend to the level of deliberately warping his facts to prove his point. It would be more charitable to consider his effusion as an illustration of the ease with which critics of the journalistic type will put forth dogmatic statements on matters of grave importance, without taking the slightest pains to inform themselves, or with any proper sense of responsibility in respect to the reputations of the past, their interest apparently being more in creating a sensation than in advancing the truth.

It is perhaps too much to expect of the modern professional critic that he should recognize that there is such a thing as a divine process in the soul of a sincerely penitent man, that either by the experience of conversion or through the mellowing influences of spiritual regeneration, to use Tennyson's fine phrase, "men may rise on stepping-stones of their dead selves to higher things," that even from a lapse of the most serious nature, one perchance extending through a series of years, the soul may emerge serene and strong, breathing a message of saving power and grace. History abounds in instances of this kind. And if some of us, on the strength of the recent discoveries, are inclined to add Wordsworth to the list, it is merely taking him at his own evaluation as indicated by the *Ode to Duty* and his consistent attitude toward sin and its consequences which we find reflected in other ways.

But of any critic it may at least be demanded that he shall realize the extreme delicacy of his task, when he undertakes to enter into the innermost recesses of a per-

sonality like the poet Wordsworth, and to trace to their
fountainhead of thought and feeling the processes which
lie back of life-decisions, and, in the long accumulation,
make for the determination of character and the expression of character in creative work. It is true there can be
no justification of looseness of thought and life on the
ground of the sensitive constitution of the poetic mind;
but that the searching of such a mind should be characterized by a humble sense of liability to mistake, goes
without saying. Certainly it will take more than the assurance of the psycho-analytic critic of our day to convince
the public that the author of the *Ode to Duty* and *Peele
Castle* made a wreck of his moral career. It is worth re-
membering that Pope begins his famous *Essay on Criticism* with the thesis: "'Tis as great a fault to judge ill as
to write ill and a more damaging one to the public."

Fortunately, of one thing we may be fairly sure, and
that is that in the long run critics of the "hard-boiled"
type will continue to annihilate one another. The Spanish
Madariaga—that veritable Euroclydon among the winds
of criticism (now ambassador to France, formerly to the
United States), in his *The Case of Wordsworth,* maintains that Wordsworth by reason of his devotion to *virtue*
rather than to art is not to be considered a universal poet,
if indeed a poet at all. As master and teacher he stands
high, especially in England, where character is still considered the principal thing. As poet he represents something that has passed. Madariaga is full of assurance on
the point. "I may perhaps be permitted to say," he remarks on a concluding page, "that in this, his predomi-
nant devotion to Virtue, Wordsworth is the prototype of
the British race and civilization. In him, as in the average
Briton, the moral comes first, and the poetical and the
scientific take what remains." Again: "And this the British virtue *par excellence*, is the bane of Wordsworth's
poetry. The British gentleman and the poet are ever in
conflict within Wordsworth's soul. Generally, the British

gentleman wins. . . . When the new type of Englishman asserts itself and its tastes, it is safe to predict that of all the great names of English literature those will suffer most which will have most intimately and adequately represented the type that passed, and of them, Wordsworth is perhaps the first."[11]

This is most interesting, since the thing that critics like Read and Fausset maintain is not to be found in Wordsworth at all, by Madariaga is found to be the leading characteristic. To him Wordsworth is virtuous or he is nothing. This is interesting, too, as a typically Latin point of view. If it is true that the reputation of Wordsworth stands or falls with the cause of virtue as the potent element in national life, the case should not be so bad. It all depends upon whether or no the English gentleman represented by Wordsworth's strong ethical note *is* to pass away. One is tempted to suggest that a century or two of emphasis upon virtue rather than upon art, and what goes with that ideal, would not be to the disadvantage of certain Latin countries that could be named. But since comparisons are odious, and oft-times misleading, we can afford to lay a consideration like this aside and to rest the case on intrinsic grounds. For Wordsworth to have attained the reputation on the continent of Europe of being *par excellence* the Poet of the moral sense, is, to say the least, a sizable achievement, and one that appears to augur well for the future. As to whether he is less of a poet on that account, the reader will have to decide according to his own tastes and proclivities of view.

[11] See chapter in *Shelley and Calderon and Other Essays on English and Spanish Poetry*, by Salvador De Madariaga. E. P. Dutton and Co., Inc., N Y., 1933.

# CHAPTER XI

# "We See Into the Life of Things"

BEYOND question Wordsworth has suffered in popular estimation from the fact that so often he is spoken of as a philosophical poet. There are those, like Coleridge, who single him out as *the* philosophical poet of modern times. This, in a distinctly non-philosophical age like the present, is a handicap of a serious nature. From the viewpoint of the average man of affairs philosophy is even farther removed from usable and reliable knowledge than is poetry. Matthew Arnold sensed the difficulty more than fifty years ago, when, in making his selections, he sought to free the reader from the necessity of wading through such bulky poems as *The Prelude* and *The Excursion,* and when, in the famous preface, he exhorted the reader to distinguish between Wordsworth as a philosopher and Wordsworth as poet. It was on this ground that he uttered his warning against the Wordsworthians. "The Wordsworthians," he remarked, "are apt to praise him for the wrong things, and to lay far too much stress upon what they call his philosophy. His poetry is the reality, his philosophy, so far, at least, as it may put on the form and habit of a scientific system of thought, and the more that it puts them on,—is the illusion."[1] This, it is known, was aimed primarily at Leslie Stephen, who had maintained that "Wordsworth's poetry is precious because his philosophy is sound," and that his "ethical system is as distinctive and capable of exposition as Bishop Butler's," that "his poetry is informed by ideas which fall spontaneously into a scientific system of thought."[2]

---

[1] *Cf.* Keats' *Lamia:* "Philosophy will clip an angel's wings."
[2] Essay: *Wordsworth's Ethics,* in *Hours in a Library.*

The issue thus joined between these master-minds of criticism has persisted to the present time, so that the critics of recent date may be divided into two classes according as they agree more with the Arnold or with the Stephen point of view. On the side of Arnold I would place: Saintsbury, Hearn, Madariaga, Bradley, Elton, Housman, Read; on the side of Stephen: Harper, Legouis, Raleigh, Garrod, de Selincourt, Beatty, Broughton, Gingerich, Bernbaum, Rice, Herford, Chapman, Batho, Sherwood, Sperry. So far as numbers go, the decision is impressively in favor of Stephen. But this at best is a rough classification, being based primarily upon whether the critic appears to be more interested in the Poet's art or the Poet's ideas. Of course the two cannot be divorced, nor would either Arnold or Stephen have argued wholly on one side of the line which they draw. In the same essay Arnold recognizes that "poetry is at the bottom a criticism of life," and that "the greatness of a poet lies in his powerful and beautiful application of ideas to life—to the question: How to live." Wordsworth he finds, must be recognized as dealing primarily with *life* "because he deals with that in which life really consists." And it is at this very point that he locates the uniqueness of Wordsworth's work, ranking him above the other English poets, except Shakespeare and Milton, because "He deals with more *life* than they do; he deals with *life* as a whole more powerfully." This comes close to a recognition of Wordsworth's philosophy as the main thing. But I take it that what Arnold objects to in Stephen's position is his insistence upon the importance of the *systematic* character of Wordsworth's thought, the appraisal involved in the comparison with Butler, and the assertion as to his ideas falling "spontaneously into a *scientific system* of thought."

Various attempts have been made to label Wordsworth as belonging to this or that school of thought. In general it has been considered that he is Platonic in his method and point of view. This was urged with great eloquence by J. H. Shorthouse (author of *John Inglesant*) in a paper read before the Wordsworth Society in 1881, entitled *On the Platonism of Wordsworth*. More recently Dean Inge has sought to maintain the Platonic basis of Wordsworth's poetry in his *The Platonic Tradition in English Religious Thought*. Shorthouse finds the likeness not in the detail of thought, but in the recognition of the general principle of Excellence which rules the formation and government of all animate and inanimate things. Inge finds his evidence in Wordsworth's passion for seeing unity behind all multiplicity, his sense of beauty as universal, but even more in his perception of Being as the all-pervading element of life. Inge appears to identify Platonism with mysticism, and Christian Platonism he considers as the philosophy of mysticism, the fundamental principles of which, now very widely accepted, especially by educated people, are avowedly the main ground of belief. This belief he finds to be an integral part of Wordsworth's creed.

Similarly, comparisons have been drawn between Wordsworth and Kant, and recently Professor Bradley of Oxford has sought to trace the likeness of Wordsworth's ideas to those of Hegel.[3] A far more explicit attempt is that of Professor Beatty, of the University of Wisconsin, who, in his *William Wordsworth—His Doctrine and Art in Their Historical Relations,* holds that Wordsworth is a philosophical poet not merely in the general sense of a contemplative poet, but one who expresses a distinctive philosophy. He would have us regard him as the poet of the English philosophy of Locke and his school, more particularly of the associationistic philosophy of David Hartley. Associationism is the theory that all our ideas and mental experiences are the result of the association together of our sense perceptions, one thing suggesting another in a steadily rising scale of com-

---

[3] *English Poetry and German Philosophy in the Age of Wordsworth,* by A. C. Bradley in his A *Miscellany.*

plexity. Not only memory, but thought, emotion, imagination, the moral sense—the most delicate processes of the mind, one and all rest back on sensation. Since the days of Locke the theory has passed through many phases and as expounded by Hartley is found in its less explicit and dogmatic form. But essentially it is a physiological and mechanistic explanation of the process of knowledge. There is no room here for the immediate perception of truth, for *a priori* or necessary truths, for the doctrine of the freedom of the will. Plainly Wordsworth could not have been both a disciple of Plato and a disciple of Hartley at the same time—since these are mutually exclusive schools of thought.

Beatty's position is that, under the influence of Coleridge, who in his early career was an enthusiastic supporter of the Hartley doctrine, even to the naming of his eldest child after the philosopher, Wordsworth accepted the associationist philosophy and adhered to it throughout the period of his greatest verse. The evidence for this he finds in *Tintern Abbey, The Prelude, The Excursion, The White Doe*—in his writings generally before 1814. This means that, in the opinion of this critic, the Wordsworth we have known and admired for the high idealism of his thought was, throughout his creative period, both a sensationalist and a necessitarian. It is a challenge which has not yet been met in any thorough-going way, and could only be met by one who is not only at home in the writings of Wordsworth, both poetry and prose, but who is at the same time versed in the literary and philosophical backgrounds of the eighteenth century. And to this should be added a painstaking, psychological mastering of literary relationships and of the transmission of influence. The best equipped critic may be pardoned for walking softly in this latter realm. When one reads that in the library of Cecil Rhodes were twenty-two different biographies of Napoleon, a fairly accurate inference is at hand. But when we consider the bearing of Plato, or

Spinoza, or Newton, or Locke, or Rousseau, or even Godwin upon the mind of an original and complex genius like Wordsworth, one may be permitted to hold his opinion somewhat in reserve. The problem of genius is the problem of richly creative thought plus human influence plus divine inspiration. Who shall say where one begins and the other ends? "The wind bloweth where it listeth." In the case of Wordsworth the problem is the more baffling from the fact that, on the philosophical side, the doctrines of Plato and of the philosophers of the German school came to him through Coleridge as a medium. In the realm of poetry Wordsworth was a student on his own account, being deeply read in the masters of English verse, especially Chaucer, Spenser, Milton, Thomson and Burns. In metaphysics his reliance upon Coleridge was conspicuous.

Professor Beatty's book, a work of painstaking, although not always accurate, scholarship, has thrown much new light upon the sources of the Poet's thought. It has provided a fresh approach to the problem of Wordsworth's mind. As a result of his investigations it may be taken as established that in the earlier period—say 1796 to 1810—the Poet was considerably influenced by the doctrine of the association of ideas, finding in this theory a helpful approach to the discussion of certain outstanding problems of life. It is possible that the conception of the three ages of man in respect to the appreciation of Nature (Childhood, the age of sensation; Youth, the age of feeling; Maturity, the age of reflection) he consciously or unconsciously took over from Hartley; although it cannot be claimed that the idea is sufficiently original to warrant any special anxiety as to its source. But that Wordsworth at any period of his life was a Hartleyan in the sense that Coleridge was, is extremely doubtful. The idealistic note which rings through his poetry from beginning to end and which has been recognized by a century of criticism as unique, is too vibrant for that. We know that after a few years Coleridge abandoned associationism in favor of the transcendentalism which we associate with his name. His conversion was characteristically sudden and complete. The temper of Wordsworth, as he found himself making progress from one phase of thought to another, was to conserve the best of the past. Continuity was the law of his being. Thus, never having committed himself to associationism, as far as Coleridge had done, he was in a better position than his friend to retain such of Hartley's approaches and ideas as served the trend of his thinking as a whole. This may help to account for the traces here and there which give to the Beatty theory a greater plausibility than the total impression allows.[4]

It cannot be said that any of the attempts to label Wordsworth philosophically have been successful. Nor can one agree with Stephen, Arnold, Beatty or the others who maintain that in any true sense Wordsworth was systematic and scientific in his philosophic verse. Distinctly he was not built upon that plan. His reliance upon feeling and imagination alone would have made system an impossibility. His function rather was to be the mystic-artist in the realm of ideas. Let us be thankful that this was so. Who wishes a poet to be philosophical in the technical sense? Who does not wish a poet to be philosophical in the vital sense? On this account the reading of a poet like Wordsworth should prove the best possible corrective of the present-day distrust of philosophy as such. It was because Wordsworth made the good-life his central theme and dealt with it in imaginative and beauty-satisfying ways that his poetry is making its appeal to so many of the strong minds of our time. Here, too, we find the secret of the attraction which Wordsworth has for men of wide diversity of philosophic view. One has but

---

[4]For an illuminating discussion of this tendency in Wordsworth, as indeed for a balanced treatment of his philosophical and religious views generally, see the section on Wordsworth in *Essays in the Romantic Poets*, 1929, by Prof. S. F. Gingerich, of the University of Michigan, especially pp. 146-7, 165. Dean Sperry, in his *Wordsworth's Anti-Climax*, 1935, supports the idea that Hartley was a dominant influence throughout the poet's career.

to mention such names as Arnold, Swinburne, Pater, DeVere, Robertson, Mill, Bagehòt, Lowell, to realize the breadth of the Wordsworth appeal. Arnold was an agnostic, DeVere a Roman Catholic, Robertson an Anglican, Lowell a Unitarian, Mill philosophically was an empiricist, ethically a utilitarian. In his essay *The Idea of God in Nature,* Mill could say, "Conformity to nature has no connection whatever with right and wrong." Yet we have seen Mill, himself a philosopher of the first rank, in an hour of darkness turning to Wordsworth as by the deepest instinct of his soul. What is it in Wordsworth that draws men of such dissimilarity of thought and taste into a common bond of appreciation and sense of obligation? Certainly it was not what Leslie Stephen calls "a scientific system of thought." The fact that we have not succeeded in extracting the system is all to the good. We have done something far better; we have uncovered the main sources of the Poet's strength. We know now that his poems were not found at the end of any syllogism, but in the innermost fountains of spiritual feeling and intuition. It is because he could assure us that

> with an eye made quiet by the power
> Of harmony, and the deep power of joy,
> *We see into the life of things,*

the building of *our own* systems of life-philosophy has become a surer task.

At the same time it must be recognized that Wordsworth thought of himself as writing not only in a philosophic mood, and with a philosophic intent, but in a philosophic way. This at least is clear so far as *The Prelude* and *The Excursion* are concerned, since we have his explicit statement to that effect. In the Preface to *The Excursion* occurs this passage: "It is not the Author's intention formally to announce a system; it was more animating to him to proceed in a different course; and if he shall succeed in conveying to the mind clear thoughts, lively images, and strong feelings, the Reader will have no difficulty in extracting the system for himself." In other words, while acknowledging no formal body of philosophic thought, he would offer the appropriate materials for such a body and trust the reader to discover what it was. This, for the most part, his readers have failed to do. Either the system is not there or the readers have been content to receive his poetry in an inspirational way. In my opinion both of these things are true. Certain outstanding attitudes and ideas have made a powerful appeal. So profound has been the impression of his mystic yet concrete idealism, that it is not too much to say, more than any other poet he has determined the trend of England's and America's philosophic thought during the past one hundred years.

In the Preface to *The Excursion,* Wordsworth also printed a portion of *The Recluse,* which he characterized as "a kind of prospectus of the design and scope of the whole poem." It may also be taken as a prospectus of the range of the Poet's philosophical views. Especially is this true of the opening lines:

> On Man, on Nature, and on Human Life,
> Musing in solitude, I oft perceive
> Fair trains of imagery before me rise,
> Accompanied by feelings of delight
> Pure, or with no unpleasing sadness mixed;
> And I am conscious of affecting thoughts
> And dear remembrances, whose presence soothes
> Or elevates the Mind, intent to weigh
> The good and evil of our mortal state.
> —To these emotions, whencesoe'er they come,
> Whether from breath of outward circumstance,
> Or from the Soul—an impulse to herself—
> I would give utterance in numerous verse.
> Of Truth, of Grandeur, Beauty, Love, and Hope,
> And melancholy Fear subdued by Faith;
> Of moral strength, and intellectual Power;
> Of joy in widest commonalty spread;
> Of blessèd consolations in distress;

Of the individual Mind that keeps her own
Inviolate retirement, subject there
To Conscience only, and the law supreme
Of that Intelligence which governs all—
I sing:—"fit audience let me find though few!"

Now in these twenty-three lines we have exactly twenty-three separate themes, arranged in a somewhat haphazard way. From the standpoint of philosophical system here is a jumble of ideas. From the standpoint of human interest and of art, here is magnificent poetry. Combined with the eighty-four lines that follow, this is one of the noblest passages in English verse, for grandeur and sweep, scarcely surpassed by Milton at his best. Here are materials and attitudes and points of view—enough for even the most hard-headed of thinkers; but the conspicuous thing is not that we are impelled toward speculation, but that we are filled with the sense of the grandeur of life. Feeling the urge of "elevated thought" we read on in the hope of appropriating the Poet's vision as our own. And this is precisely what Wordsworth had in mind when he wrote those words. His poetry is an attempt at a great and intimate sharing of his best thought and aspiration. His poetry is the quintessence of himself. Whatever else we find in the poetry of Wordsworth, we must not fail to find the soul of the man who wrote. It may be said of him as of no other poet since Milton that "Out of the abundance of the heart the mouth speaketh."

Over against these considerations, however, we are to remember that Wordsworth was never disorderly and never foggy in his thinking. Emerging from the main body of his verse are great mountain peaks of conviction to which he points with the clarity of a seer. If he leads us along the precipitous edges of ultimate ideas, it is never with faltering steps. He is always sure of himself.

When we come to look for the fundamental character of Wordsworth as a philosophical poet, I think we shall find it best expressed in the word *penetration*, in his ability to discern the inner essence lying behind all appearance. There is a certain spiritual clairvoyance which pervades his thinking on all the higher levels of his work. In one of his sermons Dr. Martineau speaks of this characteristic as belonging to Man as such. He says: "We are so constituted throughout in memory, in affection, in conscience, in intellect, that we cannot rest in the literal aspect of things as they materially come to us. No sooner are they in our possession than we turn them into some crucible of thought which saves their essence and precipitates their dross; and their pure idea emerges as our lasting treasure, to be remembered, loved, willed and believed." Exactly. And it was this very quality that Wordsworth had in mind in the line I have chosen as the title of this chapter:

> We see into the life of things,

and when he put into the mouth of the "Wanderer" of *The Excursion* the sentiment:

> Thus deeply drinking in the soul of things,
> We shall be wise perforce.

The same clairvoyance is expressed in *Peele Castle* in the line:

> And seen the soul of truth in every part.

But in each instance there is a condition laid down, in that a man shall be in harmony with his world and attuned to the moral instincts of his soul. He must know something of

> that serene and blessed mood,
> In which the affections gently lead us on.

He must be in possession of

> an eye made quiet by the power
> Of harmony, and the deep power of joy.

Undoubtedly such a power exists in every human breast. It

belongs to our richer genius. It is one of the divine qualities hidden in the soul. But for most of us it requires a
Martineau or a Wordsworth to awaken the mind to the
consciousness of the fact.

In Wordsworth the capacity for penetration existed in
such a degree that it marks him as both Prophet and *Seer.*
His was a genius for insight of an extremely high order.
We have seen it illustrated in his appreciation of the common things of earth. The success of a large part of his
most popular verse lies in this penetration of spirit into
sense, in the revelation of the hidden meaning behind the
beauty of the outer world. Here also we find the soul of
those homely descriptions of peasant life in the dales of
Cumberland and Westmoreland. It is the secret of his
understanding of men. It was by this that every casual
walk became a path of revelation, so that he could say:

> the lonely roads
> Were open schools in which I daily read
> With most delight the passions of mankind,
> Whether by words, looks, sighs, or tears, revealed;
> *There saw into the depth of human souls.*[5]

Is there any such delineation of moral fiber in the midst
of biting poverty as we find in the story of the "Leech-
gatherer? Have we anywhere a more realistic view of the
tragedies of childhood than in the much criticized *Alice
Fell,* or of the child's spontaneous enjoyment of Nature
than in the universally admired *Immortality Ode?* In
such phrases as, "thy soul's immensity," "thou best philosopher," "thou eye among the blind," "high instincts,"
"first affections," "shadowy recollections," "those first-
born affinities that fit our new existence to existing things,"
we have the marks of a mind that could plumb the very
depths of child nature and experience. And does literature
contain a keener characterization of erratic genius than
in the line in *Resolution and Independence* referring to the
youthful Chatterton:

---

[5] *Prelude,* XIII, 162-166. Italics mine.

> The sleepless Soul that perished in his pride.

This was the line of which Swinburne remarked: "There is not and will never be a greater verse in all the world of song."

Of similar power of character-penetration are the lines in *The Prelude* which describe the famous Trinity College statue of Newton:

> The antechapel where the statue stood
> Of Newton with his prism and silent face,
> The marble index of a mind forever
> Voyaging through strange seas of Thought, alone.

Here, too, we find the secret of his power of bringing the infinite into the common things of Nature, into the common life of Mankind. As to the profundity of his view of Nature in relation to God and Man, possibly enough has been said; but I will add only this: there may not be as much in Nature as Wordsworth supposed; but there is not likely to be anything more. In this realm, at least, we find him living at the center of things.

Above all, we see the Poet's genius of penetration in the analysis of his own mind, as to its nature and the processes of feeling, thought, imagination and the insight of faith and love. Philosophically the most revealing thing about Wordsworth is *The Prelude,* indicated so definitely in the secondary title, *Growth of a Poet's Mind, An Autobiographical Poem.* Here are fourteen books of the most vivid and convincing introspection that literature affords. Although in *The Recluse* the Poet speaks of "the mind of man my haunt and the main region of my song," it was in respect to his own mind that his insight, as also his art, reached the summit of its strength. Here, no less than in the objective realm, we feel that he brings us

> Authentic tidings of invisible things.

Wordsworth's penetration was more moral than intellectual. It arose less from analysis and reflection than from emotional response, singularly pure and direct, which freed him from the lower passions that blind the soul. Associated with this was a reverence which enabled him to stand before the works of God as though in the presence of God Himself. With Wordsworth the poetic insight was essentially religious. It derived from that intensity of feeling, that depth of intuition which mark the true mystic in the realm of poetic truth.

I turn now to certain favorite ideas of the Poet, which have not been touched upon, or touched upon too lightly in the preceding chapters, and which may best be taken up in connection with his philosophic sense. The first of these has to do with Man and Nature as fitted to each other by the very charter of their being. Wordsworth held that there is a subtle bond which links the whole creation together, "Through all the mighty commonwealth of things; Up from the creeping plant to sovereign Man."[*] He found a perfect accordance of the mind, so far as its essential character is concerned, with the innermost nature of things as expressed in the external world. From this arises the sense of unity and a reciprocal action highly beneficial to Man. Nothing gave him greater zest than to attempt to describe this harmonious interaction. As Professor Bradley expressed the doctrine: "The inmost principle in man's mind is also the inmost principle in everything else." The idea of universal reciprocity crops out in many places, but its best expression is in these lines from *The Recluse* where it is indicated as one of the Poet's major themes:

> For the discerning intellect of Man,
> When wedded to this goodly universe
> In love and holy passion, shall find these
> A simple produce of the common day.
> —I, long before the blissful hour arrives,
> Would chant, in lonely peace, the spousal verse
> Of this great consummation:—and, by words
> Which speak of nothing more than what we are,

---

[*] *The Excursion*, IV, 342-3.

> Would I arouse the sensual from their sleep
> Of Death, and win the vacant and the vain
> To noble raptures; while my voice proclaims
> How exquisitely the individual Mind
> (And the progressive powers perhaps no less
> Of the whole species) to the external World
> Is fitted:—and how exquisitely, too—
> Theme this but little heard of among men—
> The external World is fitted to the Mind;
> And the creation (by no lower name
> Can it be called) which they with blended might
> Accomplish:—this is our high argument.

The supreme illustration of this "cosmic law of inter-penetrating worlds," Wordsworth finds in the principle of love as proceeding from Nature to Man and from Man back to Nature and ultimately to God. From among the several passages expressing this idea, I quote the following from the last book of *The Prelude:*

> By love subsists
> All lasting grandeur, by pervading love;
> That gone, we are as dust.—Behold the fields
> In balmy spring-time full of rising flowers
> And joyous creatures; see that pair, the lamb
> And the lamb's mother, and their tender ways
> Shall touch thee to the heart; thou callest this love,
> And not inaptly so, for love it is,
> Far as it carries thee. In some green bower
> Rest, and be not alone, but have thou there
> The One who is thy choice of all the world:
> There linger, listening, gazing, with delight
> Impassioned, but delight how pitiable!
> Unless this love by a still higher love
> Be hallowed, love that breathes not without awe;
> Love that adores, but on the knees of prayer,
> By heaven inspired; that frees from chains the soul,
> Lifted, in union with the purest, best
> Of earth-born passions, on the wings of praise
> Bearing a tribute to the Almighty's Throne.

With love Wordsworth couples imagination, without which love is blind. Following immediately upon the above quotation are lines in which imagination is accorded the highest rank in all the processes of truth:

> This spiritual Love acts not nor can exist
> Without Imagination, which, in truth,
> Is but another name for absolute power
> And clearest insight, amplitude of mind,
> And Reason in her most exalted mood.

This is so much of a "presiding idea" that one is bewildered to select a passage which may be considered typical beyond the rest. But perhaps we cannot do better than quote the famous lines in which the Poet describes his sensations when, as a university student upon his first visit to Switzerland, on walking over the Simplon, most unexpectedly he found that he had crossed the Alps:

> Imagination—here the Power so called
> Through sad incompetence of human speech,
> That awful Power rose from the mind's abyss
> Like an unfathered vapour that enwraps,
> At once, some lonely traveller. I was lost;
> Halted without an effort to break through;
> But to my conscious soul I now can say—
> "I recognise thy glory": in such strength
> Of usurpation, when the light of sense
> Goes out, but with a flash that has revealed
> The invisible world, doth greatness make abode,
> There harbours; whether we be young or old,
> Our destiny, our being's heart and home,
> Is with infinitude, and only there;
> With hope it is, hope that can never die,
> Effort, and expectation, and desire,
> And something evermore about to be,
> Under such banners militant, the soul
> Seeks for no trophies, struggles for no spoils
> That may attest her prowess, blest in thoughts
> That are their own perfection and reward,
> Strong in herself and in beatitude
> That hides her, like the mighty flood of Nile
> Poured from his fount of Abyssinian clouds
> To fertilize the whole Egyptian plain.[7]

---

[7] *Prelude*, VI, 592-616.

In order to understand Wordsworth in the higher ranges of his thought, we must realize that he uses the word imagination in a peculiar sense, as something far beyond the coloring and shaping function to which the romantic poets in all ages have been devoted. To Wordsworth, imagination is more than fancy, more than feeling, more than reasoning. Once he called it "the feeling intellect." In one of the above passages he characterizes it as "Reason in her most exalted mood." At other times he identifies imagination with intuition, and once at least (*Prelude*, XIV, 207) it is paired with intellectual love. It has to do not only with objects and persons, but also with truth in the abstract; it has a discovering function in both the intellectual and moral realms. And it possesses a cleansing function as well, since it is capable of redeeming the faculties from their otherwise low level of absorption in "the things of the flesh." With Wordsworth, imagination, more than any other faculty, is the medium of reality. It is at once the essence and the atmosphere of spiritual perception. It was through this super-faculty of mind that, standing that day at the summit of the Simplon Pass, he became conscious of the spiritual worth of Man —"I recognize thy glory. . . ." "Our destiny, our being's heart and home, is with infinitude, and only there." In the same passage he speaks of it as "that awful power." In his *Answer to the Letter of Mathetes* (Christopher North), in referring to the *Ode to Duty,* he states that it was "in the transport of imagination" that he discovered the operation of moral law in the physical realm. As near as one can make out, according to the Wordsworth usage, imagination is the totality of mind in its farthest reaches of interpretation, exploration and creation. This alone would be sufficient to explain a certain lack of system in Wordsworth's philosophic thought. Philosophy, as taught in the schools, should be made of sterner stuff.

Wordsworth considered himself in some special sense both poet and prophet of imagination. When issuing an edition of his works in 1815 he separated many of his finest poems, including *Tintern Abbey* and other nature pieces, and gave them the caption *Poems of the Imagination,* in distinction from certain others which he called *Poems of the Fancy.* In *The Prelude,* two books, the twelfth and thirteenth, are devoted to a discussion—not too easily followed it must be confessed—of *Imagination and Taste.* It is noteworthy that for vividness and creative strength in the use of the imaginative faculty, Coleridge ranked Wordsworth second only to Shakespeare. Are we to consider that this is inconsistent with our modern scientific point of view? In one of his last addresses, President Eliot, of Harvard University, emphasized the large place of imagination in the scientific world of our time, declaring that as never before the play of the human imagination pervades science in all its processes of invention and discovery. "Quite recently," he remarked, "such subjects as chemistry and physics have illustrated vividly that influence." On this account, he argued, we are coming to a state where the old conflict between science and religion is disappearing, partly because scientific methods approach those of theology and those of theology approach those of science. With equal force might he have contended for imaginative literature as an incentive to the discovery of truth. I think President Eliot would have agreed that in this respect Wordsworth belongs distinctly to our age.

There is such a thing as imaginative reality. Sometimes it is acquired by the man of business, more often by the man of science, occasionally by the philosopher, always it must be sought by the poet who would shape the current of the world's thought. One need not accept Wordsworth's too finely drawn distinction between fancy and imagination, and we certainly cannot follow his argument for imagination as a function transcending reason, an illumination proceeding from the soul wherein the ultimate secrets of the universe are revealed. Both he and

Coleridge defined imagination in a manner peculiar to themselves. The labored defense of their thesis, found in Coleridge's *Biographia Literaria,* has failed to convince the world. We are content today to regard imagination as the vivid apprehension of things in the unseen realm, the highest of the faculties, yet subject to all the laws of thought. To the modern psychologist imagination is the eye of the mind. On this basis, Wordsworth fits comfortably into our scheme. Exactly because he dealt in realities rather than in fictions and dreams, through his deeper insight he is able to save us from the thraldom of sense. As Dr. van Dyke so well puts it: "The peculiar and precious quality of his best work is that it is done with his eye on the object and his imagination beyond it."

Today we need imagination not only in the realms of science, literature and art, but in the sphere of human relationships, and most of all in our interpretation of God. The vindication of the Golden Rule waits upon an exercise of the imaginative faculty such as Wordsworth exhibited in respect to characters like the Old Cumberland Beggar, Michael the Shepherd, Simon Lee the Old Huntsman, Margaret, whose sorrows he fathomed and depicted in such a marvelous way. A wholesome application of imagination would help greatly in solving the problems of capital and labor, possibly being needed about equally on both sides of the line. The same is true in international affairs. One is inclined to feel that more imagination on the part of the American nation would have prevented the discourteous treatment of a sensitive people like the Japanese in the matter of immigration. Many in these days are reading their Bible without the aid of this "faculty divine," and thereby they miss not only the beauties but the deeper significance of the inspired Word. Dr. Horace Bushnell said a true and helpful thing when he remarked: "The Bible is God's great gift to the human imagination." It should be a matter of historical and literary information that the Bible—cer-

tainly in its best portions—was written by the Miltons,
the Herberts and the Wordsworths of the early time.
This being the case, there is danger that the secrets of
the Most High will be missed by men who deal with the
Scriptures as they would with a text-book on logic, or with
the Statutes of Massachusetts. Particularly would it en-
rich our lives if, through the exercise of a refined and
disciplined imagination, we came to regard Nature not
merely as a symbol, an analogy of things divine, but as
itself divine, because infilled with the spirit of the Living
God. With more imaginative insight we might even be
able to say with our Poet:

> To me the meanest flower that blows can give
> Thoughts that do often lie too deep for tears.

Next in this exalted progression of ideas is the problem
of suffering. There was no aspect of life that received
more attention in his poems than this. One has but to
recall such pieces as: *The Female Vagrant, The Affliction
of Margaret, Ruth, The Sailor's Mother, The Complaint,
Her Eyes Are Wild, Alice Fell, Lucy Gray, The Leech-
gatherer, Michael, The Brothers, The Last of the Flock,
Surprised by Joy, Brougham Castle,* to realize how large
a place sorrow, disappointment, defeat and pain occupied
in the mind of this poet. Certainly there was no hiding of
his face from the stern realities of life. We have seen that
when he turned from the love of Nature to the love of
Man, it was "the still *sad* music of humanity" that caught
his ear. What the reader does not always discover is that
in a great many instances the fact of suffering is intro-
duced for the express purpose of indicating how it may
become the vehicle of joy. I find that in my desk-copy I
have marked twenty-six poems or passages which deal
with the transfiguration of sorrow. Probably the list could
be extended. Here, then, is one of the Poet's root-ideas.[6]

---

[6] No critic has more clearly discerned the message in respect to the transmutation of
suffering in Wordsworth's verse than Leslie Stephen. After the death of his wife, in
writing to Prof. Charles Eliot Norton, of Harvard, Stephen said, "Do you sympathize
with me when I say that the only writer whom I have been able to read with pleasure
through this nightmare is Wordsworth? I used not to care for him specially, but now
I love him."—*Life and Letters of Leslie Stephen*, by William Maitland.

For the reader who would pursue this aspect of Wordsworth's philosophic thought I would recommend that he
begin with *Elegiac Stanzas, Suggested by a Picture of
Peele Castle in a Storm,* as having to do with the Poet's
personal grief in the loss of his brother John; that he pass
to *The White Doe of Rylstone* (this, on account of its
length, will be a test of the earnestness of his search), as
picturing sorrow in its bearing upon the tender heart of
woman; that, as an offset, he re-read *The Happy Warrior*
as indicating the response of the masculine mind; and that
for the sake of what may be called the Poet's theory of
suffering, he take up in succession the fourth and fifth
books of *The Excursion, To Toussaint L'Ouverture, The
Immortality Ode, The Force of Prayer,* and *At the Grave
of Burns.*

From such a wealth of material I shall have to content
myself with a few of the more characteristic lines, together with a brief indication of their place in the Wordsworth scheme. *Peele Castle,* which bears the full accent of
the Poet's genius, written two years after his brother's
death, in every stanza throbbing with autobiographical
significance, by means of the symbolism of a stormy sea
conveys the lesson of the humanizing effect of sorrow and
of the acceptance of the tragic as a part of the universal
plan. The poem marks an epoch in the Poet's life:

> So once it would have been,—'tis so no more;
> I have submitted to a new control:
> A power is gone, which nothing can restore;
> A deep distress hath humanized my Soul.

The closing note is one of courageous resignation:

> But welcome fortitude, and patient cheer,
> And frequent sights of what is to be borne!
> Such sights, or worse, as are before me here.—
> Not without hope we suffer and we mourn.

*The White Doe,* which Jeffrey characterized as "the
worst poem ever written," from the standpoint of art is

not to be defended as a satisfactory piece of work; but it is the most romantic (in the Sir Walter Scott way) of all of Wordsworth's poems; it contains many beautiful lines, and, in the story of the pure-souled Emily and her patient acceptance of the loss of her father and her nine brothers as the result of a foolish adherence to a hopeless cause, we have an extremely interesting portrayal of unmerited grief. The poem has been mistakenly interpreted as inculcating the relentlessness of fate. What it inculcates is plainly set forth in the closing stanza of the *Dedication*—lines which deserve far more recognition than they have received:

> Action is transitory—a step, a blow,
> The motion of a muscle—this way or that—
> 'Tis done; and in the after-vacancy
> We wonder at ourselves like men betrayed:
> Suffering is permanent, obscure and dark,
> And has the nature of infinity.
> Yet through that darkness (infinite though it seem
> And irremoveable) gracious openings lie,
> By which the soul—with patient steps of thought
> Now toiling, wafted now on wings of prayer—
> May pass in hope, and, though from mortal bonds
> Yet undelivered, rise with sure ascent
> Even to the fountain-head of peace divine.

The lines from the *Character of the Happy Warrior* which bear on this theme are:

> Who, doomed to go in company with Pain,
> And Fear, and Bloodshed, miserable train!
> Turns his necessity to glorious gain;
> In face of these doth exercise a power
> Which is our human nature's highest dower;
> Controls them and subdues, transmutes, bereaves
> Of their bad influence, and their good receives.

The philosophical treatment of adversity, what we might call Wordsworth's theodicy, runs like a golden thread through all the books of *The Excursion*. In this poem much is made of the healing touch of Nature. But this is not the whole story, since "Within the soul a faculty abides," capable of turning evil to good account; while without the soul abides a Power Divine ready to lift the soul from the depths of gloom and to establish it on a throne of joy. It would be correct to say that the outstanding lesson of the poem is the transmutation of sorrow into joy by the alchemy of fortitude and faith. It is in this poem that Wordsworth "contests the ground inch by inch with all despondent and indolent humors." The closing lines of Book V may be taken as conveying the message of *The Excursion* as a whole:

> Life, I repeat, is energy of love
> Divine or human; exercised in pain,
> In strife, in tribulation; and ordained,
> If so approved and sanctified, to pass
> Through shades and silent rest, to endless joy.

To read the fifth book thoughtfully is to realize how abundant was the answer Wordsworth received to the prayer uttered in the *Preface* to *The Excursion* that he might become the Poet

> Of blessèd consolations in distress.

Toussaint L'Ouverture, in the well-known sonnet, is made the hero of the transmutation of sorrow as applied to the social and political movements of the time:

> Thou hast left behind
> Powers that will work for thee; air, earth, and skies;
> There's not a breathing of the common wind
> That will forget thee; thou hast great allies;
> Thy friends are exultations, agonies,
> And love, and man's unconquerable mind.

When we come to *The Immortality Ode* we find ourselves approaching the conception of a future life as affording compensation for the misery of earth. While *The Ode* does not actually enter this realm, it prepares the way by offering the high consolations of both philosophy and faith. There are compensations to be reckoned with here and now:

> In soothing thoughts that spring
> Out of human suffering;
> In faith *that looks through death,*
> In years that bring the philosophic mind.

Perhaps the most revealing passage of all is the closing stanza of *At the Grave of Burns,* since here Wordsworth has in mind not only the misfortunes but also the misdoings of a brother-poet whom he loved and admired:

> Sighing I turned away; but ere
> Night fell I heard, or seemed to hear,
> Music that sorrow comes not near,
>     A ritual hymn,
> Chanted in love that casts out fear
>     By Seraphim.

Taking these passages collectively, we may say that what they offer is something more than what Emerson had in mind when he wrote *Compensation,* something more than a balancing of accounts in favor of happiness as the ultimate thing. They deal with suffering as an integral part of the human lot, as an experience led on by God toward the goal of the abundant life, and therefore as something inherently excellent. It is to this heroic faith that in *The Prelude* he attributes his freedom from care and his progress toward

> that peace
> Which passeth understanding, that repose
> In moral judgments which from this pure source
> Must come, or will by man be sought in vain.[9]

In a noteworthy passage—the one leading up to his ascription to Love, dealing with "the adverse principles of pain and joy," he characterizes evil as a term "rashly named by men who know not what they speak."[10] In another place he speaks of "Sorrow that is not sorrow but

---

[9] *Prelude,* XIV, 126 ff.
[10] *Ibid.,* XIV, 167.

delight." It will be recognized that in all this Wordsworth is as far as possible removed from the shallow
philosophy of our day which finds in pain and sorrow only
"an error of mortal mind."

Wordsworth has been criticized as implying that a
purifying and hallowing influence arises from suffering as
such, and that he attributes too much to the recuperative
forces inherent in the individual soul, without dependence
upon immediate divine help.[11] The criticism possibly has
a certain force when applied to poems like *The White
Doe* and *The Happy Warrior;* but it is not valid in respect to *The Force of Prayer,* or to *The Excursion.* Certainly no one can ask for a more definitely religious reference than this, from the fourth book of *The Excursion,*
where the "Wanderer" is made to say:

> One adequate support
> For the calamities of mortal life
> Exists—one only; an assured belief
> That the procession of our fate, howe'er
> Sad or disturbed, is ordered by a Being
> Of infinite benevolence and power;
> Whose everlasting purposes embrace
> All accidents, converting them to good.
> —The darts of anguish *fix* not where the seat
> Of suffering hath been thoroughly fortified
> By acquiescence in the Will supreme
> For time and for eternity; by faith,
> Faith absolute in God, including hope,
> And the defence that lies in boundless love
> Of his perfections; with habitual dread
> Of aught unworthily conceived, endured
> Impatiently, ill-done, or left undone,
> To the dishonour of his holy name.

Wordsworth achieved his optimism in respect to the
forces of evil less by the processes of intellect than by the
compulsions of a rich inner life. And here an instructive
parallel may be drawn with Tennyson and Browning. In

---

[11] See Principal Shairp's *Aspects of Poetry,* p. 373.

the case of all three it is noteworthy that the poem which carries the largest measure of comfort for stricken souls is one arising from the experience of personal bereavement. With Wordsworth it is *Elegiac Stanzas,* inspired by the death of his brother John; with Tennyson it is *In Memoriam,* dealing with the loss of Henry Hallam, his dearest friend; with Browning it is *Rabbi Ben Ezra,* which reflects the processes of consolation upon the death of his wife. In each case it was the problem of loss in a universe ruled over by a beneficent God, who had revealed his nature through a *suffering* Son. Who shall say what it means to an age like the present that the three greatest poets of the former century built their message upon a foundation of Theistic and Christian belief?

# CHAPTER XII

# "The Light That Never Was on Sea or Land"

AS OUR discussion draws to a close, the thing that emerges is that Wordsworth has become a "Mighty Voice" to our age. The deeper we go into his philosophy of Nature and Man the clearer it becomes that he belongs to us in a peculiar way. He is the prophet of a future that lies on the horizon of the world of today. Practically every great lesson of Wordsworth's verse may be brought to this test. Take for example his conception of Nature as instinct with divine purpose and power, the generator of joy and peace as well as of physical well-being; or his doctrine of the supreme worth of individual Man, of Man in his capacity to transmute evil into good, of Man in his at-homeness with the divine, of the grandeur of the most elementary feelings, of the moral sense as reflecting infinite beauty and truth; or his doctrine of the eternal kinship of the soul with God as the under-girding of the immortal hope; or the prophetic nature of child instinct and imaginative sense; or, turning in another direction, take his view of poetry and science as ordained to walk hand in hand in the quest of truth, with natural religion coming once more into its own; or his teaching that the progress of society is bound up with the development of national and international relations as an inseparable unity; take any of his fundamental ideas "On Man, on Nature, and on Human Life," and we find ourselves thinking in terms of today. These are universal truths, but one and all they bear heavily upon the problems of the post-war world. If, as some of us believe, the need of this age of confused thinking and of disjointed living is to get back to first principles, the message of the contem-

plative Poet of the Lakes is calculated to make a powerful appeal.

Even more is this apparent when we consider what
Wordsworth has to offer in the way of practical suggestion for the attainment of the good-life of society under
the conditions of the modern world. It is an impressive
list, including as it does such items as these: the practice
of solitude as a healing art; integration of life through
the cultivation of tranquillity in the midst of distracting
scenes; the naturalizing of our educational program to
the point where men of high and low degree become appreciative of the finer things of life; the planned economy
of leisure and of ordered seasons of rest; the exercise of
the imagination in the understanding of Nature, Man and
God; the reading of poetry not only as a solace for the
restlessness and the mechanical prosiness of the age, but
as a means for the regeneration of society; the acceptance
of love as the law of happiness and of successful living.
It is by majestic ideas like these that Wordsworth is being
drawn into the main currents of our thinking. Here is a
mine of practical idealism, a body of sociological teaching
of extraordinary scope and applicability. Here is a poet,
a prophet and a priest conjoined in single personality.

Beyond question, Wordsworth was over given to
didacticism and heavy moralization, especially in the way
of a direct pressing of his views upon the reader's mind.[1]
But a defect of this nature should not blind us to the solid
worth of his achievement in the realm of ideas. His own
defense is well known. In writing to Sir George Beaumont
he once remarked, "Every great poet is a teacher. I wish
to be considered a teacher or as nothing." To attack
Wordsworth for inculcating moral ideas is like calling
Amos, Isaiah and St. Paul to account for proclaiming
"The Word of the Lord." He too had his "heavenly
vision," concerning which he could affirm "I was not dis-

---

[1] For a well-considered discussion of this tendency, see Lowell's essay on Wordsworth, in his *Among My Books*, Second Series.

obedient." If the comparison is bold, it is not too bold, for the Poet himself in a noteworthy passage, does not hesitate to bracket the modern Poets of Truth with the Ancient Line of Seers:

> If thou partake the animating faith
> That Poets, even as Prophets, each with each
> Connected in a mighty scheme of truth,
> Have each his own peculiar faculty,
> Heaven's gift, a sense that fits him to perceive
> Objects unseen before, thou wilt not blame
> The humblest of this band who dares to hope
> That unto him hath also been vouchsafed
> An insight that in some sort he possesses,
> A privilege whereby a work of his,
> Proceeding from a source of untaught things,
> Creative and enduring, may become
> A power like one of Nature's.[1]

Moreover we are to remember the spirit of the times. It was preëminently a preaching age. Not only every cleric, but every teacher, every philosopher, every essayist, every poet had the burden of a message to proclaim. Cowper's *Task* is a lengthy sermon—really six sermons—on the value of the devout and simple life in an age of pretension and frivolity. Gray's *Elegy* is a sermon on the pathos of mortality, and no less a beautiful poem on that account. In *In Memoriam*, what else is Tennyson doing than discoursing upon faith and doubt in respect to the future life? Browning, in his *Christmas Eve, Easter Day*, and in many another piece, is sharing his Christian and philosophic creed with the world. Lamb once remarked that he never heard Coleridge do anything else than preach. In *The Sensitive Plant*, Shelley has a matchless sermon upon Life, Love and Death, and Keats in his *Ode on a Grecian Urn* gives expression to a great moral idea. In my opinion, the grandest sermon of them all was written by that scapegrace Robert Burns, in his *Cotter's Saturday Night*. When we turn from verse to prose, Carlyle and

---

[1] *Prelude*, XIII, 300-312.

Ruskin were the most incorrigible evangelists of their time. It was the way of the age. The poems that live, the poems that people love, are the poems that preach; and let the critics make the most of it. In one of his essays, Swinburne calls our attention to the fact that it was Matthew Arnold who flung down as a challenge from the ethical critic to the æsthetic that "a school of poetry divorced from any moral idea is a school of poetry divorced from life."[2]

After all, it is not so much a question as to whether a poet should preach or not—how can he forbear in a time like the present?—but whether he has a message worth preaching, and whether he is able to put it across in terms which the men and women of our age will understand and enjoy.

A more serious criticism arises from those who are troubled by what appears to be the excessive egotism of Wordsworth in the assumption that he was the Lord's Anointed in the realm of poetic truth. It cannot be denied that he held a lofty opinion of his own ability. This is reflected in his scorn of criticism, his sublime and oft-reiterated confidence in the favorable judgment of the ages upon his work, and his slighting allusions to the younger poets of his time, not only Byron, but Shelley and Keats. Even Coleridge at times did not escape the censure of a certain superiority implied by neglect. I have recently come across an illustration of this in an unpublished letter of Wordsworth to R. P. Gillies, the Scottish editor and author, to be found in the Amherst College Collection of Wordsworthiana. In this letter bearing the date of

---

[2] For a refreshing discussion of the whole question of truth as the prime object of the poet, as opposed to the theory of "pure poetry," or poetry for its own sake, see Max Eastman's *The Literary Mind, Its Place in an Age of Science*, Scribners', 1931, especially pp. 142-147. Eastman quotes Blake as saying: "God's prophets are the poets who have the courage to take their own imaginings for truth." He adds: "That is the 'Art of Poetry,' according to William Blake. And Wordsworth is little behind him in this embattled reëntry into the lost realms of knowledge. Not only is the poet alive to nature, according to Wordsworth, but nature is alive to the poet, and by him only and his diligent sympathy to be reached unto and understood. If poetry is not perhaps the 'quintessence' it is nevertheless the 'breath and finer spirit of all knowledge; it is the impassioned expression in the countenance of all science.' . . . It is this great and conscious declaration of war on the division of labor between poetry and science—this heroic attempt, by mysticism or by metaphysics, to return to the attitude of the Elizabethans, that inaugurated the new era which we call 'romantic' in English poetry."

1817, referring to a request for his opinion of the *Biographia Literaria*, the Poet replied: "I have not read Mr. Coleridge's 'Biographia,' having contented myself with skimming parts of it." When we consider that Coleridge was his most intimate friend, that he owed more to him than to any other human being, that he once addressed him as "O Friend! O Poet! brother of my soul!" and that the work in question, while registering high praise for Wordsworth's verse, contained nine chapters of scholarly and discriminating criticism of his theory of versification, the fact that the older poet could content himself with a skimming process reveals, to say the least, an extraordinary state of mind.

Some may gain comfort from the reflection that poets, as a rule, are built on the egoistic, if not the egotistic plan, and that this trait of character must be accepted as an indispensable element in a large personality. My own feeling is that Wordsworth's self-esteem, which was by no means a dominant characteristic and expressed itself in occasional rather than in habitual ways, may be accounted for as an over-stressing of the note of authority and self-containment which so easily goes with the richly endowed yet single mind. Since all genius is aware of itself, we may consider Wordsworth's egotism a fault of his qualities, rather than a defect nourished by choice. Not for a moment is it to be mistaken for intellectual or spiritual pride. In respect to Nature, Man, Beauty, Truth, and God, Wordsworth was essentially a person of "a contrite and humble spirit."

Having dwelt at such length upon the prophetic side of Wordsworth's work, it is a pleasure in this closing section, to turn to the artistic qualities without which his message would never have found lodgment in the human breast. However much we may admire Wordsworth as philosopher, moralist, educator, humanitarian, and patriot, the obvious reason for his persistent hold upon the

general reading public is the fact that he was a great *poet.*
Here, too, lies a sure hope of his influence in days to come.

> The truly great
> Have all one age, and from an invisible space
> Shed influence! They, both in power and act
> Are permanent, and Time is not with them,
> Save as it worketh for them, they in it.

Such was Coleridge's tribute to his brother poet as he
received into his heart "that more than historic that prophetic lay." History and prophecy alike are fulfilled in
our time. Some one has said, "It takes a great deal of
history to make one poet." If that be a disheartening
word, comfort may be found in the fact that a poet, a real
poet, when once made, will never wear out. The man who
wrote *Tintern Abbey, Peele Castle, Song at the Feast of
Brougham Castle, The Affliction of Margaret, Hartleap
Well, Michael, The Happy Warrior, Ode to Duty,* and
what has come to be known as *The Immortality Ode,* had
nothing to fear as to the appraisal of men through the
ages. His place would appear to be secure in "Art's timeless realm."

Nor are we restricted to accredited and beloved poems
like the above. Many a lesser piece, such as *The Green
Linnet, My Heart Leaps Up, The Tables Turned, She
Dwelt Among Untrodden Ways, The Solitary Reaper,*
and, best of all, certain of the *Miscellaneous Sonnets,*
speak the universal language of the human heart. It is to
be noted that his poetic genius revealed itself not only in
nobility of thought and purity of diction, but also in the
small details of composition: the shining line, the frag-
ment of imagery, the sharpened and inevitable word, the
summary phrase where conjunction between idea and expression is perfect. Even some of the poems which the
general reader has neglected, and the critic has scorned,
yield evidence of an amazing insight and an individual
art. Take his characterization of Nature as an example.

Turning my Wordsworth almost at random, I run across such lines as these:

> The gloom
> Spread by a brotherhood of lofty elms.
> *(Excursion)*

> And birch-trees risen in silver colonnade.
> *(Duddon Sonnets)*

> Clothed in the sunshine of the withering fern.
> *(Prelude)*

> Of flowers that with one scarlet gleam
> Cover a hundred leagues, and seem
> To set the hills on fire.
> *(Ruth)*

> This lawn, a carpet all alive
> With shadows flung from leaves.
> *(This Lawn)*

> The river glideth at his own sweet will.
> *(Westminster Bridge)*

> The cataracts blow their trumpets from the steep.
> *(Ode)*

> Fair as a star, when only one
> Is shining in the sky.
> *(She Dwelt)*

> Like a fair sister of the sky
> Unruffled doth the blue lake lie
> The mountains looking on.
> *(The Sylvan)*

> Lady of the Mere,
> Sole-sitting by the shores of old romance.
> *(A Narrow Girdle)*

> The swan on still St. Mary's Lake
> Floats double, swan and shadow.
> *(Yarrow Unvisited)*

> No motion but the moving tide, a breeze,
> Or merely silent Nature's breathing life.
> *(Peele Castle)*

# THE LIGHT THAT NEVER WAS ON SEA OR LAND

The lightning, the fierce wind, and trampling waves.
*(Peele Castle)*

the bloom
And all the mighty ravishment of spring.
*(To Lady Beaumont)*

The witchery of the soft blue sky.
*(Peter Bell)*

These are lovely and flawless creations. They illustrate what the moderns call the "texture" of verse.

An equally impressive list can be made of lines that deal with the inner significance of natural objects. I find I have marked these arrows of poetic meaning:

The ghostly language of the ancient earth.
*(Prelude)*

Breathless Nature's dark abyss.
*(Loud is the Vale)*

This silent spectacle—the gleam—
The shadow—and the peace supreme!
*(Evening Ode)*

The holy time is quiet as a nun
Breathless with adoration.
*(Sonnet)*

The sounding cataract
Haunted me like a passion.
*(Tintern)*

Earth breathed in one great presence of the spring.
*(Vaudracour and Julia)*

The sea that bares her bosom to the moon.
*(The world is too much with us)*

The winds come to me from the fields of sleep.
*(Ode)*

Whose dwelling is the light of setting suns.[3]
*(Tintern)*

---

[3] Of this line from *Tintern* Tennyson said, "It is almost the grandest line in the English language, giving the sense of the abiding in the transcient." See *Life*, by his Son.

# THE REDISCOVERY OF WORDSWORTH

When we come to Wordsworth's craftsmanship in the depiction of personality and experience we find the same magical effect, the same lightning-flash of revelation:

> Thy soul was like a Star and dwelt apart.
> > *(Milton)*

> And homeless near a thousand homes I stood,
> And near a thousand tables pined and wanted food.
> > *(Guilt and Sorrow)*

> Her eyes as stars of Twilight fair;
> Like Twilight's, too, her dusky hair;
> But all things else about her drawn
> From May-time and the cheerful dawn.
> > *(She was a Phantom of Delight)*

> Love had he found in huts where poor men lie;
> His daily teachers had been woods and rills,
> The silence that is in the starry sky,
> The sleep that is among the lonely hills.
> > *(Brougham Castle)*

If one asks as to Wordsworth's power to convey moral sentiments—"thoughts that breathe and words that burn" —he may find it in lines like the following:

> Wisdom is oft-times nearer when we stoop
> Than when we soar.
> > *(Excursion)*

> Brooding above the fierce confederate storm
> Of sorrow, barricadoed evermore
> Within the walls of cities.
> > *(Recluse)*

> One great society alone on earth:
> The noble living and the noble dead.
> > *(Excursion)*

> The primal duties shine aloft—like stars;
> The charities that soothe, and heal, and bless,
> Are scattered at the feet of man—like flowers.
> > *(Excursion)*

> No motion has she now, no force;
>   She neither hears nor sees;
> Rolled round in earth's diurnal course,
>   With rocks, and stones, and trees.
>         *(A Slumber did My Spirit Seal)*

> Like thoughts whose very sweetness yieldeth proof
> That they were born for immortality.
>         *(Ecclesiastical Sonnets)*

>           The Gods approve
> The depth, and not the tumult, of the soul.
>         *(Laodamia)*

> Our noisy years seem moments in the being
> Of the eternal Silence.
>
>         *(Ode)*

But where is one to stop in such a treasure-house of song! To apply Saintsbury's phrase, Wordsworth taught us that "style is not merely the dress but the body of thought." Our standard books of quotations would seem to indicate that no other poet since Shakespeare has so abounded in lines "in which paragraphs have been put into sentences and then given wings." And this is borne out when we are interested enough to list the Wordsworth phrases which either have become proverbial forms of speech or have passed into the vocabulary of educated men. Among such may be mentioned:

>         Nature never did betray
> The heart that loved her.

The child is father of the man.

Our birth is but a sleep and a forgetting.

Trailing clouds of glory.

Thoughts that do often lie too deep for tears.

That inward eye which is the bliss of solitude.

Plain living and high thinking.

We must be free or die.

The world is too much with us.

The harvest of a quiet eye.

We live by admiration, hope and love.

Joy in widest commonalty spread.

Not too bright or good for human nature's daily food.

The light that never was on sea or land.

Almost any book of Wordsworth Selections (and more than a dozen of these have been published during the past twenty years), will afford evidence enough as to Wordsworth's poetry glowing with meaning for the man of today.

What was the innermost secret of Wordsworth's power? On this point the Poet has not left us in doubt. It is best summed up in the word *consecration*, and all that draws to that word from the familiar lines of *Peele Castle:*

> The light that never was, on sea or land,
> The consecration, and the Poet's dream.

It is in the note of dedication to a divinely imparted and divinely supported poetic career running through his verse early and late, that we shall find the deepest source of his strength. One recalls at once the famous passage in the fourth book of *The Prelude,* dealing with the first long vacation from Cambridge, in which he shares with his friend "The memory of one particular hour." There had been a night of revelry in connection with a country dance, when, in the early hours of morning, in a mood of emptiness and dissatisfaction, he started on his homeward way, alone. With the burst of dawn came the great reaction:

> Magnificent
> The morning rose, in memorable pomp,
> Glorious as e'er I had beheld—in front,
> The sea lay laughing at a distance; near,
> The solid mountains shone, bright as the clouds,
> Grain-tinctured, drenched in empyrean light;

And in the meadows and the lower grounds
Was all the sweetness of a common dawn—
Dews, vapours, and the melody of birds,
And labourers going forth to till the fields.
Ah! need I say, dear Friend! that to the brim
My heart was full; I made no vows, but vows
Were then made for me; bond unknown to me
Was given, that I should be, else sinning greatly,
A dedicated Spirit.

Wordsworth never outlived the thrill of that moment. It was more than the recognition of beauty as universal and supreme, more than the going out of his soul in a passion of joy. Experiences of that quality had been his before. Rather it was the coming into his soul of a Power from without, the compulsion of the conscious admission of the Divine—"Vows were then *made for me*," "Bond unknown to me *was given*." There were to be lapses, of course, but that vision of a glorified world persisted to the end of life. Some ten years later, as described in the opening section of *The Prelude,* following his experiences in France and the subsequent period of storm and stress, there was to be a rekindling of this early fire of devotion, and he records a day when

. . . poetic numbers came
Spontaneously to clothe in priestly robe
A renovated spirit singled out,
Such hope was mine, for holy services.

These two passages need to be taken together and in the order I have named, if we are to get back to the inner source of Wordsworth's power. And with them we should associate the sonnet, which, with deep significance, is used as an introduction to all his works:

If thou indeed derive thy light from Heaven,
Then, to the measure of that heaven-born light,
Shine, Poet! in thy place, and be content:—
The stars pre-eminent in magnitude,
And they that from the zenith dart their beams,
(Visible though they be to half the earth,
Though half a sphere be conscious of their brightness)

Are yet of no diviner origin,
No purer essence, than the one that burns,
Like an untended watch-fire, on the ridge
Of some dark mountain; or than those which seem
Humbly to hang, like twinkling winter lamps,
Among the branches of the leafless trees;
All are the undying offspring of one Sire;
Then, to the measure of the light vouchsafed,
Shine, Poet! in thy place, and be content.

There is yet another sonnet of autobiographic significance which belongs in this connection, and which is
worthy of quotation on the ground of artistic perfection
alone. Being written late in life, it indicates that "the consecration and the Poet's dream" had not lessened with
the years. I refer to the sonnet which Wordsworth placed
at the end of his *Itinerary Poems of 1833*:

Most sweet it is with unuplifted eyes
To pace the ground, if path be there or none,
While a fair region round the traveller lies
Which he forbears again to look upon;
Pleased rather with some soft ideal scene,
The work of Fancy, or some happy tone
Of meditation, slipping in between
The beauty coming and the beauty gone.
If Thought and Love desert us, from that day
Let us break off all commerce with the Muse:
With Thought and Love companions of our way,
Whate'er the senses take or may refuse,
The Mind's internal heaven shall shed her dews
Of inspiration on the humblest lay.

This sonnet, which Palgrave, in his *Golden Treasury*,
calls *The Inner Vision*, with its happy blend of philosophic
thought and  poetic expression, its delicate infusion of
fancy and meditation into the processes of sense perception, and its emphasis upon Love as the inseparable companion of Thought, is Wordsworthian to the core. It
would be difficult to name an equal number of lines more
characteristic of the Wordsworth point of view.

The note of self-dedication, of reliance upon "a higher

something outside the poet's self," breathes through all of Wordsworth's greater verse, being especially impressive in *Tintern Abbey* and *Wisdom and Spirit of the Universe.* His was the spiritually vital soul. It is the complete missing of this fact on the part of recent critics of the left that accounts in large measure for their blindness as to the inwardness of the Poet's life. Fortunately we have the witness of so modern a critic as Professor Harper, who, in dealing with the Hawkshead vacation experience, remarks:

> It was the hour of his baptism with the fire of poesy, an hour memorable in his life and in the history of literature. It was the supreme religious moment of his life, the point when solitude closed in on all sides of him, and his being stood cut off for the first time from every other human soul, distinct in conscious self-hood; the point, too, when by this very isolation his soul lay bare to divine influence, and he communed with God, submissive to the heavenly voice.[4]

This is a timely and wholesome return to the earlier view of Wordsworth as essentially a poet of the spiritual sense. I have not seen a better statement of the case, alike for Wordsworth and for all poetry of the higher range, than in the words of Aubrey De Vere, himself a poet of no mean distinction. He remarks:

> True poetry is less a creation of the poet's intellect than the embodied *progeny* of his total spiritual being. . . . It is not a single faculty of the mind that originates a true poem, though the imagination is specially needed for that end. It is the whole mind, and not the mind only, but the whole moral and emotional being, including those antecedent habits and experiences which fitted the being for its task. In this respect the highest poetry has some analogy to religious faith. . . . It is this also which gives to great poetry, and especially to Wordsworth's, its extraordinary influence over *as many as enter into vital relations with it.* They find in it more than beautiful thoughts, vivid images, valuable conclusions, melodious cadences; they find these things, and many more, not apart and isolated, but fused into a living and personal union. . . . It is their whole being that

---

[4] *William Wordsworth,* edition of 1929, pp. 42, 43.

is challenged by a brother man, and to that challenge they respond.[5]

The fruitage of Wordsworth's self-dedication is most easily detected in those poems which deal directly with the spiritual meanings of external things; but two of the sonnets afford perhaps a more subtle evidence of this higher inspirational mood. The first is the too-little-known lines on *The Trosachs*. So many Americans have motored, or better stage-coached, or still better tramped through this lovely bit of the Scottish Highlands that they will be in a position to appreciate the deep, spiritual impression that came to the Poet of the English Highlands and Lakes, as he strolled through the Trosachs in the glory of autumn days:

> There's not a nook within this solemn Pass
> But were an apt confessional for One
> Taught by his summer spent, his autumn gone,
> That Life is but a tale of morning grass
> Withered at eve. From scenes of art which chase
> That thought away, turn, and with watchful eyes
> Feed it 'mid Nature's old felicities,
> Rocks, rivers, and smooth lakes more clear than glass
> Untouched, unbreathed upon. Thrice happy quest,
> If from a golden perch of aspen spray
> (October's workmanship to rival May)
> The pensive warbler of the ruddy breast
> That moral sweeten by a heaven-taught lay,
> Lulling the year, with all its cares, to rest!

The other sonnet is the well-known and universally admired *Upon Westminster Bridge*, in which the city, at early dawn, as seen through the eyes of consecrated imagination, becomes a vision of loveliness and calm not less satisfying than that arising from "Nature's old felicities:"

> Earth has not anything to show more fair:
> Dull would he be of soul who could pass by

---

[5] *Essays Literary and Critical*, pp. 320-321. This noteworthy essay was originally a paper read before the *Wordsworth Society* in 1883, and may be found in the printed record for that year, and in the single volume *Wordsworthiana*.

> A sight so touching in its majesty:
> This City now doth, like a garment, wear
> The beauty of the morning; silent, bare,
> Ships, towers, domes, theatres, and temples lie
> Open unto the fields, and to the sky;
> All bright and glittering in the smokeless air.
> Never did sun more beautifully steep
> In his first splendour, valley, rock, or hill;
> Ne'er saw I, never felt, a calm so deep!
> The river glideth at his own sweet will:
> Dear God! the very houses seem asleep;
> And all that mighty heart is lying still!

Here we have Wordsworth in one of his high moments. I can think of no lines of his which better illustrate the difference between the surface light of sagacity and the deep inner glow of inspiration. Certainly as we read a sonnet like this the Poet's emotion becomes our own, and in the process we are changed.

It is worthy of note that the two sonnets, *Upon Westminster Bridge* and *The Trosachs*, were singled out by Walter Bagehot as models of purity in poetical composition. In an essay entitled *Wordsworth, Tennyson and Browning; or Pure, Ornate and Grotesque Art in Poetry*, England's great economist, who was also one of the keenest critics of his age, named Wordsworth as best representing the element of purity in modern verse. Bagehot's characterization of *pure* literature is "that it describes the type in its simplicity—we mean, with the exact amount of accessory circumstance which is necessary to bring it before the mind in finished perfection, and no more than that amount." He cites the two sonnets, the one dealing with the city, and the other with Nature in the rough, as perfect examples of this type of art.[6] This is a piece of genuine critical acumen, but with equal truth it may be said that they are perfect examples of the insight of a mind at harmony with itself and with the totality of the world's spiritual life. What we have in both of these sonnets is genius conjoined with a high order of consecration.

---

[6] *Literary Studies*, by Walter Bagehot, 1879.

In the last analysis, Wordsworth's sense of beauty and his sense of mission were one and the same thing. He was an artist in verse because he was an artist in truth. What he perceived and felt he proclaimed. It was from an experience of deep inner satisfaction that he devoted his life to the promulgation of a brighter and happier, because a spiritually conditioned world. He believed such a world to be possible, and that he was to have an honorable part in the great consummation. In this confidence he brought the long story of *The Prelude* to an end. In a passage of great nobility he pictured a world in which mankind was to climb to undreamed of heights of beauty and truth. Generously associating Coleridge with himself, he pledged that, speaking "A lasting inspiration sanctified by reason, blest by faith," they would forward the day of "firmer trust," since

> What we have loved,
> Others will love, and we will teach them how;
> Instruct them how the mind of man becomes
> A thousand times more beautiful than the earth
> On which he dwells, above this frame of things
> . . . . . . . . . . . . . . .
> In beauty exalted, as it is itself
> Of quality and fabric more divine.